A DREAM DEFERRED

A DREAM DEFERRED

How Social Work Education Lost Its Way and What Can Be Done

DAVID STOESZ
HOWARD JACOB KARGER
TERRY CARRILIO

ALDINETRANSACTION
A Division of Transaction Publishers
New Brunswick (U.S.A.) and London (U.K.)

Library of Congress Catalog Number: 2009048704
ISBN: 978-0-202-36380-6
Printed in the United States of America

Library of Congress Cataloging-in-Publication Data

Stoesz, David.
    A dream deferred : how social work education lost its way and what can
    be done / David Stoesz, Howard Jacob Karger, and Terry Carrilio.
        p. cm.
    Includes bibliographical references and index.
    ISBN 978-0-202-36380-6 (alk. paper)
        1. Social work education. I. Karger, Howard Jacob, 1948- II. Carrilio,
    Terry Eisenberg. III. Title.

HV11.S833 2010
361.3071--dc22

                                                    2009048704

DS: To Audrey, the consummate professional.
HJK: To the students who made the journey worthwhile.
TC: To my husband, David, for hanging in and reminding me through his example of the best ideals of social work.

Contents

Preface

This is a critical examination of social work education. More than a century after its creation late in the nineteenth century, social work continues to struggle not only for public credibility but also stature within the academy. Social work's ambiguous status is ironic in light of the enormous expansion of social programs during the twentieth century. The creation of the American welfare state as well as the growth of the service economy should have augured well for American social work, but that has not been the case. After assessing social work's performance on several indicators , we conclude that many of the profession's travails can be attributed to the poor quality of professional education as overseen by the Council on Social Work Education (CSWE).

CSWE's poor stewardship of social work education is evident in several indicators: the weak scholarship of its board and commissions, the absence of scholarship of deans and directors of schools of social work, the lack of publications by editors of social work journals, the low test scores scores of applicants to Masters of Social Work (MSW) programs. Compounding these has been a disregard for conventional research standards within professional education, evident in social work's enthusiasm for postmodernism, constructivism, and "alternative ways of knowing." This anti-empirical orientation to social reality has compromised the profession's ability to generate knowledge about social work practice, the context in which it occurs, the circumstances of vulnerable populations, and plausible policy and program alternatives.

Our analysis indicates CSWE's overexpansion of social work programs coupled with inferior professional education has created an "educational bubble." Not unlike the housing bubble that preceded the recession beginning in 2008, social work's educational bubble is evident in the profession's inability to generate sufficient faculty to teach in its accredited programs and the acute problems confronted by social work students who not only sustain high loan debt but also face deteriorating job prospects upon graduation. The likelihood is that the Great Recession will puncture social work's educational bubble with predictable results: social work programs will be demoted or consolidated with other departments, tenured lines will evaporate or be converted to adjunct positions, tuition increases will cause students to question the economic viability of a career in social work, social agencies will look elsewhere when they fill positions because social work graduates are less skilled than those from other disciplines. In the absence of structural reform, a descending vortex thus jeopardizes social work education, presaging its demotion to vocational status. Because CSWE sustains a network of leaders in social work education who benefit from the status quo, establishing what is essentially a patronage system, we propose alternative accreditation as a way to assure that social work education prospers in the twenty-first century.

Undoubtedly, the analysis that follows will be disputed by apologists of the status quo. In an open society where citizens enjoy their First Amendment rights and professors enjoy academic freedom, we welcome a discussion about the future of social work education. Historically, social work education has witnessed little internal dissension. Aside from *Unfaithful Angels* by Harry Specht and Mark Courtney,[1] one is hard put to find a critical assessment of social work practice, let alone a rigorous examination of social work education. After a century of questionable quality, such an investigation is long overdue. In that regard we are heartened that "Reinventing Social Work Accreditation," appearing in *Research on Social Work Practice* prompted a healthy discussion from a cross-section of social work educators.[2]

Given the breadth of our critique we understand that some defenders of the status quo will prefer personal vilification to civil discussion. In that regard we are obliged to present our *bona fides*. Among the three of us, we have over seven decades of experience in professional education. We have written a dozen books on social welfare, two of which have received national prizes, as well as scores of refereed journal articles. We have managed the accreditation of two undergraduate social work programs, developed two doctoral programs, managed a social work policy institute, and directed a prominent school of social work. One has received two Fulbright awards. Aside from being educators, we have practiced in public welfare, child welfare, and border affairs; one was recognized as "Social Worker of the Year" by a regional chapter of NASW. In sum, having dedicated our careers to social work, we have an abiding faith in the capacity of social work education to fully exploit its quite ample opportunities.

*   *   *   *   *   *   *

We are appreciative of the assistance that many colleagues have made to this work. Confirming our patronage thesis in social work education, most have been unwilling to be identified, fearing adverse career consequences; these include a particularly capable doctoral student, a journal editor, and several academics. Others have been less discreet. The transparency of the book has been enhanced by Bill Epstein who reviewed the entire manuscript, Bob Green whose research on the productivity of social work faculty was central to the book, Harry Chaiklin whose contributions to social work history were invaluable, Bruce Thyer who arranged the discussion on accreditation in *Research on Social Work Practice*, and Maria Anderson of Academic Analytics who answered many queries about its ranking of schools of social work. To all of them, we offer not only our sincere thanks, but also the assurance that the conclusions in this book are ours alone.

Notes

1. Harry Specht and Mark Courtney, *Unfaithful Angels* (New York: Free Press, 1994).
2. David Stoesz and Howard Karger, "Reinventing Social Work Accreditation, *Research on Social Work Practice*, 19, 1 (January 2009).

1

Slouching into the Twenty-First Century

Social work education is at a tipping point between the abundant opportunities of the last century and the formidable challenges of the future. As a result of the unprecedented infusion of resources accompanying the New Deal and the War on Poverty, twentieth century social work anticipated continued expansion of its professional project. Accordingly, social work education promised altruistically minded college graduates not only a ticket to upward mobility, but a promise to advance a liberal agenda in social and economic justice as well. That agenda grounded to a halt as an ascendant conservatism during the final decades of the twentieth century, followed by the Great Recession early in the twenty-first century, stymied the progressive trajectory in public policy. Ominously, these events cast doubt about the inevitability of social progress, a fundamental assumption of the profession's leaders since social work's inception. Despite dramatic changes in the nation's political economy during the closing decades of the twentieth century, social work education failed to change course: the accreditation of programs continued apace with little regard for the quality or relevance of social work education. Rather than upgrade professional education, the Council on Social Work Education, the dominant force in accreditation for a half-century, ignored the movement towards accountability that has surged through American higher education. The consequences of this failure in leadership were evident in the growing disparities between social work and other disciplines that flourished after the Progressive Era, teaching, nursing, and public health. Instead of preparing social workers to deal confidently with the challenges of the future, social work education continued the suboptimal education that typified professional training in the past.

The incongruence between social work's promise and its performance warrants a critical review of professional education. For the past half-century, the fortunes of social work have been controlled by the Council on Social Work Education (CSWE), which oversees accreditation of the nation's schools of social work. Has CSWE's regulation of professional education elevated the stature of social work? Have salaries been sufficient to attract the best students to the profession? Have journal editors selected the best knowledge to distribute to practitioners? Has the leadership of schools of social work and CSWE represented its best scholars? These and related questions are the basis for this book.

Social Work

Throughout human history some members of every society have been excluded, oppressed, or marginalized for reasons ranging from ethnicity, race, ideology, religion, and class to personal failures and eccentricities. Over time various societies have managed the treatment of "out-groups"[1] differently; yet, in most cases accommodations are made so that the following functions are carried out: (1) direct ameliorative intervention with individuals, (2) effective control of individuals so that they do not unduly disrupt the social order, harm themselves or others; and (3) reform efforts to alleviate the burdens of excluded groups by developing social welfare policies and programs. These functions tend to emerge organically from within a society and can be carried out by actors holding varying roles. So it is that wise men and women—police, politicians, journalists, businessmen, clergy, and academics among others—have played these roles in different times and places. The tension between nurturing those who are vulnerable and punishing them for their weaknesses has been present since the first alms were offered to the poor. Ameliorative and social reform efforts have evolved in the course of events, varying with feudal, industrial, and post-industrial eras. These helping roles have emerged informally, but have evolved into formal occupations as societies become more industrialized.

With the rapid changes associated with industrialization, these functions were formalized in order to contend with the massive cultural, economic and social dislocations associated with advanced capitalism. During the industrial era, a new profession—social work—emerged to fulfill these essential functions. Social work education developed alongside the emerging profession as a means of assuring the transmission of specialized knowledge and practice methods.

Crisis of Identity

From its inception social work has struggled with carrying out the complex, sometimes contradictory functions associated with reducing suffering, enhancing social order, and social reform. Questions about whether social work was a catalyst for change, a preserver of the social order, or a palliative for the hopelessly impaired, led to polarization and unresolved dialectics. Attention on public institutions and social reform diverged from a more individualized approach emphasizing the repair of those who had already been damaged. On the one hand social change via reform relied on a data-driven approach that demonstrated to lawmakers and other leaders that tweaking institutions and improving conditions for the disadvantaged would reduce social ills and lead to a more productive, just society. On the other, application of compassionate, values-based methods of intervention with the victims of society could help them to help themselves, and improve their social functioning; the art of engaging and interacting with the disadvantaged required the development of important listening and diagnostic skills. One perspective tended towards viewing problems as having been caused by unequal social conditions that induced pathology, while the other assumed that the problem was in the individual, who needed to change in order to be eligible for, and able to maximize extant opportunities.

The person-in-environment perspective emerged as an attempt to reconcile the issue of the locus of the problem. In 1958, the National Association of Social Workers (NASW) Commission on Practice stated:

> The social work method is the responsible, conscious, disciplined use of self in relationship with an individual or group. Through this relationship the practitioner facilitates interaction between the individual and his social environment with a continuing awareness of the reciprocal effects of one upon the other. It facilitates change: (1) within the individual in relation to his social environment; (2) of the social environment in its effect upon the individual; (3) of both the individual and social environment in their interaction.[2]

Despite the effort to understand the dynamic relationship between person and context through person-in-environment, an emphasis on social pathology has further confounded social work in the United States. Kathryn Cornell observed that, "The concept of "person-in-situation" or "person-in-environment" stemmed from the beginning of social work and its dual focus on both individual assistance and social reform."[3] A series of questions evolved that animated social work education: Was social work's professional mission change or adjustment? Should the

Table 1
Dualism in Social Work

Unit of Attention—Individual	Unit of Attention-Society
Cause	Function
Practice (Art-Based Apprentice)	Research (Empirical Research)
Vocation	Profession
Social Control	Social Change

inculcation of knowledge be through apprenticeship or research? Was social work ultimately a vocation or profession? Did social work attempt social change or social control? Thus, from the beginning, what came to be called 'social work' has been conflicted.

Internal dissension notwithstanding, by the early twentieth century those who were doing good works, improving social conditions, salving suffering, and pushing for reforms, consistent with the emergence of professionalism during the Progressive era, became interested in having their work recognized as being "professional." Addressing the changing identity of social work, Margaret Gibelman noted that, "The definition of the profession and its boundaries, then, is a mirror reflection of the values, priorities and technologies of American society in interaction with the social work profession at any given point in time."[4] Alterations in the social, political, economic, and cultural context of the United States have influenced social work considerably since the profession emerged in the early twentieth century. In recent decades, globalization has not only transformed economic structures, but also altered culture and the popular psyche with a rapidity that requires adaptation on the part of the profession. The twenty-first century now poses challenges for social work and its educational institutions quite unlike anything witnessed in the century before.

In response to a diverse membership, social work educators have preferred to resolve its historic dualisms by justifying their pedagogy on the basis of values imparted through practice wisdom as opposed to demonstrating efficacy through empirical research. Thus, moral pronouncements have often provided the basis for social work education. Moral metaphysics have an advantage in that they are often universally endorsed; however, they can also devolve into propaganda, in which event education more resembles indoctrination than impartial training. While members of any occupational group may subscribe to moral metaphysics in professional training, doing so at the exclusion of empirical research runs the risk of attracting objections from opposing groups. This was essentially the perception by a conservative legal rights organization when it brought a successful suit on behalf of Emily Brooker, a social work student at Missouri State University, for violating her free-speech rights. Embarrassed by the incident, the Provost of Missouri State University placed the social work program under the direction of an English professor and commissioned two social work deans, Karen Sowers of The University of Tennessee and Michael Patchner of Indiana University, to evaluate it. Released in the Spring of 2007, the report portrayed a nightmare in professional education. "It appears that faculty have no history of intellectual discussion/debate," which may have contributed to their "bullying" of students and colleagues as well.[5] Symptomatic of a preoccupation with internal procedures, "committees are used to interminably process and debate issues with little problem solving or resolve."[6] Not surprisingly, committee activity subverted scholarship at Missouri State's School of Social Work: "Overall, the faculty are incredibly underproductive particularly in the areas of research, scholarship and service,"[7] the site visitors concluded. The absence of scholarship notwithstanding, faculty felt at liberty to indoctrinate students, resulting in "possible bias against students who are faith based."[8] Meanwhile the School was not particularly vigilant about those who were admitted: "It also appears that MSW applicants who clearly do not meet admission standards are admitted to satisfy enrollment expectations."[9] The dysfunctional ambiance of the social work program was so advanced that both students and faculty actually felt unsafe at the School. Among the alternatives proposed by the reviewers was actually closing the school long enough for the offending faculty to be removed, a draconian step which might jeopardize the accreditation of the program. The gravity of the option was not lost on the reviewers who offered a gratuitous observation:

> Both external reviewers have extensive experience in several institutions of higher education and both have conducted numerous site visits for reaccreditation. Neither of the reviewers have ever witnessed such a negative, hostile and mean work environment. Persons with administrative roles are held in contempt by the faculty; faculty colleagues are disrespectful to one another, and some faculty are disrespectful and demeaning toward students. The consequence is a dysfunctional and hostile work and learning environment.[10]

In response to the report, the President of Missouri State University, Michael Nietzel, promptly threatened to close down the social work program within a year and a half if its problems were not resolved. "I was embarrassed by the things that were said in this report," he explained, "but it was not a difficult decision to make it public."[11]

Lost Opportunities

As early social workers, motivated by idealism and morality, engaged with the significant personal and social problems of early industrialism, they very quickly realized that training and standard-setting in the new field would be essential to assure competence and accountability. Social work education developed as a way to provided specialized training, teaching new social workers the skills needed to perform the essential functions of alleviating suffering, maintaining social controls, and promoting social justice. Once the idealistic reformers of the Progressive Era began professionalizing, they sought to establish social work's status as a modern profession. Unlike the classic professions, such as the military, divinity, and law, the modern professions, including engineering, psychology, and medicine, base their practice on knowledge derived from science. Yet, social work and its educational establishment struggled to fully exploit the professional opportunities attached to the emergence of the American social welfare state.

As will be noted in Chapter 2, a dispute between rival organizations of social work academics subverted the new profession's ability to take advantage of the opportunities at hand. The underlying premises of public welfare were in conflict with the clinical orientation that had shaped professional education up to that point. The clinical orientation relied heavily on a medical model and over time evolved to support the delivery of clinical social work services through private practice. The conflict between private practice and public welfare practice is not a trivial one, as each represents a different delivery system and philosophy of service. So it was that "training for public social welfare, while it received greater attention during the thirties, never really challenged the dominance of the private case work tradition in social work education."[12] The inability of educators to resolve social work's internal contradictions compromised its public mission. While social work educators continued to debate issues, the new profession's ability to address pressing social problems flagged. This is illustrated with examples from two traditional concerns: public assistance and child welfare.

Public assistance

A generation after passage of the Social Security Act of 1935, the War on Poverty of the 1960s introduced a second generation of social programs, most of them benefiting the poor. Yet, while government funding to combat poverty increased, social work's attention to the poor diminished. Perhaps the clearest evidence of this disinterest is found in

Social Work Research and Abstracts. Beginning in 1965, articles about social welfare were abstracted and cross-referenced. In 1965, a pivotal year of the War on Poverty, 12 articles about poverty were published; the following year the number jumped to 22. Through the late 1960s and early 1970s, the number ranged between 12 in 1969 and three in 1970. In 1973, the editors added "the poor" to "poverty" as an entry, and the number of articles jumped to 11. Thereafter, social work's interest in poverty flat-lined; between 1974 and 1988, the year in which the first conservative reform of welfare was enacted through the Family Support Act, the number of articles appearing in the social work literature averaged fewer than four per year.[13]

Subsequently, social work would miss an enormous opportunity to influence anti-poverty policy during the debate about welfare reform that preceded passage of the 1996 Personal Responsibility and Work Opportunity Reconciliation Act (PRWORA). Having invited states to apply for waivers for the purpose of deploying alternatives to Aid to Families with Dependent Children (AFDC), the Reagan Administration had provided governors an opportunity to mount demonstration programs, but provisions of the Social Security Act required that such experiments be evaluated according to state-of-the-art research methods. For over a decade, various alternatives to AFDC were developed, the evaluations of which were funded in the tens of millions of dollars. Well distributed throughout the country, schools of social work were perfectly situated to conduct such research and secure significant funding in the process, but few did. Instead, funding was diverted to a fledgling research industry comprised of private organizations, such as the Manpower Demonstration Research Corporation, Abt Associates, and Mathematica Policy Research. During the debate on welfare reform, social work's understanding of the relationship between poverty and government assistance was dominated by the "feminization of poverty," attributing family poverty to patriarchical institutions that oppressed disproportionately minority, low-income mothers. That such a characterization had been discredited by mainstream historians, such as Theda Skocpol[14] and Linda Gordon[15], was ignored. Thus, social work academics not only missed a signal opportunity to leverage welfare policy, they deluded themselves about the origins of anti-poverty programs.

Child welfare

Social work has had primary responsibility for child welfare since passage of the Social Security Act. Despite a series of subsequent policies to enhance child well-being, child welfare has fared poorly. "The system set up to promote child welfare continues to face confusion about its purposes and methods, exacerbated by declining professionalism, and progressive disorganization," observed Alvin Schorr, "The immediate future of public child welfare is relatively clear—child welfare around the country is in a parlous state," he concluded. "In many places the debasement of services, the decline of staff, and the absence of sustained citizen engagement are so advanced that it is difficult to see how these may be reversed."[16] A small literature has depicted the deterioration in child welfare, including books by academics, such as Gelles[17] and Epstein,[18] as well as journalists. *The Lost Children of Wilder* by Nina Bernstein chronicled Marcia Robinson Lowry's valiant attempt to attain a measure of justice for foster children in New York City.[19] Lowry would found Children's Rights, a legal advocacy organization that by 2006 had secured consent decrees from ten public child welfare agencies. Two teams of journalists have won Pulitzer Prizes for their exposés of child welfare.

Systematic data from governmental agencies and private foundations indicate that child welfare is failing its mandate to serve children from troubled families. A review of the child welfare literature by the Child Welfare Workforce Task Group, which meets at the Children's Defense Fund, documented the serious personnel problems of the field: 90 percent of states experience difficulty recruiting and retaining child welfare workers, only 28 percent of child welfare staff hold a social work degree and fewer than 15 percent of child welfare agencies require professional credentials, and the average tenure of a child welfare worker is less than two years.[20] The Child and Family Service Reviews (CFSRs) released in 2005 by the Department of Health and Human Services determined that of the 50 states and the District of Columbia evaluated on seven standards of child welfare, not one state was able to assure that maltreated children had a permanent and stable living arrangement; not one state was in compliance with regard to families having improved their ability to care for their children; only one state demonstrated that it adequately met a child's physical and mental health needs.[21] Data on foster children reveal the extent to which child welfare has been compromised. A study of children who have aged out of foster care in the Northwest revealed that, within the 12 months prior to being interviewed, 20 percent had a major depressive episode, 12 percent suffered from alcohol and drug dependence, and 25 percent were diagnosed with Post Traumatic Stress Disorder.[22]

With rare exception, social work academics have been negligent in pursuing field experiments to identify optimal interventions in child welfare. The rarity of field experiments in child welfare led the authors of *Beyond Common Sense* to conclude "there is not a single intervention that has generated a published peer-review article based on a study in which they accepted referrals from a child welfare agency, randomly assigned them to a treatment condition, and evaluated the outcome."[23] The absence of field experiments in child welfare is inexplicable in light of comparable research on welfare reform and the substantial funding schools of social work receive for child welfare training. Budgeted at $280 million in 2006, federal child welfare training funds might be expected to generate rigorous research on child welfare services in general and outcomes of training in particular, but the results are typically presented through remedial case studies.[24] The lack of serious inquiry ultimately discredits child welfare in the eyes of critical decision-makers. "Given that child protection systems experience chronic failure in the achievement of their missions," concluded an international review of child welfare, "there is understandable annoyance on the part of political and bureaucratic figures that despite significant increases in scarce resources, the situation does not seem to improve, with ongoing system and practice failures evident."[25]

Social Work Accreditation

As professions have developed educational and licensing structures, the idea of assuring that educational and training programs provide minimal consistency and quality has grown into a complex accrediting process. Although accreditation of social work programs have been divisive historically, since 1952 CSWE has been the sole accreditor, holding a monopoly on the function. Unlike other industrialized nations where accreditation is conducted by the government, the United States has upheld a tradition of self-regulation in academe, relying on private organizations for this purpose. American accreditation policy has been the responsibility of the Council for Higher Education Accreditation (CHEA) that authorizes CSWE, as one of 66 "programmatic accrediting organizations,"[26] to regulate social work education.

The role of the federal government in accreditation evolved later, with the provision of federal financial aid to students through the Higher Education Act of 1952; subsequently the U.S. Department of Education recognizes programs that assure the quality of higher education.[27] During the administration of George W. Bush, Secretary of Education, Margaret Spellings employed this is in an attempt to make higher education more accountable, an effort perceived by many educators as politicization. By the first decade of the twenty-first century, federal student assistance exceeded $85 billion annually,[28] an amount that few colleges or universities could afford to ignore. Student aid thus became the carrot assuring not only that all institutions of higher education became accredited but also that the federal government had a stake in determining the quality of higher education.

Accreditation of social work programs has become controversial, as it has been for other disciplines. Despite its universality, accreditation has been problematic as tuition has outpaced the cost of living and questions have emerged about how well-prepared students are. Traditionally, accreditation bodies have elided the issue of quality, focusing instead on inputs and process. Accreditation reports are treated as confidential, thus not available to parents and prospective students who might benefit from learning more about institutional performance. Finally, accreditation reviews are conducted not by independent experts, but by academics, who may be reluctant to be severe critics of colleagues who, in turn, could be in a position to evaluate their academic programs.

During the latter decades of the twentieth century the issue of student performance erupted, despite costly and pervasive accreditation of higher education programs. "We are graduating fewer and fewer well-educated students, no matter what their field of study," complained two accreditation researchers.[29] The substitution of "distribution requirements" for core courses in the humanities, philosophy, the arts, and the natural sciences has resulted in an incoherent curriculum, they argued, one that invited frivolous courses and an academic climate that lacked intellectual rigor. Although students, faculty, and administrators might be complicit in this, the accrediting authority also benefited since it was sustained by the fees of member institutions and given legitimacy through state licensing laws. The indiscriminate accreditation authority, thus, stood to gain directly by accrediting new programs as well as refusing to discipline weak ones. By the end of the twentieth century the traditional accrediting format was no longer functional: "today accreditation does not necessarily ensure that a college or university provides students with a sound or well-rounded education," concluded George Leef and Roxana Burris, "The standards imposed by the accrediting associations focus on readily measured and observed inputs and processes. They do not endeavor to measure student learning, instructional quality, or academic standards."[30]

Early in the twenty-first century, even academics from the liberal arts were having misgivings about the intellectual tangents of the previous decades. "Banging the drum of relativism, celebrating the allegedly porous border between truth and fiction, and declaring that the 'meta-narrative' (by which we ourselves learned what we know) is oppressive to 'the Other,' we've pretzeled ourselves into the absurd stance that there's actually no knowledge out there that's dependable on anything—at least none, at any rate that can withstand our 'unpacking' of it," fumed professor Laurie Fendrich. "Lacking conviction, we relieved ourselves of making judgments, heating up grades that used to rate our student's performances to the point where, in many colleges and universities, A's are now handed out as if they were candy." Having dispensed with a reality that circumscribed the lives of most Americans, critics of the academy claimed an internal audit was overdue:

> With billions of dollars of government money being poured into higher education, why shouldn't taxpayers—and students—balk at bankrolling what often seems like a high-end welfare program for societal malcontents who get off on lording over students with the idea that nobody can ever really know anything for sure?[31]

The twentieth century not only posed unprecedented challenges for social work education but for the entire social welfare project as well. The nation's schools of social work became susceptible to the same forces buffeting higher education while social work as a professional enterprise struggled for public credibility.

Recession

The current economic downturn, the worst recession since the Depression, has exacerbated the fundamental challenges facing social work. President Barack Obama, who inherited the recession from Bush's presidency, quickly assembled an economic team and delivered a $787 billion stimulus package then constructed a $3.6 trillion federal budget.[32] Ominously, Obama also signaled that adjustments to social insurance programs, especially Social Security and Medicare, would be factored into his administration's economic recovery strategy.[33] Paralleling the New Deal and the War on Poverty, the Obama presidency seemed intent on introducing the next expansionary phase of the American welfare state. However social work was poorly positioned to exploit the burgeoning federal support for social programs, in large part because its public credibility had been weakened by its inferior performance, much of which could be attributed to a suboptimal professional education encrusted by stale accreditation and educational schema.

The consequences of the recession for social programs are significant. Assuming an unemployment rate of 9 percent, the Center on Budget and

Policy Priorities projected that by the end of 2009 the number of poor Americans will have increased by 7.5 to 10.3 million and that the number of children in deep poverty (with incomes below half the poverty line) would grow by 1.5 to 2.0 million.[34] Yet, social programs were not able to offer succor for the destitute. Only 37 percent of jobless Americans receive unemployment benefits, and only 40 percent of those eligible for public assistance programs actually receive benefits.[35] By the end of 2008, nineteen states had reduced Medicaid payments and were considering further cuts.[36] For the first time since its inception, welfare applications threatened to exceed the block grant appropriation for Temporary Assistance for Needy Families.[37]

In the queue that has formed as desperate institutions struggled to close a widening chasm between budget commitments and fiscal resources are automakers, followed by state governors, and university presidents. On December 16, 2008, readers of the *New York Times* and *Washington Post* found an advertisement from 40 leaders of higher education asking that 5 percent of economic stimulus ($40-45 billion) be dedicated to public colleges and universities.[38] Americans were lagging behind in higher education, the ad's sponsors announced: "The United States has fallen from first place among nations to tenth in the percentage of our population with higher education degrees ... for the first time in our history, the cohort of Americans ages 25 to 34 is less well educated than the older cohorts that preceded it."[39] The ad drew from the National Center for Public Policy and Higher Education's "Measuring Up 2008" report documenting that while the United States ranked seventh in the percent of young adults aged 18 to24 enrolled in college, it fell to fifteenth in the number who actually received a degree.[40] Other organizations concurred that the future for higher education was bleak, at least in the near future. The center for the Study of Education Policy reported that the 2008-2009 appropriation for higher education increased less than one percent more than the year prior, the smallest amount in the previous five years; the National Governors Association projected a gap of $200 billion in state higher education funding.[41] "This is the most challenging environment that any of us in higher education have seen in our lifetimes," concluded Molly Broad, President of the American Council on Education.[42] Thus, 2009 found social workers confronted with escalating poverty and social disorganization while social work education was less able to offer the best and the brightest students the professional quality education necessary to tackle the dislocations attendant with the economic crisis.

The Future of Professional Education

Social work is by no means the only profession whose training is under scrutiny. Since the publication of *A Nation at Risk* in 1983,[43] Americans have been informed regularly about the inferior performance of students. After two decades, growing indignation contributed to passage of No Child Left Behind, an attempt to make under-performing elementary schools more accountable. Concomitantly, Wendy Kopp founded Teach For America in order to train and place students from elite colleges in poor schools. By 2009 Teach For America was expecting over 35,000 applicants to fill fewer than 5,000 teaching positions.[44] As Teach For America expanded, questions about its efficacy prompted several foundations to fund a study of the performance of its instructors. During the 2001-2002 school year, Mathematica Policy Research, a private research firm, randomly assigned 2,000 students in five cities to classes taught by Teach For America instructors or traditional teachers. On average the Teach For America instructors were half as credentialed as traditional teachers, and they had considerably less classroom experience; yet, the reading scores of their students were comparable to those of traditionally trained teachers, but the math scores of Teach For America instructors were actually higher, comparable to an additional month of math instruction. The report concluded that Teach For America was a program "that can attract good teachers to schools in the most disadvantaged communities."[45] Subsequently, two Teach For America graduates, Mike Feinberg and Dave Levin, pioneered the Knowledge is Power Program, a model that has upgraded education in the most disadvantaged neighborhoods in America.[46]

Varying quality of professional education in social work is probably not unlike that in education; yet, critiques of social work education are rare. The Alliance for Children and Families critiqued the status quo by surveying social work administrators, faculty, and students *vis-à-vis* the need for community organizers among community service agencies. With respect to the vast majority of social work students pursuing clinical training, "agency directors expressed their frustration with social workers that have a commitment to helping families, but lack skills and experience with community-centered strategies."[47] As a result, family service agencies reported that "community-building jobs are now being filled by candidates from outside social work: young workers with graduate or undergraduate degrees in business, public, or human service administration, or the liberal arts."[48] Noting the disconnect between social work's historic mission and the preparation of contemporary practitioners, the report's authors wondered if social work was consigning itself to "the sidelines."[49]

While social work has obtained some professional accoutrements, such as licensure in all states and an extensive array of training institutions, it continues to struggle for credibility with the public and status among the professions. Like the modern professions, including engineering, psychology, and medicine, which based their practice on knowledge derived from science, social work too claimed to apply social science knowledge to the practical alleviation of social and personal problems. Since the Enlightenment, the modern professions have identified the application of scientifically-based knowledge as the *sine qua non* of their existence because it not only assures the public that its methods are optimal, but it also justifies the professional monopoly through state licensing that protects them from encroachments by competing disciplines. A modern profession prospers to the extent it uses optimal methods for developing knowledge, employs its most accomplished scholars to vet its knowledge base, elevates its most proficient scholars into leadership positions, all of which serves to build the educational infrastructure of the professional community. A strong profession assures graduates of solid career opportunities with respect to salaries and promotions, which in turn, serve to attract the best applicants.

The paradox of professional education in social work is that while substantial resources are invested in setting accreditation rules and licensing standards, performance remains in doubt. The lack of investigation into professional education represents a *de facto* ratification of an untenable status quo. Too often, social work education finds itself watching from the sidelines as other disciplines conduct both its traditional work in the field and its intellectual work in the academy. Instead of providing leadership in addressing the changing needs of post-industrial America, the leaders of social work and its educational institutions have become, in effect, curbside academics, watching passively as events unfold around them.

For the sake of the profession's future, the role that social work education has played in defining and replicating the profession and its potential for improving the current state of affairs requires critical review. Social work education is vital because it prepares future practitioners for the intellectual, social, and institutional roles they will play. In this book we will focus upon the crisis in social work education by reviewing its antecedents. Our analysis will examine polarities in purpose and epistemology, the inferior quality of education, and low standards of scholarship on the part of decision-makers, with the result that social work graduates are less and less able to articulate, much less carry out, the mission of social work. Social work education in the United States has become associated with confused epistemology, low standards, and inferior knowledge, maintained by a compromised accreditation establishment, which has contributed to the field's lowered status and relevance.

This review of current concerns in social work education is intended to inspire dialogue, encourage reflection, and raise questions: Will social work as we currently know it survive in the United States as a profession? Is the scholarship of decision-makers adequate for the survival and relevance of American social work? Can changes to the educational structure improve social work's relevance? In the following chapters we will explore the historical and structural dynamics in social work education as well as critique the promiscuous growth of programs and concurrent decreases in the quality of students, faculty, and professional leadership. It is our sincere desire that the analysis is understood as representing a concern for the future of this brave and noble endeavor that we know as social work.

Notes

1. Bruce Jansson, *The Reluctant Welfare State* (Belmont, CA: Wadsworth Brooks/ Cole, 2001): 22-23.
2. National Association of Social Workers (NASW) Commission on Practice, *Working Definition of Social Work Practice* (1958), 7.
3. Kathryn Cornell, "Person-In-Situation: History, Theory, and New Directions for Social Work Practice," *Praxis*, 6 (Fall, 2006): 50-57.
4. Margaret Gibelman, "The Search for Identity: Defining Social Work-Past, Present, Future," *Social Work* ,44 no.3 (1999): 308.
5. Karen Sowers and Michael Patchner, "School of Social Work Site Visit Report," (Springfield, MO: Missouri State University School of Social Work, 2007), p. 2.
6. Sowers and Patchner, p. 3.
7. Sowers and Patchner, p. 4.
8. Sowers and Patchner, p. 5.
9. Sowers and Patchner, p. 5.
10. Sowers and Patchner, p. 8.
11. Erik Vance, "President of Missouri State U. Threatens to Shut Social-Work School After Scathing Report," *Chronicle of Higher Education* (April 20, 2007), p. A17.
12. Leslie Leighninger, *Creating a New Profession* (Alexandria, VA: Council on Social Work Education, 2000), p. 87.
13. David Stoesz, *A Poverty of Imagination* (Madison, WI: University of Wisconsin Press, 2000), pp. 40-41.
14. Theda Skocpol, *Protecting Soldiers and Mothers* (Cambridge, MA: Harvard University Press, 1992).

15. Linda Gordon, *Pitied but Not Entitled* (Cambridge,MA: Harvard University Press, 1994).
16. Alvin Schorr, "The Bleak Prospect for Public Child Welfare." *Social Service Review* (March, 2000), pp. 124, 131.
17. Richard Gelles, *The Book of David.* (New York; Basic Books, 1996).
18. William Epstein, *Children Who Could Have Been.* (Madison: University of Wisconsin Press, 1999).
19. Nina Bernstein, *The Lost Children of Wilder: The Epic Struggle to Change Foster Care.* (New York: Vintage, 2001).
20. Child Welfare Workforce Task Group "The Research Is Clear: Child Welfare Workforce Issues Must Be Addressed," (Washington, D.C: Children's Defense Fund, 2006).
21. Department of Health and Human Services, Administration for Children and Families, "Summary of the Child and Family Services Reviews." (Author: Washington, D.C., 2006).
22. Peter Pecora, "Improving Family Foster Care: Findings from the Northwest Foster Care Alumni Study. (Seattle: Annie E. Casey Foundation, n.d.).
23. Fred Wulczyn, et al. *Beyond Common Sense: Child Welfare, Child Well-being, and Evidence for Policy Reform.* (New Brunswick, NJ: AldineTransaction, 2005), p. 155.
24. Elizabeth Collins, Maryann Amodeo, and Cassandra Clay, "National Evaluation of Child Welfare Training Grants," (Boston: Boston University School of Social Work, 2007).
25. Bob Lonne, et al, *Reforming Child Protection* (London: Routledge, 2009), p. 154.
26. "About CHEA;" "Recognized Accrediting Organizations," (Washington, DC: Council on Higher Education Accreditation, 2009).
27. Anne Neal, "Dis-Accreditation," *Academic Questions*, vol. 21, no. 4 (Fall 2008).
28. Amit Paley, "Student Loan Overhaul Advances," *Washington Post* (June 21, 2007): A1.
29. George Leef and Roxana Burris, "Can College Accreditation Live Up to its Promise?" (Washington, DC: American Council of Trustees and Alumni, 2003): 17.
30. George Leef and Roxana Burris, "Can College Accreditation Live Up to its Promise?" (Washington, DC: American Council of Trustees and Alumni, 2003): 49.
31. Laurie Fendrich, "A Pedagogical Straitjacket," *Chronicle of Higher Education* (June 8, 2007): B7.
32. Lori Montgomery, "In $3.6 Trillion Budget, Obama Signals Broad Shift in Priorities," *Washington Post* (February 27, 2009), p. A1.
33. Jeff Zeleny and John Harwood, "Obama Promises Bid to Overhaul Retiree Spending," *New York Times* (January 8, 2009), p. A1.
34. Sharon Parrott, "Recession Could Cause Large Increases in Poverty and Push Millions Into Deep Poverty," (Washington, DC: November 24, 2008), p. 1.
35. Seven Greenhouse, "Will the Safety Net Catch the Economy's Casualties?" *New York Times* (November 16, 2008), p. WK3.
36. Amy Goldstein, "States Cut Medicaid Coverage Further," *Washington Post* (December 26, 2008), p. A1.
37. Amy Goldstein, "Welfare Rolls See First Climb in Years," *Washington Post* (December 17, 2008), p. A1.
38. Valerie Strauss, "Higher-Education Leaders Press Congress for Chunk of Stimulus Funds," *Washington Post* (December 16, 2008), p.A17.

39. Vartan Gregorian, Thomas Kean, Richard Riley, "Higher Education Investment Act," *Washington Post* (December 16, 2008), pp. A8-A9.

40. "Measuring Up 2008" (San Jose, CA: National Center for Public Policy and Higher Education, 2008), p. 6.

41. Eric Kelderman, "Colleges See Slowest Growth in State Aid in 5 Years," *Chronicle of Higher Education* (January 16, 2009), p. 1.

42. Susan Kinzie, "Market Losses Tighten Screws on Colleges," *Washington Post* (January 27, 2009), p. A7.

43. National Commission on Excellence in Education, *A Nation at Risk* (Washington, DC: author, 1983).

44. Megan Greenwell, "Applicants Flock to Teacher Corps for Needy Areas, " *Washington Post* (December 6, 2008), p. A1.

45. Paul Decker, Daniel Mayer, and Steven Glazerman, "The Effects of Teach for America on Students," (Princeton, NJ: Mathematica, 2004), pp. xi-xvi.

46. Jay Mathews, *Work Hard, Be Nice* (New York: Algonquin Paperbacks, 2009).

47. Wendy Jacobson and William Ryan, "Aligning Education and Practice: Challenges and Opportunities in Social Work Education for Community-Centered Practice," (Milwaukee: Alliance for Children and Families, 2000): 6.

48. Jacobson and Ryan, 14.

49. Jacobson and Ryan, 9.

2

Legacy Lost

The promise of social work education has been unfulfilled primarily because of the profession's inability to reconcile the tension between empirical methods and normative theory, exacerbated by lack of internal coherence within a dynamic society. In the United States social work emerged as an identifiable profession in the late nineteenth century, a period in which competing visions of human perfection proliferated. Proponents of natural rights drew from the abolitionist movement and fought for equality for African Americans and later for women. Religious and ethical motives offered not only the promise of achieving a perfectible world, but a vision of the common good.[1] The period was an epoch of moral crusades, often theologically inspired. The social gospel movement, a powerful driver for many reformers, encouraged the middle class to improve the lot of the poor and disempowered and provide them with skills, education and resources to help themselves. In 1910, the Presbyterian Church declared, "The great ends of the church are the proclamation of the gospel for the salvation of humankind; the shelter, nurture, and spiritual fellowship of the children of God; the maintenance of divine worship; the preservation of truth; the promotion of social righteousness; and the exhibition of the Kingdom of Heaven to the world."[2] There was an underlying sense that people could and would help themselves, and an assumption that the millennium could not come until the world had been perfected.

Other reformers drew their inspiration from the Enlightenment, arguing that the application of scientific methods could rid industrial society of extensive misery. The eradication of contagious disease, through early public health measures, reinforced a belief that other social problems could be overcome through science. In the United States, the Progressive Era, following the Civil War, demonstrated how social engineering could advance the public welfare by eliminating corruption in government, implementing essential services for the public including education, health, and charity, and building a university-based network of professional education. Social work and its professional schools were direct descendents of the Progressive promise.

To be sure, critics of progressive social reform held a different perspective. Social Darwinists argued that those who could not or would not help themselves were inferior and should be cast aside since there would be no place for them in a competitive capitalist economy.[3] A powerful negative narrative emerged regarding the poor, the vulnerable, and the excluded, which placed responsibility for their sufferings on their own shortcomings. Early twentieth century social crusaders convinced of the perfectibility of people and society, thus opposed this caricature of the socially vulnerable, and engaged with issues of poverty and injustice by employing the best methods of the social sciences of the times.

Through the protean brew accompanying late industrial capitalism, American social work came to be associated with the application of a variety of activities aimed towards improving social conditions, reducing injustice, and helping individuals to adapt better to their social contexts. Using data obtained primarily through interviews and early survey methodology, social activists were able to demonstrate on both economic and moral grounds, that a variety of social conditions could be positively addressed. Thus were born regulatory reforms such as housing codes, licensing laws for professional practice, and controls over working hours for women and children, at local and national levels.[4] These early reformers wedded pragmatism, social research, and a moral imperative into a powerful movement, Progressivism. Social work as a defined field of interest emerged as efforts to formalize, develop standards, and share methods grew among the reformers. At the same time, divergent forces impeded the ability of the new profession to develop a consensus. A series of disagreements served to confound social work's emergence as a unified field, and these disagreements carried over and compromised professional education: the superiority of individually focused casework versus reform, empirical methods versus experience as a basis for knowledge, and undergraduate versus graduate education. The inability of educators to resolve these problems would impair social work's ability to establish itself as a profession.

The Professions Emerge

Modern professions evolved during the Progressive Era, a time of pragmatism and optimism about the uses of the scientific method to improve the human condition. The key components of a profession included: philosophy, theory, research, and their practical application. As the modern professions emerged, so too did an educational structure designed to replicate and expand the necessary knowledge of practitioners. Importantly, competing European visions shaped professional education in the United States: a British model emphasizing the humanities versus a German model which focused on research.[5] These differences became institutionalized through undergraduate education being based on the English tradition, and graduate training based on the German regime, although inelegantly. "At American universities, the undergraduate college remained essentially a descendant of the Oxbridge college,[6] while the graduate schools emerged as a superstructure of German faculties or departments that were added to the undergraduate college," concluded William Clark. "After the 1870s, the new graduate schools cultivated research, while the college had a traditional pedagogical mission."[7] Although England lagged behind Germany's experiment in social welfare under Bismarck, the employment of social empiricism to evolve a social infrastructure was readily evident. "The 1830s, indeed, was the decade in which the foundation of the modern [British] state were laid," noted Richard Reeves, "investigating, rationalizing, regulating, inspecting, democratizing and secularizing—had been firmly established before the decade was out."[8]

The founding of Johns Hopkins University in 1876 imported the German research model into American graduate education, which was soon adopted by the University of Chicago, Harvard University, and Columbia University in the 1880s.[9] Professional associations in America soon followed.

American Historical Society	1884
American Economic Association	1885
American Mathematical Society	1890
American Psychological Association	1892
American Philosophical Association	1901
American Sociological Society	1905
American Political Science Association	1906

How to put science to social benefit was a primary concern within the new professional associations. Proponents of the professions debated fundamental issues, such as universal versus idiosyncratic strategies of reform, and the value of quantitative data versus direct experience as a basis for improving the plight of the destitute.

Central to these discussions was Franklin Benjamin Sanborn, a Unitarian social reformer. A founder of the American Social Science Association (ASSA) immediately after the Civil War, Sanborn also edited its journal from 1867 to 1897. As the ASSA expanded, Sanborn proposed to Daniel Coit Gilman, an ASSA member and President of Johns Hopkins University, that it be incorporated into Johns Hopkins as a complement to courses in "social ethics and applied anthropology."[10] But Gilman demurred preferring to develop academic departments in the social sciences. Sanborn's appreciation of social surveys to document need, a method that was congruent with the preoccupation of the emergent social sciences with measurement, would distinguish several premier schools of social administration at the University of Chicago, the University of Wisconsin, and the University of Michigan, which continued a strong emphasis in social scientific methods. Eventually, the ASSA morphed into the National Conference of Charity and Corrections, which Sanborn had also founded, a precursor of the National Conference of Social Welfare.[11]

From its inception, social work grafted poorly onto the stalk of American higher education. Evolution of the 1898 summer program of the New York School to an eight-month curriculum at Columbia University as well as other emergent social work schools illustrated the difficulty. Under the influence of Mary Richmond, Charity Organization Societies (COS) had established casework as the primary method of social work and their growth dictated much of the emergent labor market in human services. The COSs preferred an apprenticeship model of education whereby students acquired necessary skills by working alongside skilled workers. Thus, the COS model of training was fundamentally vocational. In contrast, social reformers, such as Edith Abbott and Sophonisba Breck-inridge, who had leveraged legislation and become program administrators, understood that an industrial society required research in order to establish and expand social programs. The social administration model of education was perforce professional. Roy Lubove described how the fissure between apprenticeship and professional education confused an incipient, educational movement.

> An uneasy alliance between academician and practitioner ... blurred the goals and objectives of social work education. Both groups agreed upon the superiority of school to apprenticeship training, and both agreed that a social work curriculum had

to combine the academic and the practical, but social workers placed greater weight upon field work and the vocational goals of training.[12]

Casework might well have merged with social administration to develop a truly social profession in America, but European influences intruded. Before World War I, COSs had become ubiquitous in American cities, and the work of "friendly visitors" sufficiently extensive to prompt Mary Richmond to write *Social Diagnosis*, an exhaustive inventory of the systemic problems encountered by COS clients.[13] American intellectuals, however, were captivated by the psychoanalytic approach developed by Sigmund Freud and his followers. Because Freudian and related methods were predicated on the unconscious, they defied empirical substantiation. As social workers embraced psychoanalytic methods, the prospect of an empirically verifiable practice technique became increasingly remote. Additionally, Freudian approaches emphasized individual functioning, leaving the social context and larger social justice concerns out of the elaborate studies of human behavior they claimed to offer. Later formulations, such as constructivism and postmodernism, would actually denigrate empiricism, further impeding the development of verifiable methods of professional practice.

The Flexner Report

The nation's social casework agencies organized the National Conference of Charity and Corrections in 1874 in order to attend to "the more practical organizational issues" that they faced.[14] TheConference had drifted from the orbit of the professional associations of the day, which were affiliated with university graduate research programs, and came under the influence of agencies. Acutely aware of this, in 1915 the Conference invited Abraham Flexner to speak on social work's professional status. A graduate of Johns Hopkins University, Flexner had conducted an investigation, published in 1910, for the American Medical Association of the quality of medical education. Educated in the German research tradition, Flexner advocated culling those medical schools which were vocational in focus; subsequently, by 1915 the number of medical schools in the United States had fallen from 131 to 95, although this was not a steep enough reduction for Flexner who concluded that only 31 actually met scientifically-based standards of medical education.[15]

In light of Flexner's earlier proposal that medical education be sharply attenuated, his comments about the professional status of social work were decidedly diplomatic. Flexner's synopsis of what constitutes a profession remains relevant:

professions involve essentially intellectual operations with large individual responsibility; they derive their raw material from science and learning; this material they
work up to a practical and definite end; they possess an educationally communicable
technique; they tend to self-organization; they are becoming increasingly altruistic
in motivation.[16]

To what extent did early twentieth-century social work comply with
these requirements? According to Flexner, not particularly well. Much
of social work, he mused, appeared to involve routine activity, and much
of the activity seemed not to originate in social work but with other
disciplines. Much of social work's knowledge was derivative. Social
work, Flexner suspected, "appears not so much a definite field as an
aspect of work in many fields."[17] Ever the academic diplomat he asked,
"Would it not be at least suggestive therefore to view social work as in
touch with many professions rather than a profession in and by itself?"[18]
Even then, the quality of professional education was suspect. Instead of
rigorous study of various aspects of professional practice, "the education
is not technically professional so much as broadly cultural in a variety
of realms of civic and social interest."[19] Compounding these problems,
were the low wages that typified agency work. In Chapter 7 we will examine the impact of social work's developmental links to volunteerism,
its essentially nurturing mission, and its connection to the greater good
as contributing factors to the depressed wages and relatively low status
of the profession.

Flexner likened social work to journalism:

a profession needs ... a form of expression and record that is scientific rather than
journalistic in character. The newspapers, the weekly and monthly periodicals, more
or less serve social work as far as journalistic publicity is concerned. But while it is
doubtless still advisable to concentrate this material in journals expressly devoted to
social work for news-propaganda and agitation, it is important to remember that we
[i.e. professions] do thus rise above the journalistic to the scientific and professional
level.[20]

If social work was not a profession in the same sense of medicine
or engineering, Flexner concluded that it was like journalism. Just as
journalists relay the news generated by others, social work facilitated
the knowledge produced by other disciplines. Instead of developing a
unique and irreplaceable body of knowledge, social work behaved like
an acquisitive occupation, borrowing knowledge from others. The result
may have been a fragrant stew but it hardly qualified as a distinctive
cuisine. To what must have been an audience poignantly disappointed by
his remarks, Flexner offered a tactful bit of advice: "To some extent the
evolution of social work towards the professional status can be measured

by *the quality of publication put forth in its name.*"[21] Flexner suggested that regardless of social work's derivative nature, it could elevate its status by cultivating a professional literature, an empirically-based approach to integrating a variety of social science theories and research traditions, becoming in effect *applied social science.*

Despite Flexner's discouraging observations about social work's status, his audience drew some consolation from the realization that the new discipline had gained momentum during the Progressive Era. Social workers were developing an identity that led them to organize to promote their interests. In rapid succession, professional groups emerged replicating the academic associations earlier in the Progressive Era.

American Association of Medical Social Workers	1918
National Association of School Social Workers	1919
American Association of Social Workers	1921
American Association of Psychiatric Social Workers	1926

Paralleling expanding employment opportunities, the number of schools of social work grew from 15 to 40 between 1915 and 1930.[22]

The demand for expertise to ameliorate social problems associated with urbanization, immigration, and industrialization transformed colleges and universities from tidy institutions which had trained clergy according to the classic texts of philosophy, Latin and Greek, and theology, to the engines of social betterment, spawning graduate programs in education, public health, urban planning, and social work. Philosophical pragmatism wedded to the scientific method proved a powerful combination in charting the nation's course through the latter part of its industrial revolution, and the professions benefited accordingly. In attracting altruistically motivated students, graduate education not only promised professional status and upward mobility, but it offered professionals the opportunity to contribute to social progress. "Pragmatists join action and thought," proclaimed John Dewey with uncharacteristic brevity. [23]

Subsequently, social work attracted legions of young, forward thinking progressives. The field incorporated a wide array of activities and social reform efforts—the Charity Organization Society, Settlement House, and juvenile court movements. The emerging profession offered the promise of applying current methods of data collection and analysis to ameliorate the critical problems associated with rapid expansion of manufacturing attendant with industrialization, massive waves of immigration, and a flood of people from rural communities to cities. Urban squalor, rural isolation, class division, immigrant illiteracy, family stress, and extensive poverty provided daunting challenges, as did public corruption on the scale of Tammany Hall. At the same time, a modernizing society carried the potential and promise of the financial resources and innovative ideas to overcome these problems.

Pioneering leaders like Jane Addams and Mary Richmond provided role models and guidance to the cadres of idealistic, reform-minded social workers. In her best-selling memoir, *Twenty Years at Hull House,* Jane Addams served to instruct and inspire. Among the supporters of the Hull House project were leaders like John Dewey, who introduced pragmatism, a philosophy that provided intellectual support for the systematic application of research findings to resolve social problems. In *Social Diagnosis*, Mary Richmond presented an exhaustive taxonomy for virtually every social affliction. While Addams and Richmond differed in their approaches, they both subscribed to a systematic collection of data on human suffering through methods such as social surveys, using the findings to demonstrate the magnitude of problems and offer programmatic suggestions to law-makers. Programs such as state "widow's pensions" attested to the political savvy that progressive reformers had attained. As a result of the progressive's effective use of information prominent Republicans, such as Governor of Wisconsin Robert La Follette and President "Teddy" Roosevelt were enthusiastic boosters of government as an engine for social progress.

By integrating pragmatism, empiricism, and compassion, social work promised to not only provide a balm for the hard-pressed but also a rigorous philosophy of generosity. Social work was thus more than a job; it was part of a greater social project. For young Progressives, the future was redolent with opportunity, providing an auspicious context for employing effective methods to enhance social welfare. These ambitious reformers, while motivated by lofty ideals, were able to avoid the marginality of utopianism by maintaining a focus on effective and pragmatic social change. In "The Second Coming," William Butler Yeats had voiced his apprehensions about the enthusiasms of the time, so evident with the rise of Communism and Fascism in the aftermath of World War I. "The ceremony of innocence is drowned;" he wrote, "The best lack all conviction, while the worst are full of passionate intensity." In this respect, the humanistic empiricism proposed by social work seemed to be the ideal antidote to the excesses of the emerging totalitarian ideologies.

Confounding Social Work Education

Despite the unprecedented opportunities of the Progressive Era, educators were unable to develop a unified educational strategy that would position the newborn profession to exploit these opportunities. In 1919 seventeen training programs representing private agencies formed the Association of Training Schools for Professional Social Work, later renamed the American Association of Schools of Social Work (AASSW). During the 1920s AASSW "moved aggressively toward limiting formal accreditation to two-year graduate professional education programs."[24] Despite the German research model that had been imported by professional schools in the United States, social work continued to be defined by casework and the staffing needs of private agencies. The vocational nature of casework training clashed with the research priorities of university-based academicians. The popularization of psychoanalysis, evident in the creation of a psychiatric social work training program at Smith College in 1918, further fragmented professional education. Acknowledging that intra-psychic practice *sui generis* dealt with matters that could not be demonstrated empirically, proponents of psychoanalysis depicted their practice as an art. Paradoxically, psychoanalysis reinforced the vocational nature of social work education; as an art, it could only be learned by a lengthy apprenticeship.

Within a decade of Flexner's assessment leaders from six national welfare organizations tried to resolve issues of professional education, later published as "the Milford Conference Report." In attempting to reconcile competing visions of social work, the report awkwardly straddled a philosophical fence ultimately subsuming science to art:

> Nowhere does the fact that social casework is an art appear more clearly than in treatment. Here there is the blending of scientific knowledge, training and experience as in the finished picture. Here, too, the vision of the artist is made an actuality through his ability to combine in effective use—not only with skill but with genius—the separate units of his knowledge. But the social case worker has no passive canvas on which to paint his picture. The client himself must be a participant in the art of social casework.[25]

The Report also addressed issues related to professional education. Ultimately, social work education was lodged within the casework agency as apprenticeship training, the efforts of which would be enhanced by the evolving schools of social work.

> We make our recommendations for the development of apprentice training without reservations. Nevertheless, we believe that the only sound ultimate development

must be the organization of professional education in schools of social work. Such schools must always be allied with agencies for social case work in order to provide the field training which we believe to be indispensable. We look forward, therefore, to a system of professional education under the schools of social work but in alliance with agencies for social case work, the two having co-operative responsibility for one program for professional education and sharing the same educational objectives and standards.[26]

The favoring of casework that had evolved under the auspices of private agencies was not well received by Progressives who had larger ambitions and were more likely to see the value of data collection and systematic research into best practices. To the chagrin of activists who had organized the New Deal in response to the Depression, social work education was failing to address the demands of new, federal social programs: first, schools of social work were located in cities while much need was rural; second, many more graduates were needed than those being trained. Because social work education, as managed through the AASSW, was inadequate for the staffing requirements of government programs authorized under the Social Security Act of 1935, other disciplines began training workers and managers in public welfare. In 1942, the National Association of Schools of Social Administration (NASSA) was created by eleven representatives of disciplines outside of social work. The work of NASSA was in part motivated by actions taken by AASW and its members. AASSW had restricted membership to graduate education in social work, while NASSA supported undergraduate education. Moreover, as a vestige of the COS antipathy toward public assistance, the AASSW looked askance at the new federal welfare programs, while the NASSA embraced them as an essential public function.[27] With respect to social change, the *sine qua non* of Progressivism, the NASSA saw itself as charting the future, while the AASSW represented the past.

Social work's attempt to establish itself meant that it would forsake more radical options; thus, social work education as presented by AASSW was decidedly more institutionally conservative than that promoted by NASSA.[28] Ultimately, social work would conform to market dictates on professional development. "Social work in the 1930s and 1940s devoted itself almost single-mindedly to maintaining and extending its professional enterprise," concluded Stanley Wenocur and Michael Reisch. "Even as it advocated a public interest, it shaped its public concerns to fit its self interest."[29] The definition of professional activity was narrowed to the level of individual therapy, resulting in an emphasis on the primary role of the social worker as therapist and placing the social reform role in a secondary position.

A fault line ran between AASSW and NASSA along all aspects of professional education. AASSW's members were graduate programs in private, urban universities and had a historic aversion to public assistance. By contrast, NASSA's members were undergraduate programs in public, rural universities and were committed to public welfare. AASSW represented an elitist old guard, while NASSA symbolized a democratic future. Eventually, AASSW's hegemony in social work education was challenged in 1943 when the Association of Land-Grant Colleges and Universities and the National Association of State Universities recognized NASSA as an accreditation organization for social work programs.

Leaders in social work education realized the continuing fissure between AASSW and NASSA could sabotage professional education, so they proposed merging the organizations. In anticipation of the merger of AASSW and NASSA, an interim organization, the National Council on Social Work Education, commissioned a study to examine the status of professional education. Significantly, the study, under the direction of Ernest Hollis from the U.S. Office of Education, and his assistant, Alice Taylor Davis, a social worker from the Bureau of Public Assistance, called for a rigorous labor market study of social workers and asked talented teachers to bridge the chasm between undergraduate and professional education. While the Hollis-Taylor Report served to bridge the distance between AASSW and NASSA, it provided few details through which to resolve the issues that had animated the members of the competing organizations. The Report sparked conflict by questioning social work's focus on casework, its weak conceptual development, and the limited development of research. Notably, the statistical analysis of labor market needs for social workers was never conducted.[30]

Eventually, differences between AASSW and NASSA would be covered over by the creation of the Council of Social Work Education (CSWE) in 1952. But, two contrary themes persisted: "the academic social science model and the practitioner-apprentice training model—that is, between social work education as an 'academic discipline' and as 'professional training'."[31] Vestiges of the dispute have continued to color professional education in subsequent decades. The historical evolution of graduate schools at prominent universities as training programs further compounded the problem. As other social science disciplines embraced the German research agenda in graduate professional education, American social work education was not only invested in an apprenticeship, vocational model, but its enthusiasm for psychoanalysis subverted the prospect of empirically-based practice.

Accreditation

The new Council on Social Work Education was responsible for overseeing professional education at all levels. Initially consisting of 59 graduate and 19 undergraduate programs as well as seven practice organizations and 18 agencies, CSWE represented the interests of a broad spectrum of stakeholders.[32] Yet, the absence of specifics about what would constitute sufficiently rigorous professional preparation clouded its accreditation function. A decade after its creation, a CSWE board committee undertook an extensive review of its activities, which was later accepted by the full board. The first three objectives of the report reflected concern about the quality of professional education:

> To improve the quality of social work education.
> To expand resources for social work education of high quality.
> To increase the number of people of high quality interested in social work careers.

Katharine Kendall summarized the committee's concerns: "What emerged clearly from this review and acceptance of a new statement of functions and priorities was a call for quality along with quantity, more and better social workers, excellence with expansion."[33]

Yet, accreditation of new programs continued apace, despite the board's concern about the quality of professional education, reflecting early on the primacy of expansion over quality. Shortly before the report was finalized, the number of graduate and undergraduate social work programs had already swollen to 115, an increase of 49 percent within the decade.[34] Such expansion during a period when the quality of professional education was being questioned highlighted the importance of accreditation. One of the external members of CSWE's new Accreditation Council was Ewald Nyquist, an education official in New York State and chair of the Commission on Institutions of Higher Education for the Middle States Association of Colleges and Secondary Schools, one of the six primary accrediting organizations in the United States. In 1970 after ten years of service on CSWE's Accreditation Council, Nyquist was less than sanguine about the quality of professional education. He concluded that the "first phase [of accreditation] placed emphasis more on the letter than the full spirit of qualitative standards and has concerned itself largely with the maintenance of minimal standards and the establishment of an accredited list [of programs]." Nyquist proposed a second phase of accreditation, conceding that its introduction would be discomfiting: "Part of the pain in making the transition may be a low level of expectations, an occupational hazard of social work, a lack of familiarity with the real function of accrediting, or a combination thereof." He doubted that accreditation could be upgraded if the function were the province of practitioners as opposed to the most accomplished social work academics.[35]

Nyquist's concerns notwithstanding, the War on Poverty of the 1960s had expanded the American welfare state, providing new opportunities for social workers in the public sector as well as those working for nonprofit contract agencies. As it had during the New Deal, the demand for social workers in public social programs increased dramatically. Subsequently, in 1974 CSWE authorized the accreditation of undergraduate social work programs, a decision that would result in the accreditation of more than four hundred undergraduate social work programs within the next three decades. Once established, the number of undergraduate programs continued to increase. As the number of accredited undergraduate programs accelerated, a burgeoning number of BSWs sought to bolster their credentials and incomes by earning Master of Social Work (MSW) degrees. As more BSWs were graduated, difficulty in discerning the difference between undergraduate and graduate degrees became an issue. CSWE addressed to this by insisting that graduate programs give credit for those students with undergraduate preparation in social work, further blurring the distinctions between graduate and undergraduate education.

The skyrocketing number of undergraduate programs increased the demand for faculty to teach in them, propelling the growth doctoral programs. Between 1986 and 2001 the number of graduate social work programs increased 70 percent, and the number of those offering doctorates 28 percent.[36] Yet, CSWE had opted not to accredit doctoral programs, leaving it the responsibility of the institutions electing to mount them. In reviewing her lengthy experience in social work education including having been Executive Director of CSWE, Katharine Kendall specifically targeted doctoral education as a problematic feature of professional education.

> Research competence was expected of all doctoral students, but again there were problems in how to achieve that objective. The schools had to cope with inadequacies in the previous research preparation of many of the doctoral students and few of the faculty were themselves engaged in research endeavors of their own.[37]

Having focused on the accreditation of graduate and later undergraduate programs, CSWE had evaded any responsibility for doctoral education, the incubator through which the modern professions prepared new generators of knowledge. Not only was doctoral education of irregular quality, it also flew under CSWE's radar. Even then, the number of social work doctorates failed to keep pace with expanding undergraduate social work education and subsequent demand for faculty.

Unrestrained expansion of social work programs would continue to raise concerns, especially about the quality of professional education:

> the rapid growth in the number of social work degree programs is having a profound impact on the academic quality of many students admitted into social work programs, the quality of instruction, the readiness of graduates to contribute to the profession, salaries for social work graduates, and the overall future of social work practice and education.[38]

Regardless, CSWE continued its unchecked accreditation of social work programs. The result was of direct benefit to CSWE since much of its revenues were derived from fees paid by social work programs it had accredited. In this respect, CSWE was not unlike any enterprising venture exploiting a virgin market: opportunism was a virtue because it resulted in organizational growth. After its first two decades Kendall admitted that CSWE had behaved in the best tradition of American commerce: "with its very large staff the Council had all the earmarks of a departmentalized company."[39]

The Quality of Social Work Education

As CSWE has been reluctant to develop measures of the quality of professional education, others have addressed the omission.[40] Primary among these has been *U.S. News & World Report*, which began publishing an annual ranking of institutions of higher education, including professional schools, among them schools of social work. Relying on a technique that sampled the reputation of social work programs, the business magazine ranked the nation's schools of social work. A *USN&WR* questionnaire simply asked deans, administrators, and selected faculty to evaluate accredited programs on a five-point Likert scale. Although the survey was not without controversy, schools of social work which were ranked highly by social work peers put their notoriety to good effect, using it to advertise their standing. The most recent ranking can be found in Table 1.

Questioning the validity of a reputational method for ranking schools of social work, researchers sought other criteria. One solution was to use journal publications, an approach facilitated by the data collected through the Social Sciences Citation Index (SSCI). Subsequently, SSCI analysis of faculty publications for purposes of ranking schools of social work became a cottage industry. The method was not without its detractors who

Table 1
Ranking of schools of social work by
U.S. News & World Report, 2009

Rank	School	Score
1	Washington University, St. Louis	4.6
2	University of Michigan	4.5
3	University of Chicago	4.3
4	Columbia University	4.2
4	University of Washington	4.2
6	University of California-Berkeley	4.1
6	University of Texas-Austin	4.1
8	University of North Carolina-Chapel Hill	3.9
8	University of Southern California	3.9
10	Case Western Reserve University	3.8
10	University of California-Los Angeles	3.8
12	University of Wisconsin-Madison	3.7
14	Boston College	3.6
14	University of Pennsylvania	3.6
14	University of Pittsburgh	3.6
14	Virginia Commonwealth University	3.6
18	Fordham University	3.5
18	University of Illinois-Urbana/Champaign	3.5
18	University of Kansas	3.5
18	University of Maryland-Baltimore	3.5
22	Boston University	3.4
22	New York University	3.4
22	Smith College	3.4
22	University of Illinois-Chicago	3.4
26	CUNY-Hunter College	3.3
26	Indiana University	3.3
26	University of Minnesota-Twin Cities	3.3
26	University of Tennessee-Knoxville	3.3
30	Bryn Mawr College	3.2
30	Florida State University	3.2
30	Michigan State University	3.2
30	Ohio State University	3.2
30	Rutgers University-New Brunswick	3.2
30	University of Georgia	3.2
36	Portland State University	3.1
36	Simmons College	3.1
36	University at Buffalo-SUNY	3.1
36	University of Denver	3.1
36	University of Houston	3.1
36	University of Kentucky	3.1
42	Arizona State University	3.0
42	Howard University	3.0
42	Loyola University Chicago	3.0
42	San Diego State University	3.0

Table 1 (cont.)

42	St. Louis University	3.0
42	University of Alabama	3.0
42	University of Connecticut	3.0
42	University of Louisville	3.0
42	University of Texas-Arlington	3.0
42	University of Wisconsin-Milwaukee	3.0
42	Yeshiva University	3.0
53	Adelphi University	2.9
53	Catholic University of America	2.9
53	College of St. Catherine/University of St. Thomas	2.9
53	Tulane University	2.9
53	University of South Carolina-Columbia	2.9
53	University of Utah	2.9
53	Wayne State University	2.9
60	Baylor University	2.8
60	California State University-Long Beach	2.8
60	California State University-Los Angeles	2.8
60	Colorado State University	2.8
60	Syracuse University	2.8
60	University of Hawaii-Manoa	2.8
60	University of Iowa	2.8
67	California State University-Sacramento	2.7
67	San Francisco State University	2.7
67	University of Vermont	2.7
71	Barry University	2.6
71	Georgia State University	2.6
71	Louisiana State University	2.6
71	Ohio University	2.6
71	SUNY-Stony Brook	2.6
71	San Jose State University	2.6
71	Temple University	2.6
71	University of Missouri-Columbia	2.6
71	University of South Florida	2.6
71	Western Michigan University	2.6
82	Brigham Young University-Provo	2.5
82	Eastern Washington University	2.5
82	George Mason University	2.5
82	Monmouth University	2.5
82	Rhode Island College	2.5
82	Southern Illinois University-Carbondale	2.5
82	University of Arkansas-Little Rock	2.5
82	University of Maine-Orono	2.5
82	University of Minnesota-Duluth	2.5
82	University of Missouri-St. Louis	2.5
82	University of Montana	2.5
82	University of North Carolina-Charlotte	2.5
82	West Virginia University	2.5

Source: http://grad-schools.usnews.rankingsandreviews.com/grad/sow/search/

noted that a single variable hardly captured the entirety of professional education: publications captured by the SSCI omitted other scholarship, such as monographs, books, journals not captured by the Web-of-Science, and government reports. Nor did SSCI analysis incorporate grant-funded research. Regardless, it was a convenient metric, readily available. Publication of articles in the refereed literature had become not only the primary method for exchange of ideas among disciplines, but it was also used as criteria for evaluating the scholarship of faculty for purposes of promotion and tenure. Table 2 compares the rankings received in the *USN&WR* with a ranking based on faculty publication rates over the same period.

The relationship between reputational rankings and rankings based on publications was further explored in a survey of social work deans, faculty, and graduates according to three objective criteria: admissions selectivity, faculty publications, and program longevity. The admissions selectivity of doctoral programs, the length of time that graduate programs had been extant, and faculty scholarship productivity were consistent with *USN&WR* rankings.[41] Both reputational and refereed-publication studies suggested a ranking of schools into tiers, but such lists are inherently limited. Noting the value of multiple factors in ranking educational programs, Ronald Feldman suggested a more comprehensive inventory of factors, including federal research funding as well as scholarly awards and prizes.[42]

Rankings of schools of social work have evolved largely because CSWE has failed to identify valid indicators of program performance. After a half-century of regulation of social work education, the nation's only accreditation authority, CSWE has neglected to publish data through which to determine the quality of professional education. Extant data reveal that there is significant variation in the perceptions of administrators about schools of social work as well as the productivity of their faculties.

Progressive Education for the Twenty-First Century

By 2004, CSWE had accredited 459 BSW and 182 MSW programs. In the same year more than 70 doctoral programs in social work had been mounted independently of CSWE; social work education employed 6,857 faculty and graduated 9,889 BSWs and 15,473 MSWs. Aside from unrelenting expansion, social work education resembled less and less the priorities that had so animated young altruists of the Progressive Era. While critical thinking was encouraged in professional education,

Table 2

Reputational Scores of Schools of social Work Compared to Scholarship Scores*

UNIVERSITY OR COLLEGE	Ranking Based on Publications (2000-2004)		Us News & World Report Reputational Ranking (average 1997 and 2000)
	RANK	MEAN ARTICLES/ YEAR	RANK
Columbia University	1	30.00	4
University of Michigan	2	27.40	1
Washington University	3	23.20	2
University of Washington	4	21.20	6
University of North Carolina	5	19.60	7
University of Pennsylvania	6	16.20	14
University of Tennessee	7	15.60	27
University of California at Berkeley	8	15.00	3
University of Illinois–Urbana	9	14.80	23
University of Southern California	10	14.00	7
Boston University	11	13.40	18
State University of New York-Albany	12	13.20	20
Case Western University	13	12.80	--(not listed)
University of Maryland	14	12.40	23
University of Texas at Austin	15	12.00	9
Rutgers University	15	12.00	34
New York University	17	11.80	30
Fordham University	18	10.80	11
University of Chicago	19	10.40	5
Florida State University	20	10.00	26
University of Illinois–Chicago	20	10.00	25
UCLA	23	9.80	12
Virginia Commonwealth University	23	9.80	16
Yeshiva University	24	9.40	40
University of Kansas	24	8.80	20
University of Wisconsin–Madison	26	8.60	9
University of Minnesota	26	8.60	--(not listed)
Ohio State University	28	8.20	32
University of Iowa	30	8.00	45
Smith College	30	8.00	15
University of Pittsburgh	31	7.80	16
Boston College	32	6.80	18
City University of New York-Hunter	33	6.60	--(not listed)
Arizona State University	34	6.40	55

Table 2 (cont.)

University of Indiana	36	6.20	--(not listed)
University of Georgia	36	6.20	45
University of Kentucky	37	6.00	--(not listed)
State University of New York-Buffalo	38	5.40	32
University of South Carolina	39	5.00	--(not listed)
University of Connecticut	40	4.60	52
University of Texas at Arlington	40	4.60	49
Bryn Mawr College	42	4.20	20
University of Houston	42	4.20	55
Loyola University	43	3.40	41
Simmons College	43	3.40	32
Michigan State University	45	3.20	41
Portland State University	45	3.20	31
University of Denver	47	2.80	50
Catholic University	48	1.60	39
Howard University	49	1.20	37
TulaneUniversity	50	1.00	41

Sources: Ronald Feldman, "Reputations, Rankings, and Realities of Social Work Schools," *Journal of Social Work Education*, 42, 3 (Fall): 493-94; Robert Green and Frank Baskind, "The Second Decade of the Faculty Publication Project," *Journal of social Work Education* 43, 2 (Spring-Summer):288-89.

Note: some schools are tied so there may be more than one school at a given rank level.

with few exceptions, little of it was directed at social work and virtually none at professional education. Stanley Wenocur and Michael Reisch provided an historical explanation why social reform had given way to commercial interests in social work. Harry Specht and Mark Courtney concurred "Social work has abandoned its mission to help the poor and oppressed and to build communality," they contended. "Instead, many social workers are devoting their energies and talents to careers in psychotherapy: A significant proportion of social work professionals—about 40 percent—are in private practice serving middle-class clients."[43]

Ultimately, social work was a profession that emerged during the Progressive Era, capitalizing on the notion that experts could be trained to apply the scientific method to ameliorate social problems, thereby enhancing public well-being. The social welfare project, as it evolved with the American welfare state, was to demonstrate how empiricism wedded to pragmatism could mitigate suffering, expand potential, and extend compassion to distressed Americans. The success of that venture has been borne out by the expansion of public social programs complemented by an extensive network of nonprofit agencies. Yet, social work has failed to fully exploit these most propitious circumstances. Much of that can be attributed to the expansion of accredited social work programs far beyond the requisites for professional education. The reach of social work education had simply exceeded its grasp.

Notes

1. Barbara Levy Simon, *The Empowerment Tradition in American Social Work: a History* (New York, Columbia University Press, 1994), 57.
2. Jack B. Rogers, and Robert E. Blade, "The Great Ends of the Church: Two Perspectives," *Journal of Presbyterian History* 76 (1998): 181-186.
3. Bruce Jansson, *The Reluctant Welfare State* (Belmont, CA: Wadsworth Brooks/Cole, 2001), 118.
4. Bruce Jansson, *The Reluctant Welfare State* (Belmont, CA: Wadsworth Brooks/Cole, 2001), 123-165.
5. C. Wright Mills, *Sociology and Pragmatism* (New York: Oxford University Press, 1966): 71.
6. A conflation of Oxford and Cambridge Universities.
7. William Clark, *Academic Charisma and the Origins of the Research University* (Chicago: University of Chicago Press, 2006): 28.
8. Richard Reeves, *John Stuart Mill: Victorian Firebrand* (London: Atlantic Books, 2008), p. 88.
9. Clark: 463.
10. David Austin, "The Institutional Development of Social Work," *Journal of Social Work Education*, 33, 3 (Fall): 600.
11. Harris Chaiklin, "Franklin Benjamin Sanborn," *Research on Social Work Practice*, 15, 2 (March 2005), 2-7.
12. Roy Lubove, *The Professional Altruist* (New York: Atheneum, 1965), p. 144.
13. Mary Richmond, *Social Diagnosis* (New York: 1917).
14. Austin: 600.
15. Paul Starr, *The Social Transformation of American Medicine* (New York: Basic Books, 1982): 118, 121.
16. Abraham Flexner, "Is Social Work a Profession?" proceedings of the National Conference of Charities and Corrections, 1915: 581.
17. Flexner: 585.
18. Flexner: 586.
19. Flexner: 587.
20. Flexner: 589-90.
21. Emphasis added, Flexner: 590.
22. Stanley Wenocur and Michael Reisch, *From Charity to Enterprise* (Urbana, IL: University of Illinois Press, 2001), pp. 89-90.
23. Mills: 51-60, 206.
24. Austin: 604.
25. *Social Case Work: Generic and Specific* (New York: American Association of Social Workers, 1929), 30.
26. *Social Case Work: Generic and Specific* (New York: American Association of Social Workers, 1929), 90.

27. Katharine Kendall, *Council on Social Work Education: Its Antecedents and First Twenty Years* (Alexandria, VA: Council on Social Work Education, 2002), p. 4.
28. Stanley Wenocur and Michael Reisch, *From Charity to Enteprise* (Urbana, IL: University of Illinois Press, 2001).
29. Wenocur and Reisch, p. 259.
30. Kendall, pp. 62-73.
31. Austin: 607-8.
32. Kendall, p. 95.
33. Kendall, p. 120.
34. Kendall, p. 95.
35. Kendall, pp. 149-50.
36. Karger and Stoesz: 286.
37. Kendall, p. 204.
38. Karger and Stoesz: 289.
39. Kendall, p. 209.
40. Academic Analytics ranks doctoral programs in social work; however, their methodology has yet to be perfected, so that ranking is included in the book's appendix.
41. Robert Green, Frank Baskind, Andreas Fassler, and Anne Jordan, "The Validity of the 2004 *U.S. News and World Report* Rankings of Schools of Social Work," *Journal of Social Work Education*, (2006) 51(2).
42. Feldman: 487, 500.
43. Harry Specht and Mark Courtney, *Unfaithful Angels* (New York: Free Press, 1994), 4.

3

Good News Gospel

As Abraham Flexner observed almost a century ago, the stature of a discipline is contingent on its intellectual sentinels, the gatekeepers of the knowledge through which a profession does its work. Typically, professions utilize their most accomplished scholars to perform a gatekeeping function as referees of manuscripts and journal articles. Good editorial practice takes into account that such scholars will likely be busy with their own research, and recognizes the importance of disseminating new knowledge in a timely fashion. Scholarly disagreements and open debate in most fields help to refine knowledge and encourages intellectual rigor. The quality of the gatekeepers and the vigor of intellectual debates exert a powerful influence over the status and success of the modern professions. Editorial practices that do not support quality or gatekeepers who are not the most highly accomplished scholars in their fields pose a problem for the long term success of a profession.

When weak scholars become referees and editors, their lack of accomplishment is likely to result not only in errors in evaluating manuscripts, but also defensive reactions to the prospect of debate within the discipline. Weak referees and editors are not likely to be versed in current methods, often preferring the familiar, and these tend to be articles that celebrate the virtues of a discipline. Rather than publishing rigorous research about a discipline's successes and failures, such journals become repositories of good news. Aside from compromising professional prosperity, the institutionalization of inferior editorial practice has several unintended consequences: Accomplished scholars are likely to be baffled by evaluations of their submissions which are logically incoherent or factually wrong. Because multiple submissions to refereed journals are disallowed, accomplished scholars find their work effectively embargoed by the journal to which it is submitted; recognizing its perishable nature, they will be disinclined to submit again. As a result of inferior scholarship, journals are devalued, and their use diminishes. Being devalued, such journals find it difficult to attract accomplished scholars to serve as referees and editors. Rather than contributing to the timely distribution of state-of-the-art knowledge, such journals descend into mediocrity. Aware of their vulnerability, insecure referees and editors of inferior journals are unlikely to invite debate within the discipline; instead the tendency is to circle the wagons and vilify critics. When editorial practices persist in confirming the values of a discipline over and above more rigorous analyses, they run the risk of promulgating ideology as professional knowledge. Editorial practices, then, not only figure prominently in the ascent, or descent, of a discipline, but affect its public credibility as well.

The relationship between editorial practices and the stature of social work is evident in the citations of a journal's articles in other publications, e.g., their impact scores. Of the ten social work journals with the highest impact scores promulgated by the Web of Science, only three are distinctly products of American social work (*Health and Social Work* [0.800], *Social Work Research* [0.763], *Social Service Review* [0.755]), while four are produced by other disciplines (*American Journal of Community Psychology* [1.922], *Child Abuse and Neglect* [1.627], the *Journal of Community Psychology* [0.732], *Family Relations* [0.687], and three are foreign (*Journal of Social Policy* [1.037], *Health and Social Care in the Community* [0.869], *British Journal of Social Work* [0.707]. The flagship journals of American social work, the *Journal of Social Work Education* [0.647] and *Social Work* [0.598] have become second-tier journals, ranked number 12 and 14 respectively.[1] Among American educators who were familiar with social work journals, *Social Work* was ranked number 16 and the *Journal of Social Work Education* number 26. The prestige of the vast majority of social work journals declined between 1990 and 2000.[2]

Editorial Practices in Social Work

The quality of social work journals has been negatively affected by editorial practices that permit less accomplished scholars to serve as gatekeepers of knowledge. The editors of the *Journal of Social Work Education*, the flagship journal of social work educators, averaged 2.8 total publications between 1987 and 1990, according to an analysis of several social work journals.[3] A study of editors of *Social Work*, the flagship journal of the profession, revealed a similar problem: from 1990 to 1995,

50% of the editorial board and 19.1% of the consulting editors did not have a single article listed in the abstracting resources reviewed over the six year period of this study. Twelve and one-half percent of the editorial board and 17 percent of the consulting editors had only one article from 1990 to 1995. The data clearly suggest that a significant percentage of the editorial board and consulting editors of *Social Work* did not appear to be active scholars in the area of journal publishing during the first half of the 1990s.[4]

The researchers observed that "when the qualifications of reviewers is suspect, the selection of articles published in journals are open to question"(sic).[5]

"How is it that a publication record that would not warrant even consideration for tenure at most colleges and universities is sufficient for appointment to the editorial board of our field's major peer-reviewed journals?" asked Duncan Lindsey,[6] editor of the *Children and Youth Services Review.* The denigration of scholarship in the field raised questions about the purpose of having a refereed literature at all. Lindsey noted, "What I found indicated an apparent guild mentality that was mainly concerned with promoting, bolstering, or rewarding the careers of administrators, deans, and organizational leaders to the detriment of a serious commitment to critical inquiry and research."[7] Other researchers have suspected that "an old boy and old girl professional acquaintance influence might be involved in the selection process [of editors]."[8] Compared to the editorial standards of other disciplines, social work resembles less an academic profession and more a system of patronage typical of an occupational guild.

The late John Pardeck compared the scholarship of social work editors with those of psychology between 1992 and 2001, finding that social work editors demonstrated significantly less scholarship (by a factor of seven) than psychology editors.

The differences between social work and psychology journals tell a tale. Not only are editors of psychology journals published more often, but their scholarship is more often a sign of its importance. Not one of the social work journals matched the weakest psychology journal with respect to the average number of articles published by editors. Gary Holden, a researcher in the field of bibliometrics, wrote a review of such studies that included the unflattering light that it cast on social work education.[10] He later became Editor-in-Chief of the *Journal of Social Work Education*; but, perhaps indicative of the structural problems in editorial procedures, resigned after only eleven months.

COMPARISON OF SOCIAL WORK AND PSYCHOLOGY EDITORS[9]

Social Work Editors		
Journals	No. Articles Published by editor	Citations
Families in Society	2	0.0
Social Service Review	5	17.4
Child Welfare	0	0.6
Journal of Social Work Education	10	18.8
Social Work	0	9.6
Mean	**3.40**	**9.28**
Standard Deviation	4.22	8.92

Psychology Editors		
Journals	No. Articles Published by editor	Citations
Journal of Counseling Psychology	21	53.5
Journal of Applied Psychology	26	83.6
Journal of Abnormal Psychology	20	18.7
Journal of Educational Psychology	40	131.4
Journal of Personality and Soc. Psych	15	97.0
Mean	**24.40**	**76.82**
Standard Deviation	9.50	42.89

Another factor that compromises the editorial quality of social work journals is the tendency of editors to take an extraordinary amount of time to get issues into the field. For the April 2004 issue of *Social Work*, for example, the average time from submission to publication was 40.8 months, or 3.4 years. Even if the article had been accepted, the time between acceptance and publication was 27.7 months, or 2.3 years. Social work had not advanced much since its poor showing in 1986, when *Social Work,* ranked dead last among professional journals in the time from submission to acceptance/rejection as well as the period from acceptance to publication. At that time the most-timely journal was the *American Bar Association Journal* which conducted the entire process in 4.5 months; the *American Journal of Nursing* required 15 months, while the *American Journal of Public Health* needed only eight months.[14]

Text Box 1
Good News Sells—The Experiments of William Epstein

Two experiments were conducted by a social work academic, William Epstein, in an endeavor to identify the standards by which journals evaluated submissions. He found that the reviewers were not able to adequately assess methodological and statistical aspects of submissions, and that acceptance or rejection were influenced by ideological congruence and current professional orthodoxy, or "confirmational bias."[11]

Employing an experimental method, Epstein constructed two fictive studies, then randomly distributed the positive version to 74 journals, the negative manuscript to 72. Editors and reviewers preferred the positive article at a statistically significant level. After reporting his findings, Epstein was shunned by the organized social work community. His findings that editors and referees of social work journals were more ideological than scientific lead to stories in the *New York Times, Washington Post,* and *Chronicle of Higher Education* in 1989 and 1990.

In a follow up study Epstein constructed two fictitious interventions around family preservation and pregnancy prevention, and randomly distributed these to social work journals. Independent raters scored the comments by reviewers, and determined that 73.5 % of these were inadequate. Fifty-four percent of the reviews were rated as extremely deficient in that they were personal and reflected opinion rather than objective evaluation of the scientific merits of the submissions.[12] Epstein concluded that "the publication decisions of social work journals are biased to accept confirming papers and routinely rely on the uninformed enthusiasms of referee reviewers."[13]

By 2005 the field's editorial problems had reached critical mass, if not in the board rooms of *Social Work* and *JSWE,* then at least among social work researchers. Fourteen scholars met in Miami to discuss "peer review and the publication process." The result of their deliberations was "The Miami Statement," an extensive list of flaws in social work's knowledge dissemination procedures.[15] The Miami Statement established that "scholars in social work are concerned with the overall quality and impact of social work journals as well as the processes of publication and peer review."[16] Among the problems identified were

- More accomplished scholars avoid social work journals because of the "limited impact" of the journals.

- Reviewers of articles are unknowledgeable, a problem when authors of other disciplines encounter social work editors through a multiple-authored manuscript.

- The slow processing of submissions compromises currency and impedes the careers of authors seeking promotion and tenure.

- The editorial staff capriciously interferes with content of articles after the article has received a final review.

- Several journals have yet to take advantage of information technology in order to expedite manuscript review and reduce errors.

- Many journals evade accountability by failing to publish dates of submission and acceptance as well as their acceptance rates.

- Some journals fail to offer readers and authors opportunities to publish comments on topical articles.

- Journal editors should adopt the practices established by the American Psychological Association and the International Committee of Medical Journal Editors.

- Because of its breadth of publishing in the profession, NASW should assume leadership in up-grading review and publishing practices.[17]

The Miami Statement documented fundamental problems about the way in which social work acquired its knowledge, but omitted the issue of confirmational bias, or a tendency to publish those items that fit ideologically with the editors' preferences. As a result of the types of problems identified in the Miami Statement, the most productive social work scholars began to seek other venues to publish their work.

Weak Scholarship of Editors

In the decade since Pardeck's study, the scholarship of social work's editors has remained problematic. In 2006, the consulting editors of *Social Work* and *JSWE* averaged 15.7 and 9.3 lifetime articles, respectively. Critics could target the large number of weak scholars who are vetting what is published in social work's flagship journals. Among *Social Work*'s consulting editors, 10.8 percent had zero articles recorded by the Social Sciences Citation Index; for *JSWE* the comparable figure was 32.7 percent.

Another way to capture the scholarly inexperience of consulting editors is to liken their productivity to standards for promotion to associate professor with tenure. Hypothetically, if a minimal standard were six publications in SSCI journals, then 35.1 percent of consulting editors for *Social Work* and 61.8 percent of *JSWE* consulting editors would not likely have been promoted or tenured based on their scholarship. Considering that *JSWE* is a journal for educators and *Social Work* is geared for practitioners, these figures are actually inverted; academics would be expected to have <u>stronger</u> publication records.

A comparison of social work's editorial performance with that of a closely related profession, psychology, provides some context for evaluating social work's relatively weak performance. Of the psychology journals evaluated by Pardeck, the *Journal of Counseling Psychology (JCP)* ranked in the middle of journals for that discipline. For 2006, the average number of articles published by consulting editors of *JCP* was 23.5, far above comparable figures for *Social Work* or *JSWE*. *JCP* consulting editors were also less likely to be scholastic novices: only 5.4 percent had zero SSCI publications with 12.5 percent having published between one and six SSCI articles. Based on these figures, it would be fair to conclude that the consulting editors of *JCP* were twice as productive as those of *Social Work* and *JSWE*. Among *Social Work*'s Editorial Board, one member had no SSCI publications and two between one and six; the average number of lifetime publications was 8.25. In order to evaluate data-based articles more adequately, *JSWE* appointed statistical reviewers, two of whom had no SSCI publications and one between one and six; the average number of publications for these special reviewers was 4.8.

These data shed light on the weak editorial practices uncovered by Epstein (see Text Box 1). If the consulting editors of social work's flagship journals are so green that they would probably not be promoted or tenured at a mid-level social work program, what would be expected of their ability to evaluate submissions? Editorial inexperience is likely to result in a failure to comprehend the theory and methods of submitted papers, or their importance to the profession. In cases of uncertainty in rendering a verdict on a submission, odds are high that the article would be forwarded to another consulting editor equally inexperienced. As a result, submissions that confound reviewers are unlikely to get a reasoned review if that means a careful screening by someone well-versed in the theory and methods involved. Such erratic editorial reviews may account for more established scholars avoiding social work journals in favor of periodicals with more capable reviewers. Consulting editors who are not well-grounded in social science theory, social programs, and statistical analysis are likely to look more positively on submissions that avoid such content.

Censorship

A publishing process that insists on good news risks crossing the line into censorship. The example of Jim Midgley demonstrates the vulnerability of weak editorial practices to political and ideological pressures.

A former Dean of the School of Social Welfare at Berkeley, Midgley is an international expert on social development, a regular contributor to the professional literature, and a life-long member of NASW. The new editor of *Social Work*, Jorge Delva, had invited Midgley to submit an editorial on the challenge that globalization presented to international social work. After addressing those issues, Midgley presented "unipolarism"—a strategy pursued by the presidency of George W. Bush—as inconsistent with social development. Unipolarism, as defined by Midgley, sought to disperse American values internationally, using political influence, economic power, and military force, if necessary. Midgley identified by name several neoconservatives who had been central to the Bush administration's aggressive foreign policy: Charles Krauthammer, Paul Wolfowitz, and William Kristol.

Robert Leighninger, Jr., the editor of the *Journal of Sociology and Social Welfare* picked-up the story from there:

> This provocative, though hardly incendiary, thesis was designed to start a discussion in the two international social work meetings held this summer. But in the headquarters of NASW it did more than that: it set off alarms. When the copy-edited manuscript was returned to its author, a number of names of neoconservatives and Bush administration officials had been removed. Thinking this was just capricious editing, Jim [Midgley] insisted that they be reinstated. He was told by NASW Press that a "final" decision had been made denying his request. He withdrew the manuscript.
>
> In the course of the discussion, it became apparent that this was not an isolated instance of administrative involvement in NASW journal publications. Review by NASW administrative staff, apart from editorial and peer review, is established procedure.[18]

Midgley's article subsequently appeared in the *Journal of Sociology and Social Welfare.*[19]

The resulting brouhaha reverberated throughout the profession. In printing Midgley's essay, Leighninger invited readers to submit other incidents of "self censorship."[20] Subsequently, Rick Hoefer, editor of the *Journal of Policy Practice*, judged that

> if NASW considers itself an organization that demands advocacy of its members, NASW and its related organization, NASW Press, should support the advocacy that emerges, so long as it is well-grounded in facts and falls within other professional parameters. It appears that what has happened to Dr. Midgley's manuscript is an example where diffusion of professional research and advocacy has been lessened for invalid reasons. As a result NASW members have been needlessly deprived of information that would help them in fulfilling their professional responsibilities.[21]

Former editor of *Social Work*, Stanley Witkin, wondered about the implications of deferring to an administration that had run roughshod over professionals who had objected to its policies in education, foreign affairs, and scientific research: "if academic journals do not resist such tendencies, they can have a chilling impact on the integrity and legitimacy of such publications. Perhaps most chilling is when, even in the absence of specific regulations, journals begin to exercise censorship of information they believe might be offensive to an administration."[22] In reply NASW Executive Director Elizabeth Clark invoked the tax code as an excuse for the tawdry affair.[23]

The Midgley incident underscored the amateurish manner in which NASW manages its editing. Rather than viewing it as an essential instrument through expanding the intellectual discourse vital to the profession, NASW sought the excuse of its tax-exempt status. Within the broader context of social work journals, the incident was consistent with the lack of standards, weak scholarship, and inept management that appear to be characteristic of social work editorial practices. NASW attempted to sweep the Midgley incident under the editorial rug rather than view it as indicative of the need to reform its procedures. The mettle of editors should not be tested by their promulgation of good news, but their ability and willingness to enhance a profession's literature. In the Midgley affair, *Social Work* simply failed to bring its decision-making in line with its values. It would have been one thing had the editorial staff simply been maladroit, but the fact that the Board and Executive Director weighed-in on the matter and voted for censorship is an embarrassment to the profession. *Quis custodiet ipsos custodes?*[24]

Ideological Vulnerability

It is poignantly ironic that social work editors would attempt to muzzle a reasoned and accurate critique written by one of its most accomplished educators to avoid confronting unpleasant political reactions from a conservative administration. For the last quarter of the 20th century, the Right has been criticizing faculty of American universities as well as professionals beholden to the welfare state for their unalloyed liberalism. Yet, social work's editorial standards served to validate the Right's critique of higher education.

Towards the end of the twentieth century, American academics were confronted with criticism from conservative intellectuals who launched a fusillade at higher education. The first salvo was drafted by Lewis Powell, a corporate attorney who advised the Chamber of Commerce to take seriously the Left's challenge to "the free enterprise system." In a

1971 memo, Powell targeted the university as the source of left-wing criticism, and admonished conservatives to take aggressive action: "The first essential is to establish the staffs of eminent scholars, writers and speakers, who will do the thinking, the analysis, the writing, and the speaking. It will also be essential to have staff personnel who are thoroughly familiar with the media, and how most effectively to communicate with the public."[25] Although Powell had urged the Chamber of Commerce to mount a counter-attack to the Left, that object would eventually be assigned to several think tanks that evolved as parallel institutions to the nation's colleges and universities. Instead of working within the cloistered confines of academe, Powell urged conservatives to be more assertive, engaging the electronic media as well as writing articles and books for public consumption. "If you wish to make a productive investment in the intellectual and educational worlds," Irving Kristol would later suggest to corporate executives, "you find competent intellectuals and scholars—'dissident' members, as it were of the 'new class'—to offer guidance."[26]

In order to be competitive in "the marketplace of ideas", conservatives recognized the need to develop an alternative to liberal universities and colleges. "If the Right was going to have a hard time getting its voice heard in universities, then it would invent conservative institutions of its own," observed two British journalists, "And instead of teaching students, it would teach politicians."[27] Thus, during the final decades of the 20th century, conservatives embellished existing policy institutes or established new think tanks as a strategic network to counter the nation's colleges and universities which they perceived were the province of the Left. By century's end, conservative policy institutes, including the American Enterprise Institute, the Heritage Foundation, the CATO Institute, the Manhattan Institute, and the Hoover Institution, had challenged liberal hegemony in public affairs.

During the 1990s conservatives also began a prolonged assault on higher education. Dinesh D'Souza accused radical African Americans, Latinos, feminists, and homosexuals of elevating their agendas over the traditional virtues of higher education, compromising truth.[28] Similarly, Roger Kimball warned that leftist groups were deliberately subverting the superior values of Western culture by attacking the humanities.[29] While these diatribes sparked indignation among liberal academics, the Right remained frustrated in its attempts to attain more influence within higher education, an institution that, aside from a handful of economic departments and law schools, remained bastions of liberalism.[30] Particular indignation was reserved for higher education which conservatives contended had been degraded; from their perspective the nation's colleges and universities had been responsible for the world-wide diffusion of the West's supreme virtues: democratic-capitalism as the model political-economy, civil rights as the basis for individual freedom, and a secular aesthetic in the fine arts. The Right's strategic funding of conservative think tanks increased to the point that, despite liberalism's stronghold in American higher education, public opinion–indeed, the nation's public philosophy—were becoming more conservative.

Ultimately, conservatives resorted to reforms geared towards reducing supposed liberal influences in education. During the Reagan presidency, the National Commission on Excellence in Education famously warned about "a rising tide of mediocrity that threatens our very future as a Nation and a people;" then added: "If an unfriendly foreign power had attempted to impose on America the mediocre educational performance that exists today, we might well have viewed it as an act of war."[31] In the early 1990s, a group of leaders in higher education, the Wingspread Group, reported that more than half of American-born college graduates could not consistently "perform simple tasks, such as calculating the change from $3 after buying a 60-cent bowl of soup and a $1.95 sandwich."[32] The Educational Testing Service (ETS) released a study of college graduates reporting that only 35 percent could do such things a write a letter to explain a billing problem, and that only 42 percent were capable of writing an argument contrasting two views from newspaper articles. ETS noted that college graduates demonstrated "levels of literacy [ranging] from a lot less than impressive to mediocre to near alarming, depending on who is making judgment."[33] Paradoxically, while American college students tested worse than their foreign classmates in many academic categories, they consistently ranked first in self-esteem.[34] A decade later American higher education continued to produce a shoddy product. A 2003 study of proficiency in prose literacy, such as reading a newspaper, declined from 40 to 31 percent while document literacy, such as reading a medical prescription fell from 37 to 25 percent during the previous decade. A 2006 study of American history found college seniors getting only 53 percent of items correct, only slightly above that of freshmen, 51.7 percent.[35] The producers of a 2005 Public Broadcasting System documentary on higher education placed the nation's colleges and universities adrift "in a sea of mediocrity."[36] Employing multiple data sets, Mark Bauerlein documented the striking degradation of knowledge on the part of today's college-age young people with respect to history, civics, mathematics, and the fine arts.[37]

President George W. Bush's campaign to reform higher education was facilitated by several organizations that had been established during the 1980s and 1990s to reverse perceived liberal excesses in academe. In 1985 the National Association of Scholars was launched to promote the free exchange of ideas in a democratic society, subsequently publishing its own journal, *Academic Questions,* and establishing affiliates in most of the states. David Horowitz inaugurated the Center for the Study of Popular Culture in 1988, which morphed into the David Horowitz Freedom Center promoting the Academic Bill of Rights, an initiative to inject ideological diversity into higher education. In 1994 35 evangelical ministers founded the Alliance Defense Fund to eliminate barriers to religious freedom in higher education. A year later, the American Council for Trustees and Alumni was established to "support liberal arts education, uphold high academic standards, safeguard the free exchange of ideas on campus, and ensure that the next generation receives a philosophically-balanced, open-minded, high-quality education at an affordable price."[38]

Thus, when Margaret Spellings, the Bush administration's Secretary of Education, introduced the Commission on the Future of Higher Education, a 19-member panel assigned the task of making higher education more efficient and accountable at the beginning of 2005, she had ample institutional support. In the preamble to its draft report, the Commission cited critical failings of the nation's colleges and universities, including the reluctance of many poor students to pursue post-secondary education, the remedial education needed for many matriculating students, and the absence of data on the performance of institutions of higher education, including evidence of proficiency for students who were graduating. Ominously, the Commission warned about an academy adrift:

> History is littered with examples of industries that, at their peril, failed to respond to—or even to notice—changes in the world around them, from railroads to steel manufacturers. Without serious self-examination and reform, institutions of higher education risk falling into the same trap, seeing their market share substantially reduced and their services increasingly characterized by obsolescence.[39]

The Commission reported that, while the U.S. was once preeminent in higher education, among the two-dozen industrialized nations belonging to the Organization for Economic Cooperation and Development, it ranked ninth.[40]

Suspecting the Bush administration had ideological designs for the nation's colleges and universities, liberal academics immediately accused the Commission of politicizing higher education.

Yet, leaders in higher education recognized the problem of the lack of accountability of their institutions. If the primary objectives of the Department of Education under the second Bush Administration were to "establish minimum expected levels of student performance" for the professions, including such factors as rates of job-placement rates and percent passing licensing exams,[41] the nation's college and university presidents were crafting more nuanced methods for assessing the performance of their institutions. Described in Chapter 10, these performance assessments have been adopted by large numbers of educational institutions, although their influence has yet to become evident in social work education. Unwilling to adopt the accountability methods that were emerging in American higher education, social work education continued to justify its performance on the authority of accreditation. Emphasizing professional values at the expense of instructional outcomes, social work education became vulnerable to critics who opposed the profession's alleged indoctrination of students. In 1999 the Foundation for Individual Rights in Education (FIRE) had been created to advance individual freedom in higher education. FIRE soon developed a track record challenging schools of social work for violating the free speech rights of students. In 2007, FIRE successfully sued Missouri State University for violating the rights of Emily Brooker (noted in Chapter 1). In 2008, FIRE sued Rhode Island College for discriminating against a student, Bill Felkner, who professed conservative values. The same year, FIRE successfully defended a student, Andre Massena, from dismissal from Binghamton University's School of Social Work after he lobbied against the retention of an adjunct faculty member.[42] As these cases attest, at least some social work educators can no longer presume that they are immune from scrutiny. Indeed, a professional education that has emphasized liberal values while shorting rigorous research is bound to be perceived as indoctrination, inviting reprisal from organizations, such as FIRE, which defend student free speech rights.

Denouement

The stature and relevance of a modern profession rests with the quality of its specialized knowledge, and its ability to communicate this knowledge to other professionals and to the public. Despite developing a formidable education establishment, social work's impact has been minimal. The failure to establish standards of research and publication has weakened the profession. Editorial boards have not been filled with the field's best scholars, but instead have been populated with relative novices, the majority of whom have contributed only modestly to the professional literature.

The pool of weak scholars vetting manuscripts for *Social Work* and *JSWE* has compromised the quality of material that entered those journals, contributing to the observed confirmational bias within the refereed literature, and disseminating a politically correct version of good news: social work's methods were effective, the profession was nobly battling oppression, and its work was instrumental in advancing human well-being. One consequence of the low standards of editorial practice has been that the best scholars are often driven away and end up publishing their works in journals of other disciplines. Instead of confronting its internal problems, social work's journals have encouraged self-deception. Matters of editorial missteps have contributed to social work's vulnerability to accusations by the Right that professional education is nothing less than indoctrination. In an open society in which the First Amendment is paramount, professions are obliged to justify their instructional content by state-of-the-art research.

Having failed to generate a valid body of such research, social work's values have become the primary basis for justifying and evaluating professional education. This may be fine for liberal students, but it can offend conservative students who may resort to legal advocacy organizations to protect their free speech rights. The blow-back from such episodes extends far beyond a school of social work. University administrators must expend resources defending social work from litigation, and interdisciplinary committees are often impaneled to investigate ambiguous incidents. Regardless of the merit of any given case, capitulation by the school of social work ultimately reflects poorly on the profession, sometimes to the embarrassment of the social work program. Rather than securing social work's purchase in American higher education, inferior editorial practices have sabotaged the profession's status, effectively driving the quality of professional social work education and practice down. Social work may be virtuous by championing its moral values; but, in the absence of empirically validated knowledge, these are little more than normative, metaphysical assertions. For its supporters, social work consists of "good people" proclaiming "good news" about people and society; but, to its critics, social work education has degenerated into dogma and indoctrination.

Notes

1   http://admin.isiknowledge.com/JCR/JCR?RQ=LIST_SUMMARY

2   Sherrill Sellers, Sally Mathiesen, Robin Perry, and Thomas Smith, "Evaluation of Social Work Journal Quality," *Journal of Social Work Education*, 40, no. 1 (Winter 2004), pp. 149, 152.

3   John Pardeck and Roland Meinert, "Scholarly Achievement of the *Social Work* Editorial Board and Consulting Editors: A Commentary," *Research on Social Work Practice*, 9, 1 (January 1999): 88-89.

4   Pardeck and Meinert: 89.

5   Duncan Lindsey, "Ensuring Standards in social Work Research," *Research on Social Work Practice*, 9, 1 (January 1999): 117.

6   Lindsey: 116.

7   Pardeck and Meinert: 90.

8   John Pardeck, "Scholarly Productivity of Editors of Social Work and Psychology Journals," *Psychological Reports*, 90: 1054.

9   Gary Holden, G. Rosenberg, and K. Barker, "Tracing Thought through Time and Space," *Social Work in Health Care*, 41, ¾: 1-34.

10   William Epstein, "The Sleeping Sentinels of Social Work," *Academic Questions* (Summer 1990): 41.

11   Epstein, "The Lighter Side": 16.

12   Epstein, "Conformational Bias": 19.

13   David Stoesz, "Time Capsule," *Social Work*, 31: 480-81.

14   The scholars were Robert Schilling (convener), Judith Baer, Rick Barth, Mark Fraser, Dan Herman, Gary Holden, Gordon MacNeil, Elaine Maccio, Jeanne Marsh, Ann Nichols-Casebolt, Enola Proctor, Dale Ronbinson-Rogers, Trina Williams Shanks, and David Tucker.

15   "Peer Review and Publication Standards in Social Work Journals: The Miami Statement," (Society for Social Work Research, February 15, 2005), p. 1.

16   "The Miami Statement,"

17   Robert Leighninger, Jr., "The Perils of Self-Censorship," *Journal of Sociology and Social Welfare*, 33, 4 (December 2006): 9-10 (emphasis added).

18   James Midgley, "International Social Work, Globalization, and the Challenge of a Unipolar World," *Journal of Sociology and Social Welfare*, 33, 4 (December 2006): 11-19.

19   Leighninger, "Perils":10.

20   Rick Hoefer, "Letters to the Editor Regarding NASW Press Censorship Issue," *Journal of Sociology and Social Welfare*, 33,4 (December 2006): 22-23.

21   Stanley Witkin, "Letters to the Editor Regarding NASW Press Censorship Issue," *Journal of Sociology and Social Welfare*, 33,4 (December 2006): 25.

22   Elizabeth Clark, , "Letters to the Editor Regarding NASW Press Censorship Issue," *Journal of Sociology and Social Welfare*, 33,4 (December 2006): 27-28.

23   Who is watching the sentinels?

24   Lewis Powell, "Attack on American Free Enterprise System," (memo to Eugene Sydnor, August 23, 1971), 7.

25   Quoted in Barbara Ehrenreich, *Fear of Falling* (New York: HarperCollins, 1989), 157.

26   John Micklethwait and Adrian Wooldrich, *The Right Nation* (New York: Penguin, 2004), 9-10.

27   Dinesh D'Souza, *Illiberal Education* (New York: Free Press, 1991).

28   Roger Kimball, *Tenured Radicals* (New York: Harper & Row, 1990).

29.   Michael Berube,"The Academic Blues," *New York Times Magazine* (September 17, 2006): 23.

30.   National Commission on Excellence in Education, *A Nation at Risk* (Washington, DC: US GPO, 1983),:5, 11.

31.   The Wingspread Group on Higher Education, *An American Imperative: Higher Expectations for Higher Education* (Racine, WI: The Johnson Foundation, 1993),.15.

32.   Cassandra Burrell, "Study Finds Variation in College Grads' Skills," *Idaho Statesman* (December 10, 1994), A8.

33.   Russell Jacoby, *Dogmatic Wisdom* (New York: Doubleday, 1994),.89.

34.   Thomas Reeves, "The Spellings Report," *Academic Questions*, vol 20, no. 1 (Winter 2006-7): 57.

35.   Richard Hersh and John Merrow, *Declining by Degrees* (New York: Palgrave MacMillan, 2005), p. 9.

36.   Mark Bauerlein, *The Dumbest Generation* (New York: Targer/Penguin, 2008).

37.   http://www.goacta.org/about_acta/mission.html, (Accessed April 24, 2007).

38.   "Preamble to the Final Draft Report of the Commission on the Future of Higher Education," *Chronicle of Higher Education*, vol. 53, no.2 (September 1, 2006),: A39.

39.   Preamble to the Final Draft Report of the Commission on the Future of Higher Education," *Chronicle of Higher Education*, vol. 53, no.2 (September 1, 2006),: A39.

40.   Burton Bollag, "U.S. and Accreditors Reach Impasse after 2nd Negotiating Round," *Chronicle of Higher Education*,(April 6, 2007)::A23.

41.   Downloaded January 29, 2009 from http://www.thefire.org/index.pphp/case/

4

Spinning Out of Control:
The Runaway Growth of Social
Work Programs

Social work education benefited from a convergence of two develop-
ments accompanying industrialization: the evolution of higher education
following the Civil War and the application of scientifically-based expertise during the Progressive Era. The former deposed a stuffy education in
the classics with a more flexible menu of electives; the latter promised to
apply research to social problems. These were buttressed by the Morrill
Act of 1862, which established a network of public universities, and the
Pendleton Act of 1883, which replaced the practice of appointing civil
servants through patronage with the civil service. With the emergence
of philosophical pragmatism, higher education emerged as a powerful
institution that trained experts in the methods essential to enhance the
general welfare. Early in the twentieth century, colleges and universities
in the United States rivaled those of Europe; among industrial nations, it
became "an article of faith that America's higher education [had become]
the best in the world."[1]

Professional education emerged during the twentieth century to meet
the demand for expertise in a variety of fields. Extension work was
introduced in 1889 in rural as well as urban environs: the Wisconsin
Agriculture College offered classes in adult education as did Columbia
Teachers College in New York City. By 1919, two million Americans
had enrolled in adult extension courses, compared to 35,000 who pursued
formal courses of instruction.[2] All of this inchoate interest in adult education was soon organized into fields by nascent professional associations,
as noted in Chapter 1, among them social work. Among the activities
addressing industrialization, immigration, and urbanization, social work

was complemented by ventures in education and health care. The Progressive Era spawned a vibrant mental health movement, activities to improve public sanitation, the creation of juvenile courts, and scientific philanthropy, unprecedented organizational innovation.[3]

Social work, public administration, and related disciplines expanded with the elaboration of the American welfare state, an institution that not only prized expertise but also provided tens of thousands of civil service jobs. The New Deal and enactment of the Social Security Act of 1935 followed by the Great Society War on Poverty of the 1960s guaranteed secure employment for human service professionals in federal and state government as well as contracting organizations. Although the American welfare state lagged behind its European counterparts, Progressives and later liberals held, as an article of faith, that it would eventually assure basic protections as a right of citizenship. Indeed inexorable expansion of social programs was codified in social philosophy on both sides of the Atlantic. In broad strokes, the British philosopher T.H. Marshall had reflected that while the eighteenth century assured *civil* rights to citizens and the nineteenth guaranteed *political* rights, the twentieth would deliver *economic* rights.[4] In the United States, Harold Wilensky and Charles Lebeaux thought that "under continuing industrialization all institutions will be oriented toward and evaluated in terms of social welfare aims. The 'welfare state' will become the 'welfare society', and both will be more reality than epithet."[5] Social worker Leon Ginsberg echoed the refrain:

> the development of the welfare state is a natural and parallel outgrowth of the industrialization of the world. Just as physical things became more complicated following the Industrial Revolution, so did social relations. The rise of metropolitan areas, the decline of the extended family, the recurring incidence of economic crises, and the increasing need for objective help from strangers in the form of government aid, all made the welfare state and its current patterns inevitable.[6]

With the welfare state a *fait accompli* and its various social programs growing annually at double digit rates, the demand for social workers was preordained, guaranteeing the expansion of social work education.

Growth of Social Work Education

Since 1985 the rapid growth of social work programs on all three levels—baccalaureate, master's, and doctoral—has been unparalleled since the creation of the Council on Social Work Education in 1952. In 1985 there were 89 CSWE-accredited MSW programs, 351 BSW programs, and 19 programs in candidacy.[7] By 2009 that number had exploded to

195 MSW and 470 BSW programs (660 CSWE-accredited social work programs) plus another 33 programs in various stages of candidacy.[8] This represented a 52 percent growth rate. Similarly, the number of doctoral programs grew from 47 in 1985 to 69 in 2009, a 47 percent increase.[9] Despite what appears to be a reduced, and increasingly less qualified, pool of applicants, this growth spurt impacts the quality of the pedagogy in the field and shows no signs of abating.

The number of MSW degrees awarded constitutes only a tiny proportion of all graduate degrees. In 2006, more than 400,000 masters degrees were awarded in the United States compared to about 16,000 MSWs, or about 4 percent of all graduate degrees.[10] In comparison to other graduate students, social work students are more likely to be female (85 percent versus 57 percent) and more likely to be 30 years old or older (43 percent versus 10 percent).[11]

While the number of CSWE-accredited BSW programs grew from 313 in 2000 to 470 in 2000, a 50 percent increase, the number of MSW programs jumped from 139 to 195, a rise of 40.3 percent. Nevertheless, student enrollment in both BSW and MSW programs failed to keep pace with program growth. From 1996 to 2007, the number of BSW degrees awarded dropped slightly from 12,356 to 12,018, respectively, far less than the number of new programs.[12] MSW student enrolment suffered a similar fate. Despite the growing numbers of new MSW programs, the number of MSW degrees awarded increased by only 11.5 percent from 1996 to 2007, or close to one-fourth the growth in the number of MSW programs.[13]

The rash of new MSW programs is fostering a volatile climate for student enrollment. Overall, the majority of social work programs saw moderate to sharp drops in graduate student enrollment. CSWE data (some of it incomplete) from 108 graduate social work programs found that from 1995 to 2004, 28 had program enrollments that were roughly the same size (plus or minus 10 percent) for nine years, while 35 grew, and another 45 saw enrollment declines. All told, roughly 42 percent of the 108 social work programs experienced declining enrollments between 1995 to 2004.[14] The size of MSW programs also grew smaller, dropping from 287.5 in 1990 to 257.4 in 2003.[15] Patricia Keith-Spiegel and Michael Wiederman interpret this trend as arising from the increased competition between graduate programs.[16] Given the exploding number of MSW programs coupled with the relatively stagnant pool of full-time graduate student applicants—the pool inched up only nine percent from 1995 (21,088) to 2004 (22,936)—the applicant pie had to be cut into

Figure 1

Enrollment Drops 1995-2004

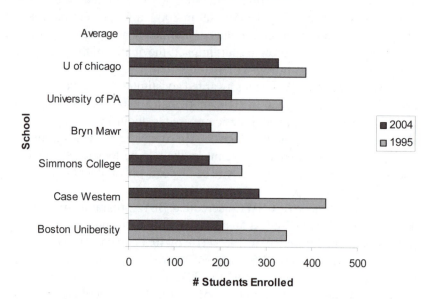

thinner slices to satisfy social work education's voracious appetite for graduate students.

Even the modest nine percent increase in the graduate pool from 1995 to 2004 may be hugely over-reported. As Peter Kindle and Ira Colby point out,

> CSWE reported a full-time and part-time actual enrollment rate of 37.6% and 53.4%, respectively, for graduate social work programs in 2003.... Calculated as the simple ratio between actual enrollment and total applications received and considered, the actual enrollment rate is often used as a proxy for selectivity in program admissions. In light of the findings in this study that the average full-time student reported applying to 2.02 ... graduate programs and that the average part-time student applied to 1.39 ... it may be that the enrollment rate is significantly understated by CSWE.[17]

The leeching of students from one program to another may be more pronounced among second- rather than first-tier social work programs. However, anecdotal evidence suggests that even first- tier schools are feeling the impact of the growth of other social work programs, which may be less expensive. For example, Columbia University's School of Social Work website announced that it is: "Still Time to Apply for Fall 2007 ... We are currently accepting applications for the fall 2007 semester....

The suggested application deadline is February 1, 2007.... We encourage applicants to submit an application at this time."[18] This invitation was posted on February 9, 2007—after the suggested deadline—and was still on Columbia's website on May 26, 2007.

Enrollment pressures may have also led Columbia University to start an accelerated 16 month Master of Science in Social Work program that allows students to start full-time study in the spring semester and complete the degree requirements in May of the subsequent year.

The Expansion of BSW Programs

As illustrated by Figure 2, the number and scope of baccalaureate social work programs grew dramatically from 1985 to 2004, with a continuing upward trajectory. By 2007 there were 459 accredited baccalaureate programs, a 31 percent increase over 1985.[19] In addition, there were 23,533 full-time baccalaureate students in 1985; by 2004 that number rose to 32,752, a 71 percent increase. In 1985, 6,347 bachelor's degrees were awarded; by 2004 there were 9,889 (See Figure 2).

The number of baccalaureate-only social work programs declined from 248 in 1985 to 239 in 2004, suggesting that many former BSW-

Figure 2
Growth of Accredited BSW Programs 1985-2004

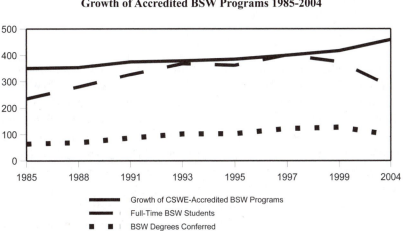

Source: Student numbers and conferred degrees are rounded off and are in thousands. Data compiled from Council on Social Work Education, Statistics on Social Work Education in the United States: 2004 (Author, 2007); and Alan Rubin (1986), Julia Hidalgo and Elaine Spaulding (1989), and Todd Lennon (1992, 1994, 1998, 2001), Statistics on Social Work Education in the United States (Sliver Springs, MD: CSWE).

only programs have started an MSW component.[20] In that sense, BSW programs are frequently viewed as a stepping-stone for starting an MSW program. This is not surprising since a master's degree piggy-backed onto an exiting BSW program requires relatively limited resources, mainly in the form of a few more faculty.

Consequently, the number of combined social work programs (i.e., offering both a BSW and MSW degree) grew by 115 percent (from 52 to 111) between 1985 and 2004. Concomitantly, the number of faculty in these joint programs rose by 111 percent (from 1,768 to 3,739) from 1985 to 2004. As a result of this growth, the number of faculty in combined programs (3,739) is almost three times higher than for BSW-only (1,400) programs, and more than twice as high as for graduate-only (1,718) master's programs. In fact, the total faculty in combined BSW-MSW programs is greater than the combined faculty of BSW- and MSW-only programs. In terms of straight numbers, CSWE is not dominated by BSW faculty, but by faculty in combined BSW-MSW programs.[21]

As noted earlier, student enrollment has not necessarily followed closely on the heels of BSW program and faculty growth. In effect, a relatively static pool of applicants is simply dispersed among more social work programs. Hence, the growth of new baccalaureate programs may well be outstripping student demand, as stagnant enrollment may be an important portent for the future success of the 12 baccalaureate programs in CSWE candidacy in 2009.[22]

The Growth of New Master's Programs

The growth of master's programs from 1985 to 2004 followed a similar trajectory to baccalaureate programs. In 1986 there were 86 CSWE-accredited master's programs;[23] by 2004, the number of master's programs climbed to 170, an increase of 97.7 percent.[24] If the number of students grew at a rate proportional to the number of new social work programs, the 22,000 full- and part-time students in 1985 would have to more than double to even begin to keep pace with program growth. Instead, from 1985 to 2004 MSW student enrollment grew by 67 percent, from 22,000 to 36,475, far below the proportional growth in the number of programs.[25]

The relative flatness of graduate student enrollment is illustrated by two indicators: the number of students enrolled and the number of MSW degrees awarded. Full-time graduate student enrollment in social work programs has been relatively static, rising from 17,672 in 1978 to 24,744 in 2004. The most significant growth trend in MSW enrollment occurred largely through part-time students, whose numbers jumped from 4,333 in

1978 to 13,539 in 2004, roughly a three-fold increase. By 2004, almost 40 percent of MSW students were part-time compared to 25 percent in 1978. Students become part-time largely because of economic issues – i.e., they cannot afford not to work – or because obligations to work and/or family often compete with professional education. Evening, weekend, or Internet classes are more convenient for them. Part-time students have similar problems to commuter students at residential campuses; namely, part-time students are less able to contribute to, and participate in, the culture of professional education.[26] They are less able to meet with faculty over lunch, attend brown-bag talks featuring guest lecturers, or participate in weekday student and faculty meetings. Increasingly, part-time education is social work training *in absentia*, at least as regards important aspects of professional socialization. In their efforts to balance competing demands, many part-time students are forced to exchange the life of the mind for the life of the grind.

The impact of part-time students is evident in the graduation numbers. For example, 9,476 MSW degrees were awarded in 1978; by 2004 that number rose to 15,473. This is striking for two reasons. First, while the number of MSW programs nearly tripled from 1978 to 2004, the number of degrees awarded rose by only 63 percent. Second, 14,484 MSW degrees were awarded in 1995 compared to 15,473 in 2004, a 7 percent increase in nine years. Consequently, the large growth in MSW programs from 1995 to 2004 did not translate into a substantial increase in the number of MSW degrees awarded.

The emphasis on the growth model is illustrated by CSWE's high rates of accreditation and re-accreditation. It is also evident by the low rates of program sanctions (See Table 1). Out of 628 BSW and MSW programs in 2006, only six were placed on conditional accreditation, while ten had their full accreditation restored. CSWE's Commission on Accreditation's Annual Report of June 2006 reported that only one MSW program was placed under the category of "Review Program for Compliance and Move to Withdraw Accreditation." Only six programs—or less than 1 percent of all social work programs—were deemed problematic in 2006. Even then, these problematic programs were merely placed on conditional accreditation. It appears that CSWE's accreditation process is driven more by revenue considerations than merit and performance, CSWE is also apparently a club that keeps its members regardless of their performance.

Growth Factors

Several factors contributed to the expansion of social work education programs. One factor was especially idiosyncratic. In the early 1980s, a

Table 1
Commission on Accreditation Decisions
– October 2005, February 2006, and June 2006

	October 2005	February 2006	June 2006
Reaffirm Accreditation			
Baccalaureate	12	14	09
Master's & Combined	03	05	04
Placed on Conditional Accreditation			
Baccalaureate	02	03	01
Master's & Combined	01	01	00
Restore Accreditation			
Baccalaureate	03	04	02
Master's	00	01	00
Grant Initial			
Baccalaureate	04	03	03
Master's	01	01	04
Grant Candidacy Status			
Baccalaureate	00	01	06
Master's	02	00	02

Total Number of Accredited Programs 628
Baccalaureate: 453
Master's: 175

Source: Council on Social Work Education, Archive of COA decisions. Retrieved May 9, 2007, from http://www.cswe.org

misadventure in investments nearly bankrupted CSWE, and there was an urgent need for revenues to sustain its functions, including accreditation. Second, state licensure of social workers is predicated on graduation from an accredited social work program, requiring students wishing to be licensed to enroll in a CSWE-accredited program. Third, futher elaboration of governmental social programs and their nonprofit contractors increased the number of positions in the social welfare bureaucracy, contributing to employee interest in upgrading their credentials. Taken together, these provided an auspicious context for mounting new professional training programs. A contributing, if often neglected, factor is the relatively low salaries commanded by social work faculty, at least as

Table 2
Average Faculty Salaries by Selected Fields and Rank at
4-Year Institutions, 2006-7

Discipline	Professor	Associate Professor	Assistant Professor
Law	121,301	91,509	78,294
Engineering	102,954	79,759	69,896
Business	98,384	82,347	75,835
Public Health	87,639	67,862	56,519
Mental & Soc. Health	83,821	63,422	52,288
Biology	82,612	62,677	52,510
Hum. Dev. & Fam. St.	81,778	60,736	50,627
Social Sciences	81,501	63,008	52,826
Public Admin.	80,073	62,978	52,643
Library Science	79,309	60,583	49,382
Psychology	76,949	60,091	50,722
Counseling	74,551	57,148	47,846
Nursing	74,391	61,942	52,033
Social Work	74,334	58,553	49,283
Special Education	73,492	57,832	49,555

Source: "Almanac Issue 2007-2008," Chronicle of Higher Education, August 31, 2007, p. 25; "2005-06 National Faculty Salary Survey by Discipline and Rank in four-Year Colleges and Universities, College and University Professional Association for Human Resources, 2007.

compared to other professional education programs. In effect, this made the enlarging of social work programs relatively inexpensive since not only are social work salaries lower than most professions, but they are among the lowest for the social sciences.

Entrepreneurial administrators in higher education likely perceived that, as regards their bottom line, the institutional investment in social work education could be easily recovered by student fees. Depending on their public versus private auspice, many college and university administrators found this cost-benefit calculation agreeable. In 2006, for example, a BSW program could be established for a minimal investment. Undergraduate social work programs could be accredited with a faculty complement of three. The salary for a new assistant professor of social work was $43,318.[27] Assuming that the other social work positions could be filled by faculty paid less than $45,000 and adding a modest amount for administrative expenses, augmenting the library collection, and orienting field instructors, the total budget for the new BSW program could be kept below $150,000.[28] This amount would have to offset by student fees, of course. In 2006, the average tuition of a four-year public university was about $16,500, while that of a private college was about $33,000.[29] At the typical public university, a BSW program would be generating revenue above costs once it had enrolled 10 students; for the typical private college, the program would be in the black with the enrollment of the fifth student.

Once the BSW program was established, evolving an MSW program would have been an attractive option since CSWE accreditation requirements mandated that a BSW applicant to an MSW program be given credit for their undergraduate education. Typically, MSW programs recognized this by offering "advanced standing" to BSW students, essentially waving their first year of study. For the entrepreneurial academic administrator, this meant that an MSW program could be added to the institution's array of graduate degrees at a modest cost. For BSW students from the host institution, an MSW could be acquired with an additional year of study. Yet, accreditation standards for the MSW required five full-time faculty. Assuming that two faculty from the BSW program have been promoted to associate professor with a median salary of $63,084 each, two new assistant professors with a median salary of $54,267 each, a field coordinator at $30,000, and adding a moderate amount for administrative costs, a new MSW program could be established for less than $300,000. For the public undergraduate institution eager to amplify its graduate credentials, that amount would be recovered with the enrollment of the nineteenth student; for the typical private college the new MSW program operates in the black once the tenth student is enrolled

The difference between having a BSW-only and a combined BSW-MSW program is as easy as employing a few more faculty members, a bargain for a small university hungry for prestige and eager to claim another graduate degree program under its belt. The modest costs of adding an MSW program to an existing BSW program is further mitigated by external funding. Small grants from community foundations and the United Way for research projects and programs for vulnerable populations can augment the social work budget while embellishing the faculty curriculum vitae. Not coincidentally, the majority of external money ($2 million to $3 million or more) generated by many social work programs often comes from Title IV-E Public Child Welfare Training Program grants. These grants are not research-oriented, but are designed to educate and train MSW students for employment as public child welfare practitioners.

Offering an MSW degree also elevates the prestige of program directors and allows them to join the National Association of Deans and Directors of Schools of Social Work (NADD). Apart from increasing the visibility of the social work program within the university, an MSW component also aids in faculty hiring. For instance, roughly 300 doctoral graduates are produced yearly, many of whom choose to teach only in social work programs that offer an MSW. (Some opt to teach only in programs that include a doctorate.) In many cases, BSW-only programs find it difficult to attract faculty with doctorates. Although the number of doctoral-degreed faculty increased slightly in social work baccalaureate programs from 1985 to 1999 (from 33 to 38 percent), by 2004 only 40 percent of baccalaureate faculty held a doctorate.[30] Some candidates who apply for teaching positions assume almost *a priori*—although often erroneously—that social work programs with an MSW component provide a more conducive research environment than BSW-only programs. In a tight academic job market, combined- or MSW-only programs clearly have an advantage over their BSW-only cohorts.

Even baccalaureate social work programs in smaller universities are experiencing increased pressure to raise the level of scholarship and research productivity. Hiring promising faculty from research-oriented doctoral programs is an important avenue for raising productivity, including the development of external grants. Hiring more research-oriented faculty can change the culture in some social work programs and help motivate veteran faculty to publish. Such baccalaureate programs are betting that, as in graduate rankings where "research money and faculty productivity" attract better students, they too can compete with more established academic units.[31]

The interests of CSWE, students, and educational administrators may converge around the growth of social work programs, but the benefits may be ephemeral. A boom-bust phenomenon can occur in areas traditionally underserved by social work education. When a new MSW program is started in an underserved geographic area, applications tend to be high for the first few years. However, with each successive year the pent-up applicant pressure is released and the pool grows smaller, eventually coming into balance with the general size of the population and the job market for social workers. In order to sustain enrollments, the application criteria change, going from more to less stringent as the top applicants have been siphoned off, forcing selection committees to choose from mid- and lower-range applicants to fill their student quotas. In the end, the long-term viability of a social work program will partly depend on whether the population base (and the demand for social work education) is sufficiently large enough to justify its continued existence.

There is also the danger of over-saturation leading to a Darwinian struggle for existence among competing social work programs. An example of this is the widespread accreditation of MSW programs in south Texas. For example, the greater San Antonio metropolitan area has a population of 1.4 million, and up until a few years, the only MSW program was the long-established Worden School of Our Lady of the Lake University. By 1995 Texas State University at San Marcos offered an MSW degree. In 2005, the University of Texas at San Antonio's MSW program was granted candidacy for accreditation, the first step toward full accreditation. All three programs are within a 50-mile radius of each other, and two are within a few miles of each other. It is unlikely that this small geographic area can sustain three MSW programs, especially when much larger cities like Houston (metro population of 5.2 million) and Dallas (metro population of close to 6 million) have only one MSW program in each city.

Perhaps an even more striking example of over-saturation is the proliferation of graduate social work programs in North Carolina. Although North Carolina has a relatively modest population of 8.8 million, it supports nine MSW programs, the same amount as Texas with a population almost three times larger (23.5 million). Seven of those MSW programs are within a radius of 200 miles or less. While this rapid program growth provides a short-term revenue boost for CSWE, in the long-term a saturated marketplace means that non-viable programs will be forced to close their doors, resulting in less future revenue for the organization, not to mention faculty lay-offs. Oversaturation will also produce a surplus of graduates that will bring down social work salaries in a supply and demand labor market. Clearly, the short-term pro-growth strategy pursued by CSWE has long-term implications for social work education and the future of the profession.

In at least one instance, the incongruence in accredited social work programs is striking. Both California and Texas boast three doctoral programs, but the similarity ends there. California has 16 MSW programs compared to 9 for Texas. Yet, the number of accredited undergraduate programs is reversed: California has 14 while Texas has 29.[32] Either Californians warrant higher-level professional services, or Texans simply require lower-level services. Regardless, the disparity between these states is stark evidence that CSWE's accreditation practices are willy-nilly, inconsistent with the human service demands of citizens.

The justification for the expansion of social work programs is that their size and number must increase to satisfy the growing demand for social workers. This is based on Bureau of Labor Statistics (BLS) data showing a strong demand for social workers in the upcoming decades, especially given aging baby boomers. Unfortunately, pro-growth advocates underestimate the flaws in BLS data and projections. For one, BLS data does not discriminate between social work and social service-type jobs that require a lower level of skill training, often counting social service aides and technicians as social workers. In fact, BLS counts anyone that calls themselves (or is labeled) a social worker, regardless of their credentials or training. Consequently, growth in the social services labor market does not correlate perfectly with growth in the number of "real" social work jobs, or more specifically, jobs that require a high level of specialized education, training, pre- and post-graduate supervision, and licensure. Instead, BLS data reflects an overblown assessment of social work personnel needs, especially since the data fail to address the growing numbers of marriage and family therapists, counseling psychologists, nurses, and others with applied degrees who are competing—and often winning—in the human service marketplace. Without sound data on labor market demands, unchecked accreditation promises to glut the human services labor market, one consequence of which is to drive wages down.

Social work education's adherence to a growth model is based on the assumption that social programs will require an infinitely elastic supply of professionals. The industrial model of social work education is thus designed to turn out widgets for the welfare state, or to be more precise, personnel to serve the social welfare bureaucracies with which social work has been associated. In replicating the industrial model of professional education, social work has chosen to stress uniformity over customization, and efficiency over competence. It is convenient that the programs accredited pay the dues that are essential for CSWE's sustenance, thus allowing CSWE to behave as if past resources (students and funding) will continue uninterrupted into the future. With those assumptions in place there are no negative consequences for expansion; indeed, it portends organizational nirvana—an ever-expanding number of social work graduates that will belong to NASW, some of who will cycle back to higher education and belong to CSWE. Among the casualties of such arrogance has been the quality of social work education.

Ramifications of Program Growth

The rapid growth of master's programs from 1985 to 2004 led to several consequences for social work education, including high rates of acceptance for prospective MSW applicants (more than 68.8 percent) nationally in 2004. Typically, academic criteria for admissions into most graduate programs focuses on GRE scores and undergraduate grade point averages, with both supposedly correlating to academic performance. Some researchers, however, have raised questions regarding the validity of GRE scores.[33] Other social work educators argue that student autobiographies may be better predictors of graduate performance, but even here little evidence exists to back up the claims.[34] These discussions are largely academic since many graduate programs in social work have essentially adopted what amounts to open enrollment.

During the 1980s Catherine Born and Donald Carroll criticized the escalation of acceptance rates that accompanied a downturn in applications.[35] Hepler and Noble affirmed the importance of maintaining admissions standards and reported that elevated admissions criteria at one school had only a minimal adverse impact on applications by the second year of implementation.[36] Both framed the graduate admission decision as an ethical issue in which the gate-keeping function of graduate admissions should prevail over enrollment goals. In many cases this has not happened.

A study by Peter Kindle and Ira Colby found higher acceptance rates for both full-time (76 percent) and part-time (74.3 percent) social work students than claimed by CSWE (68.8 percent). In 2003, 92 (60 percent) of the 153 reporting accredited and candidacy programs admitted more than 70 percent of their applicants while 26 (about 17 percent) programs admitted less than 50 percent.[37] Kindle and Colby's findings suggest that most applicants to graduate social work programs are likely to be admitted if they apply to multiple programs. For instance, the 23,498 full-time applicants adjusted by the average number of applications in their sample resulted in only 11,633 unique applicants; the 9,414 part-time applications in their study fell to 6,773.[38] Adjusting numerators to recalculate enrollment rates produced substantially higher estimates of 76 percent for full-time students and 74.3 percent for part-time students. For Kindle and Colby this suggested a decided lack of selectivity in admissions, which is especially striking when compared to admissions rates in other professions (see Table 2).

Open enrollment presents a challenge to the gate-keeping function of graduate education. According to Kindle and Colby, "Although this conclusion cannot be specifically applied to any individual program, acceptance rates at these high levels suggest that there is, in effect, an open enrollment policy for graduate social work education on a national level."[39] The authors conclude that:

> The proliferation of programs, low GRE scores among graduate social work students, and modest entry-level wages for social work graduates are consistent with a national trend toward open enrollment.[40] If high enrollment rates are escalating based on the growth of programs, it can be predicted that low GRE scores among graduate social work students, modest entry-level wages for social work graduates, and declining pass rates on the MSW licensing examination will prevail as the number of programs grow.[41]

Table 3
Graduate Application By Field, Fall 2005

Major Field	Total Applications	Accepted Applications	Applications Not Accepted
Total	1,290,635	588,510 (46%)	696,072 (54%)
Biological Sciences*	81,834	25,872 (32%)	55,692 (68%)
Business	152,147	79,313 (52%)	72,279 (48%)
Education	134,335	93,306 (70%)	40,150 (30%)
Engineering	153,102	60,682 (40%)	92,077 (60%)
Health Sciences	90,173	40,894 (46%)	48,608 (54%)
Humanities & Arts	135,696	45,870 (34%)	89,404 (66%)
Physical Sciences	141,326	52,677 (37%)	88,167 (63%)
Public Adm. & Services	42,550	26,874 (63%)	15,557 (37%)
Social Sciences	166,593	56,271 (34%)	109,665 (66%)
Other Fields*	91,365	46,869 (52%)	43,260 (48%)

NOTE: Because not all institutions responded to all items, detail variables may not sum to total. Percentages are based on total of known acceptance status.

* Biological Sciences includes agriculture.
** The category "Other Fields" includes architecture, communications, home economics, library sciences and religion.

Source: Heath Brown, Graduate Enrollment and Degrees: 1986 to 2005. Council of Graduate Schools, Office of Research and Information Services, Washington, DC.

While CSWE data includes acceptance rates for master's programs, the statistics do not provide information about the quality of student applications or the standards employed in admissions decisions. Hence, while most social work programs reported relatively constant admissions rates (from 60-68 percent) from 1985 to 2004, there is little information about the academic abilities of the students admitted. Moreover, while many MSW programs require a GRE, not all schools use these scores in admissions decisions. In short, rising numbers of new master's programs coupled with the relatively stagnant growth in student applications, suggests that many—if not most—social work graduate programs are downgrading admissions standards or employing an open admissions policy to maintain stable student numbers. The ramifications of the declining quality of the admissions process are reflected in the abysmally low GRE scores.

Social work not only falls far below graduate students who apply to study the physical sciences, but also those who are pursuing studies in related fields, such as social psychology, secondary education, public health, clinical psychology, sociology, psychology, nursing, and elementary education. The data show that students applying for graduate social work studies not only have low verbal scores, but the *lowest* mathematical scores. Every academic or applied discipline related to social well-being attracts graduate applicants who score higher than social work applicants. Applying to graduate studies is a self-selection process, of course, and it is worth noting that graduate applicants to animal management—fish studies, wildlife management, and veterinary medicine (a profession that is overwhelmingly female)—score higher than most disciplines related to their human counterpart. Evidently, some disciplines attract students whose verbal and computational skills are quite strong, while others appeal to weaker applicants. That social work attracts applicants who are among the least proficient verbally and mathematically raises fundamental questions about their promise as human service professionals.

Not surprisingly, a further reduction of admissions standards will have even more dire consequences for the future of the profession. Alice Lieberman and Margaret Severson sum up the dilemma: "Are our clients suffering, and will they continue to do so, because of the need of graduate programs to fill student slots by dipping even lower into their applicant pools?"[42] Eileen Gambrill's editorial in the *Journal of Social Work Education* summarizes the dilemma: "To the extent to which … effective programs … [do not] contribute to helping clients, we create professionals who cannot fulfill required practices and policies advocated in our accreditation guidelines and code of ethics."[43]

Table 4
Distribution of Graduate Record Examination (GRE) Scores Within Graduate Major Field (2005)

DISCIPLINE	N	VERBAL MEAN	QUANTITATIVE MEAN	TOTAL (Verbal Mean + quant. Mean)
Physics	3,785	541	744	1285
Mathematics	4,088	519	741	1260
Physical Chem	966	514	713	1227
Aerospace Engr	2,662	498	727	1225
All Phil. Fields	3,304	589	636	1225
Biomedical Engr	4,298	500	717	1217
Chemical Engr	3,725	487	728	1215
Economics	7,254	505	706	1211
Computer Engr	4,868	478	729	1207
Chemistry, Gen	1,229	499	696	1195
Electrical Engr	10,542	468	727	1195
Mechanical Engr	6,634	469	725	1194
Computer Sci	20,262	477	716	1193
Neurosciences	2,686	527	665	1192
Finance	971	476	709	1185
Ecology	2,342	535	643	1178
Linguistics	1,335	553	625	1178
Biochemistry	3,256	497	678	1175
Organic Chem	2,258	490	685	1175
Cell & Molec Bio	4,929	507	660	1167
Cognitive Psych	1,149	529	630	1159
Civil Engr	4,388	450	708	1158
Genetics	2731	500	654	1154
Music History	925	540	606	1146
Religion	844	554	584	1138
Europe History	2,341	565	572	1137
Industrial Engr	2,453	426	706	1132
Computer Prog	1,574	437	694	1131
Geology	2,297	495	630	1125
Internat. Rel	8,889	528	597	1125
Relig. Studies	617	545	578	1123
French	670	540	580	1120

Table 4 (cont.)

Eng Lang & Lit	8,564	564	555	1119
Zoology	974	501	613	1114
City & Reg Plan	1,482	505	605	1110
Environ Sci	2,858	491	617	1108
Epidemiology	1,023	492	614	1106
Archaeology	1,596	535	570	1105
Pub Policy	4,213	516	589	1105
Social Psych	1,921	511	592	1103
Biology	4,812	487	615	1102
Anthropology	3,541	530	571	1101
Creative Writing	5,467	553	548	1101
Marine Biology	1,655	489	611	1100
Art History	2,237	540	560	1100
Pharmacology	1,476	459	640	1099
Microbiology	2,658	482	614	1096
Poli Sci/Govern	3,011	519	573	1092
Architecture	5,745	469	619	1088
Information Sci	2,630	448	639	1087
Amer History	3,582	533	549	1082
Wildlife Mgmt	1,106	483	596	1079
Pathology	567	469	610	1079
Veterinary Med	6,955	477	601	1078
Medical Sci	1,695	466	609	1075
Agricult Econ	913	451	622	1073
Forestry & Rel Sci	664	477	595	1072
Library Sci	2,757	532	539	1071
Veterinary Sci	1,252	474	596	1070
Geography	1,514	488	578	1066
Exp Psych	926	492	573	1065
Secondary Ed.	7,512	485	578	1063
Public Health	6,863	479	579	1058
Design	720	469	589	1058
Physiology	1,113	457	599	1056
Urban Studies	713	488	568	1056
Drama/Theatre	1,322	512	543	1055
Music	3,014	489	564	1053
Clinical Psych	16,862	483	556	1039

Table 4 (cont.)

Develop Psych	1,644	477	560	1037
Journl/Mass Comm	5,356	491	543	1034
Sociology	4,120	487	544	1031
Psychology	3,990	477	551	1028
Radio, TV& Film	2,851	480	541	1021
Spanish	1,408	484	535	1019
Law	656	478	539	1017
Indust. & Org Psych	3,966	462	550	1012
Fine Arts	962	480	530	1010
Bus Adm.	1,986	432	568	1000
Labor/Ind Rel	503	453	546	999
Art	583	475	522	997
Physical Therapy	10,486	430	563	993
Advertising	1,250	443	546	989
Ed. Psych	1,259	451	537	988
Nursing	8,403	453	526	979
Nutrition	2,839	434	543	977
Allied Health	2,168	430	547	977
School Psych	3,000	449	528	977
Elem Ed.	6,455	443	527	970
Personnel Srvcs	630	448	522	970
Public Admin	2,445	452	513	965
Audiology	1,726	436	520	956
Occup Therapy	1,835	431	525	956
Counsel Psych	12,660	445	505	950
Pub Relations	2,087	445	505	950
Parks & Rec.	512	425	514	939
Family Counsel	717	436	496	932
Special Ed.	2,335	429	501	930
Speech/Lan Path	12,882	427	495	922
Early Child Ed	1,418	418	495	913
Cr. Just/Crmlgy	4,019	423	483	906
Social Work	9,672	428	468	896
Physical Ed.	1,450	397	497	894

Source: Education Testing Service, Retrieved from http://www.ets.org/Media/Tests/GRE/pdf/generaldistribution.pdf on September 30, 2006

To date CSWE has refused to establish metric standards for applicants of graduate programs, such as the GRE or Millers Analogies Test. CSWE could establish a minimum suggested score on these exams. While there is justification for not presuming that standardized tests like the GRE or MAT should be the sole determinants of academic performance, extremely low verbal or quantitative scores can indicate a serious learning problem. Even given the low combined verbal and quantitative GRE score of 896 for social work students, many faculty serving on admissions committees in universities that require the GRE have seen combined scores in the 400-450 range. Admitting these weaker students creates a pedagogical dilemma in terms of targeting material for different levels of students. If material is geared toward weaker students, the brightest students become bored, with some even choosing to leave the program in search of a more challenging graduate career. Conversely, if the material is targeted to the brightest students, the weaker ones are lost. The extremely wide range of student abilities resulting from open enrollment leads to a compromised learning environment and a curriculum that may be next to impossible to devise. In the worst case scenario, the choice is whether to focus efforts on retaining weaker students or challenging the brightest students. This dilemma is complicated by pressures felt by faculty members whose merit raises and promotion are influenced by student evaluations.

That rapid program growth in social work has occurred regardless of concerns about student performance has become a source of controversy in higher education. At the undergraduate level, colleges and universities have come under withering criticism for "batch processing" students.[44] In their Public Broadcasting System documentary on higher education, Richard Hersh and John Merrow noted that criticism of education in the United States has been working its way from elementary education upward.

> We found an insidious erosion of quality that we now believe places the nation at risk. The threat, it seems to us, is more serious today than it was in 1983, when the famous "A Nation at Risk" report warned that our schools were "drowning in a rising tide of mediocrity." Our K-12 system, although somewhat improved from that time, continues to wallow in mediocrity, and now higher education is suffering from the same condition. The tide continues to rise, the rot is creeping upward, and time is running out.[45]

Questions about the quality of professional education have been raised about education schools, and it is just a matter of time until such criticism targets schools of social work. Yet, candid assessments about the aptitude of social work students are rare. For example, an evaluation of composition skills possessed by entering social work graduate students found that one-third had deficits, but only 57 percent of these sought help through writing assistance that was offered them.[46] Such findings add poignancy to Gambrill's query that "we just assume our graduates do more good than harm. But do they?"[47]

Conclusion

Social work education is perched on a precipice. The unbridled growth of social work programs, a relatively stagnant applicant pool, declining student numbers in many programs, increased competition between social work programs, and the crowding of existing MSW programs by new BSW programs with aspirations of venturing into graduate education all compromise the quality of professional education. These problems are further aggravated by what has essentially become open enrollment in graduate social work education, leading to a weaker student body that is reflected in abysmally low GRE scores and rising rates of failure on social work licensing examinations. In an age of increased accountability driven by dwindling university resources, it is doubtful that these conditions can exist indefinitely. An increasingly severe recession will cause university administrators to reevaluate the status of social work programs. Some will opt to terminate the weakest social work programs. Other administrators will be inclined to merge social work with other academic units. While apologists for the status quo may cite continued growth of accredited programs, one consideration is irrefutable: virtually all of the growth has been at the lower end of the hierarchy of professional education; there have been no first-tier schools of social work established in recent memory.

The failure of many social work programs to measure up to any demonstrable standard of accountability is a secret that cannot be kept indefinitely. The increased use of university-commissioned quality studies, such as that done by Academic Analytics, will prove a challenge for under-performing social work programs. Leaders of undergraduate education have advocated various accountability measures, such as the Voluntary System of Accountability, the National Survey of Student Engagement, and the Collegiate Learning Assessment (described in Chapter 10), but these are virtually unknown in social work education. Rather than embrace accountability, the most recent EPAS misses this opportunity. If social work education will not clean its own house, there are others that will do so, but without compassion. Essentially, CSWE hides behind the rhetoric that social work is a professional program and should not be held to the same academic standards as other programs, an argument that long ago lost its currency.

The rapid growth of new social work programs has profound consequences for educational quality and salaries. While this growth can be viewed as a *de facto* attempt to curb the encroachment on traditional social work turf by counseling psychologists, family therapists, nurses, and even sociologists, the strategy has been ineffective. On the contrary, social work programs produce practitioners that are less able to compete with other disciplines. Lieberman and Severson make the point: "If we continue this dangerous trend by our failure to stop the proliferation of new programs, we will have no one to blame but ourselves when we find our tolerance for minimal standards, in both student and program quality, increasing by necessity."[48]

CSWE is unlikely to curtail program growth because its business model is predicated on fees from an increasing number of accredited programs. While some social work educators, such as Frank Raymond, argue that a moratorium is both unnecessary and illegal (a violation of the Sherman Anti-Trust Act), other social work educators like Alice Lieberman and attorney Margaret Severson contend that a such a moratorium is both necessary and is likely legal, "In reality, CSWE can be sued for anything, including a violation of the Sherman Act. Whether CSWE would lose that contest is another issue, one over which neither Raymond nor we have any special predictive powers. We once again assert our belief that a moratorium on new master's programs would not constitute an attempt to monopolize or restrain trade or commerce."[49]

The more fundamental issue is the inferior quality of social work training, a problem that is pervasive throughout professional education. Absent a strategy to upgrade the performance of existing schools of social work, a moratorium simply affirms a substandard status quo. For a half-century CSWE has not only choreographed educational mediocrity in social work education but has become economically dependent on its continuing expansion. The refusal of CSWE to adopt accountability measures that have been introduced by hundreds of institutions of higher education demonstrates how far behind the curve of professional education social work's sole accreditation authority has become. Rather than insist that schools of social work perform optimally, CSWE stamps accredited programs with an imprint of mediocrity.

References

1. Gene Maeroff, "The Media: Degrees of Coverage," in Richard Hersh and John Merrow, *Declining by Degrees: Higher Education at Risk* (New York: Palgrave MacMillan, 2005), p. 12.

2. C. Wright Mills, *Sociology and Pragmatism* (New York: Oxford University Press, 1966), p. 49.

3. Murray Levine and Adeline Levine, *A Social History of Helping Services* (New York: Appleton-Century-Crofts, 1970.

4. T.H. Marshall, *Class, Citizenship and Social Development* (Chicago, University of Chicago Press, 1964.

5. Harold Wilensky and Charles Lebeaux, *Industrial Society and Social Welfare* (New York: Free Press, 1965), p. 127.

6. Leon Ginsbert, *Conservative Social Welfare* (Chicago: Nelson Hall, 1998), p. 70.

7. Alan Rubin, *Statistics on Social Work Education in the United States: 1985* (Council on Social Work Education: Alexandria, VA, 1986).

8. Council on Social Work Education, Accreditation News, Reports and Archives. Retrieved February 28, 2009, from http://www.cswe.org/CSWE/accreditation/Accreditation+News+Reports+And+Archives

9. "Statistics on Social Work Education," (Alexandria, VA: Council on Social Work Education, 2007).

10. The Princeton Review, "Is the U.S. Right for You?" Circa 2006. Retrieved May 16, 2007 from, http://www.princetonreview.com/college/research/articles/international/usright.asp; and Council on Social Work Education, *Statistics on Social Work Education: 2004* (Author: Alexandria, VA, 2007).

11. National Center for Education Statistics, *Projections of Education Statistics to 2015,* 2006. Retrieved May 7, 2007 from http://nces.ed.gov/programs/projections.

12. From 2000 to 2004, full- and part-time BSW student enrollment actually shrank by 24 percent, dropping from 43,046 students to 32,752.

13. The number of degrees awarded fluctuates from year to year, perhaps due to variations in the failure of all accredited programs to report data. Requests to CSWE to obtain the percent of programs reporting were not returned. Much of this discussion is based on detailed data on program performance captured in a 2004 CSWE report; since that time, reports are more cursory.

14. Council on Social Work Education, *Statistics on Social Work Education: 2004.*

15. Lennon, *Statistics on Social Work Education: 1990;* and Todd Lennon, *Statistics on Social Work Education: 2003* (Alexandria, VA: Council on Social Work Education, 2004).

16. Patricia Keith-Spiegel and Michael Wiederman, *The Complete Guide to Graduate School Admission: Psychology, Counseling, and Related Professions* (Mahwah, NJ: Erlbaum, 2000).

17. Peter A. Kindle and Ira Colby, "Public and Private University Preferences Reported by MSW Students," unpublished manuscript, 2007.

18. Columbia University, School of Social Work Admissions, February 9, 2007. Retrieved May 23, 2007, from http://www.columbia.edu/cu/ssw/admissions/news/ApplyFall/index.html.

19. Rubin, *Statistics on Social Work Education in the United States: 1985*; and Council on Social Work Education, Accreditation News, Reports and Archives..

20. Council on Social Work Education, *Statistics on Social Work Education: 2004,* p. 2.

21.   Ibid
22.   Council on Social Work Education, *Directory of Colleges and Universities with Accredited Social Work Degree Programs, 2002;* Council on Social Work Education, *Statistics on Social Work Education: 2004,* p. 52.
23.   Julia Hidalgo and Elaine Spaulding, *Statistics on Social Work Education in the United States: 1986* (Alexandria, VA: Council on Social Work Education, 1987).
24.   Council on Social Work Education, *Summary Information on Master of Social Work Programs, 2001-2002.*
25.   Julia Hidalgo and Elaine Spaulding, *Statistics on Social Work Education in the United States: 1986;* Council on Social Work Education, *Statistics on Social Work Education: 2004.*
26.   Leon Botstein, "The Curriculum and College Life," in Richard Hersh and John Merrow, *Declining by Degrees* (New York: Palgrave MacMillan, 2005).
27.   *Statistics on Social Work Education,* 2006, p. 9.
28.   According to the College and University Professional Association for Human Resources, the minimum salaries for assistant and associate professors of social work in 2006 were $30,000, suggesting that social work was indeed a bargain for the frugal academic administrator. Curiously the low range of median salaries reported by CSWE for 2006 are significantly higher, $43,318 and $52,000, respectively.
29.   "Almanac Issue 2007-2008," *Chronicle of Higher Education,* August 31, 2007, p. 33.
30.   Lennon, *Statistics on Social Work Education: 2003;* Council on Social Work Education, *Statistics on Social Work Education: 2004,* p. 9.
31.   Arthur Levine, "Disconnects Between Students and Their Colleges, in Richard Hersh and John Merrow, *Declining by Degrees* (New York: Palgrave MacMillan, 2005), p. 164.
32.   *Statistics on Social Work Education* (Alexandria, VA: Council on Social Work Education, 2006), pp. 5-6.
33.   Katherine Dunlap, Mark Fraser, and H. Carl Henley, "The Relationship Between Admissions Criteria and Academic Performance in an MSW Program," *Journal of Social Work Education,* 34 (1998), pp. 455-462; Patricia Henry, Roseanna McCleary, and Marion Thomas, "Effectiveness of Admission Criteria on Student Performance in Classroom and Field Instruction," *Advances in Social Work,* 5(1)(2004), pp. 33-46; and Brenda Donahue and Bruce Thyer, "Should the GRE Be Used as an Admissions Requirement by Schools of Social Work? *Journal of Teaching in Social Work,* 6(2)(1992), pp. 33-40.
34.   Anne Fortune, "Comparison of Faculty Ratings of Applicants and Background Characteristics as Predictors of Performance in a MSW Program," *Journal of Teaching in Social Work,* 23(1/2)(2003), pp. 35-54; Dunlap, Fraser and Henley, "The Relationship Between Admissions Criteria and Academic Performance in an MSW Program"; Linnea GlenMaye and Margaret Oakes, "Assessing Suitability of MSW Applicants Through Objective Scoring of Personal Statements," *Journal of Social Work Education,* 38(2001), pp. 67-82; and Jaclyn Miller and Beverly Koerin, "Can We Assess Suitability at Admission? A Review of MSW Application Procedures," *Journal of Social Work Education,* 34(1998), pp. 437-453.
35.   Catherine Born and Donald Carroll, "Ethics in Admissions," *Journal of Social Work Education, 24(1988),* pp. 79-85.
36.   Juanita Hepler and John Nobel, "Improving Social Work Education: Taking Responsibility at the Door," *Social Work, 35*(1990), pp. 126-133.
37.   Lennon, *Statistics on Social Work Education: 2003.*

38. Ibid.

39. Kindle and Colby, "Public and Private University Preferences Reported by MSW Students."

40. Howard Karger and David Stoesz, "The Growth of Social Work Education Programs, 1985-1999: Its Impact on Economic and Educational Factors Related to the Profession of Social Work," *Journal of Social Work Education, 39*(2002), pp. 279-295.

41. D. DeAngelis, personal communication, May 18, 2005, quoted in Kindle and Colby, "Public and Private University Preferences Reported by MSW Students."

42. Alice Lieberman and Margaret Severson, "Should There Be a Moratorium on the Development of Social Work Education Programs? Yes!" *Journal of Social Work Education, 34(1998)*, p. 167.

43. Eileen Gambrill, "Evaluating the Quality of Social Work Education: Options Galore," *Journal of Social Work Education, 37*(2001), pp. 419-420.

44. David Kirp, "The Little Student Went to Market," in Richard Hersh and John Merrow, eds., *Declining by Degrees* (New York: Palgrave MacMillan, 2005), p. 126.

45. Richard Hersh and John Merrow, "Introduction," in authors, eds., *Declining by Degrees* (New York: Palgrave MacMillan, 2005), pp. 2-3.

46. Catherine Alter and Carl Adkins, "Improving the Writing Skills of Social Work Students," *Journal of Social Work Education, 37*(2001), pp. 493-506.

47. Gambrill, "Evaluating the Quality of Social Work Education," p. 419.

48. Lieberman and Severson, "Should There Be a Moratorium on the Development of Social Work Education Programs?," p. 167.

49. Lieberman and Severson, "Should There Be a Moratorium on the Development of Social Work Education Programs?" p. 182.

5

Eduscierosis

Since the Enlightenment, the university has been an intellectual commons, providing the institutional space for the development and debate of ideas. With the unprecedented wealth that accompanied industrialization and the advent of the Progressive Era, higher education's resources were also committed to public benefit. The promise of professionalism contributed to twin features that would subsequently define American higher education as a social institution: specialization and bureaucratization. Expanded with the inception of the Welfare State and the Cold War, higher education grew rapidly; during the twentieth century the *uni*versity morphed into the *multi*versity. A powerful engine of technical innovation as well as public purpose, American higher education attained international preeminence.

Yet, the genius of American colleges and universities contained an organizational hazard. In the United States, institutions of higher education have enjoyed independence from political and commercial interference, guaranteed by self-governance. Unlike accreditation in other developed nations, the quality of American colleges and universities has been assured by accrediting authorities that are separate from government. Ostensibly, this has protected universities and colleges from meddling from elected officials and the corruption of market forces, but the organizational freedom they have enjoyed invites an internal problem: unaccountable to the public by direct means, higher education can degenerate into a bureaucracy maintained by a self-perpetuating patronage system of educators and administrators. Under these circumstances, instead of assuring high quality performance, accreditation serves to institutionalize a self-serving status quo. A contradiction of its openness, accreditation contributes to the opacity of colleges and universities. "Accreditation, which could help lift the veil, has all the openness of the old Politburo," noted Gene Maeroff.[1]

Patronage vs. Merit

A hallmark of Progressivism was its opposition to political patronage that had metastasized due to immigration and urbanization. Prior to the security established by the welfare state, corrupt political machines exploited unemployed and poor immigrants who flooded American cities. Muckrakers' attempts to ferret out corruption contributed to some of the most comic moments in American history. When Lincoln Steffens investigated New York's Tammany Hall, George Washington Plunkett, one of its cronies, took umbrage: "Steffens means well, but like all reformers, he don't know how to make distinctions. He can't see no difference between honest graft and dishonest graft and, consequently, he gets things all mixed up."[2] In Chicago, political machine boss Jacob Avery described the *quid pro quo* of jobs and contracts in exchange for political support succinctly: "Politics is the art of putting people under obligation to you."[3]

Part of the Progressive project was to put an end to such mischief by establishing merit as a basis of public employment. In that endeavor reformers drew on the work of German sociologist, Max Weber, who posited the bureaucracy as an organizational form congruent with industrialization. The Weberian model of bureaucracy was organized around rational principles.[4] In a bureaucratic model offices are ranked, and their operations are characterized by impersonal rules with appointments based on specialized qualifications. Fundamental components of this bureaucratic model include:

- Specific rules bind the official functioning of an organization;

- Spheres of competence define a specialized division of labor;

- Offices are organized around the principle of hierarchy;

- Offices are regulated by technical rules or norms;

- Administration is separate from ownership of the means of production;

- All acts, rules, and decisions are recorded in writing;

- Positions constitute a career with a clearly delineated system of promotion; and

- Candidates for appointment are assessed according to technical qualifications.[5]

For Weber, bureaucracy was the antithesis of patronage that had compromised governance.

Modern bureaucracy in the interest of integrity has developed a high sense of status honor; without this sense the danger of an awful corruption and a vulgar Philistinism threatens fatally. And without integrity, even the purely technical functions of the state apparatus would be endangered.[6]

In this manner, Weber not only identified the primary organizational form that would typify business as well as government, but also the means for employment and promotion: merit. "The idea of advancement based on merit, however, presumes some independent criteria of judgment. Modern societies commonly use educational credentials and standardized tests as proxies for merit."[7]

A dramatic increase in the demand for vocational education accompanied the emergent bureaucracy, compelling institutions of higher education to augment their traditional, liberal arts focus with professional training. Higher education adapted to industrialization and urbanization relatively quickly, offering a range of vocational programs that provided unprecedented career opportunities for upwardly mobile Americans. The demand for a utilitarian education was so pronounced that colleges who rejected the trend flirted with "institutional extinction."[8] Social work was among the disciplines that capitalized on the secularization of American higher education, promising a rational method for uplifting distressed citizens and their communities. Auxiliary activities reinforced social work's claim to professional status, not the least of which was the emergence of "scientific philanthropy."[9] Collaterally, other disciplines, such as public health, visiting nursing, and juvenile services, subscribed to the Progressive belief in social engineering.[10] As these disciplines embedded themselves in metropolitan and state government, they were confronted with patronage appointments by elected officials, coworkers who had little training, and perhaps, even less sympathy for the problems encountered by fellow citizens. This obstacle was overcome by the Pendleton Act of 1883, which established the civil service in federal employment. Henceforth, merit would be the basis for employment and promotion in government.

At first glance, merit would appear to graft well onto higher education, particularly the incipient professions that were evolving with the Progressive project. After all, these were the very disciplines that based their expertise on scientific methods. As an inherently critical, self-renewing system for generating knowledge, science *should* also serve to constantly upgrade professional performance in higher education. All too often, however, disciplines crafted ways to avoid accountability in academe. This was perhaps understandable for the liberal arts, such as literature and performance arts where standards were inherently subjective, but the professions that emerged during the Progressive Era were allegedly different insofar as they employed objective criteria in assessing efficacy. Yet, the issue was elided. Two world wars followed by a Cold War served to mute and postpone discussions about the quality of American higher education. As a result of the destruction of the economic and educational infrastructure of Europe and Japan during World War II, American higher education was unrivaled.

Politicizing Higher Education

Gradually, questions about the integrity of American colleges and universities surfaced during the postwar era. College graduates in the United States compared unfavorably with those from other nations with respect to their scientific knowledge, facility with mathematics, and foreign language proficiency. Increasingly, universities in the United States began to depend on foreign students to fill classes in difficult courses that disinterested American students, particularly physics, computer science, molecular chemistry, and genetic biology, among others. What was worse, many American students perceived higher education to be an extension of adolescence, a caricature that would serve as the basis for Tom Wolfe's bestseller, *I Am Charlotte Simmons*.[11]

Questions about the life-style of students were a *cause célèbre* for conservatives during the 1960s, but subsequently the Right identified more malevolent forces at work. Conservatives took higher education to task for having become a vast, left-wing dystopia. Allan Bloom indicted American higher education for having disavowed its Western intellectual heritage.[12] Roger Kimball argued that the politicization of the university had resulted in its fragmentation: "multiculturalism" has become regnant, which "the politics of ethnic and racial redress is allowed to trump unity."[13] Dinesh D'Souza criticized universities for catering to the sensibilities of aggrieved women, Blacks, and Latinos by establishing academic programs that validated their victimhood.[14] By the end of the twentieth century these critiques were sustained by organizations, such as the National Association of Scholars, whose mission was to confront and, if possible, eradicate Leftist influences in higher education.

The conservative jeremiad against higher education as the last bastion of American liberalism, was not the figment of Right wing ideologues alone, however. Late in the 1980s, Russell Jacoby had also inveighed against the corruption of higher education for abrogating its Progressive mission of public service. In *The Last Intellectuals*, Jacoby accused professors of insulating themselves from the broad array of public issues that had been fodder of "public intellectuals" of generations before. The nation's colleges and universities had degenerated into *de facto* "private clubs for accredited members," alleged Jacoby. "That it is difficult for an educated adult American to name a single political scientist or sociologist or philosopher is not wholly his or her fault; the professionals have abandoned the public arena."[15] The university provided an ideal haven for the 1960s radical seeking a more stable career in applied ideology: higher education offered a tolerant administration, impressionable students, and a tradition of academic freedom. As Jacoby saw it, "the academization of a left-wing intelligentsia was not simply imposed, it was desired. For the leftists, appointment to state or academic bureaucracies constituted small steps on the path to power—or so they fantasized. Careerism and revolution converged."[16]

Not only had higher education become politicized, but in so doing, it became commercial. Traditional curricula based on foundation courses in the liberal arts were scrapped for a smorgasbord of electives, the summation of which appeared to defy the concept of an educated person, but they appealed directly to the specific interests of groups of students who demanded a course of study crafted to their requirements. Sympathetic faculty who reflected the preferences of student groups advocated the replacement of a traditional curriculum with an assortment of electives from which students, now educational consumers, could select. European philosophical fashions, such as postmodernism, provided the intellectual cover for deconstructing the traditional curriculum. As David Kirp reflected,

> The No Curriculum is ideologically compatible with these faculty members' rejection of the Enlightenment, or modernist, commitment to the search for truth through the exposure of error, in favor of the relativism of postmodernity. The new guard trashed the fundamental belief that their calling was to transmit knowledge to the next generation. On the contrary, they insisted, all knowledge was relative and no approach to the universe of wisdom was better than any other; for that reason, requiring students to learn any given body of knowledge was arbitrary. More pointedly, it reflected the imposition of Dead White Male orthodoxy, or embodied neocolonialism, or enshrined heterosexism, or racism, or.... —the litany of postmodern pejoratives is seemingly endless.[17]

The postmodern incursion, initially drawing fire from the Right, eventually gained traction among academic centrists who expressed misgivings about American higher education. Derek Bok, former President of Harvard University, lamented the widening chasm between the purpose of higher education and its performance: "faculties seem inclined to use research and experimentation to understand and improve every institution, process, and human activity except their own."[18] Echoing Jacoby's allegation that faculty were increasingly conducting research and publishing, not out of concern for the public, but in order to impress their peers, Bok noted that "many academic books and articles published today seem uncomfortably narrow, bound too closely by the confines and conventions of their discipline to do full justice to the problems they address."[19] Yet, the prospect of faculty assuming broader social responsibility in their work is subverted by countervailing forces. Presidents and deans are reluctant to offend faculty who may oppose an academic leader who takes liberties with professors' privileges. As Bok's predecessor at Harvard, Lawrence Summers, discovered, a disgruntled faculty could enlist alumni and donors to subvert academic leadership. After making an investment of several semesters of credit in a college, students are reluctant to exercise their prerogatives in the academic marketplace, vote with their feet, and transfer to another institution. State officials and trustees may well find academic administration an impenetrable thicket of customs, practices, and departments, the feudal nature of which is not worth the trouble of trying to understand, let alone reform.[20] Thus, by the second millennium American higher education had become a "black hole" which, despite consuming infinite volumes of resources, remained exempt from accountability.

Social Work Education

The absence of critical analysis of social work education is consistent with that of higher education as a whole; most research on social work education is rudimentary, conveniently evading any connection between faculty instruction and student performance. Since the 1970s, for example, a gender disparity in educational leadership has been identified. A study by John Gandy, Jerry Randolph, and Frank Raymond conducted between 1972 and 1976 found that deans were predominantly middle-aged males.[21] Thirty years later, the same demographics applied. According to the National Association of Deans and Directors (NADD), 61 percent of deans/directors are male, almost 74 percent are white, and 97 percent are

46 years old or older.[22] Reflecting the lack of reliability in social work information, data from the Council on Social Work Education (CSWE) found that women slightly outnumber men as chief administrative officers (deans/directors). At the graduate-only level, women make up 53.7 percent of deans/directors; 53.3 percent at the combined (MSW/BSW) level; and 62.6 percent at the baccalaureate level.[23] While the reason for the difference between the data is unclear, the NADD study had a slightly higher response rate (83 percent versus CSWE's 77 percent). Regardless, based on a proportional approach (female faculty outnumber male faculty by a 2 to 1 margin), female deans/directors should occupy a larger portion of deanships/directorships than their male counterparts.

Early research on leadership in social work education focused on administrative activities. A 1979 study by Jack Otis and Penelope Caragonne sought to identify why deans in social work programs resigned. The areas identified included budget problems, faculty problems, fund-raising, the inability to pursue professional goals, inadequate administrative support, problems with university administrations, personal concerns, and student problems.[24] Over a decade later Carlton Munson found that deans self-reported working 54 hours a week and the majority were on 11-month contracts. Deans reported 28 critical issues facing social work education, the top three being limited funding and diminished resources (25 percent), faculty recruitment to replace retirees (17 percent), and student enrollment (13 percent).[25]

Arguably, the most distinctive feature of research on the leadership of social work educators is its paucity. The absence of studies on what deans and directors actually do is striking. Since the creation of CSWE over a half-century ago, only a handful of studies have examined educational leadership in social work, and most of this consists of descriptive studies of demographics or administrative function. Conspicuously absent are references to social work's future in a competitive social services marketplace, the profession's role in assuring social justice, concern about lackluster social work research, the quality of faculty and students, or the proliferation of programs. The reedy research on educational research in social work education suggests a willful disinterest in the essential roles served by deans and directors.

Indeed, an examination of the scholarship of deans and directors suggests that this disregard may be functional. Virtually all deans and directors hold academic appointments in addition to their administrative title, and of these 93.3 percent were tenured and in senior faculty ranks; 71.1 percent were full professors.[26] Since a full professor is an academic not an administrative title it therefore implies scholarly achievement. Largely disregarding the teaching, research, or scholarly record of applicants for social work dean or director positions, the rank of a tenured full professor is often bestowed upon the successful candidate directly by the provost, thereby avoiding the scrutiny of a review by a university-wide tenure and promotion committee. In fact, as Tables 1 and 2 demonstrate, many social work deans and directors would fail a full-on university-wide review for tenure and promotion.

More than one-fourth of deans and directors of MSW programs had apparently published no SSCI-affiliated journal articles over their entire careers. Almost 52 percent had published only two or fewer articles; 70 percent had five or fewer articles. Less than 10 percent of deans/directors had 16 or more articles. Although deans/directors of MSW programs with a doctoral component scored somewhat better, their numbers were equally dismal. Almost 18 percent of these administrators had no SSCI refereed publications; 38 percent had zero to two articles; 57 percent had

Table 1

Publication Rates for Deans and Directors of MSW Programs. Refereed Journal Articles Cited in the Social Science Citation Index (SSSI)*

Number of Articles	No. of deans who published a total of:	% as total of all Deans/Directors
0	48	25.9%
1	31	16.8%
2	16	8.6%
3-5	34	18.3%
6-10	24	12.9%
11-15	15	8.2%
16-20	9	4.9%
21-35	3	1.6%
36-45	1	.54%
46-70	2	1.1%
70 plus	2	1.1%
Total = 185 deans and directors		**99.9%

* This includes BSW/MSW/PhD/DSW, MSW-only, and BSW/MSW programs
** Percentages were rounded off

Source: Table developed using the Social Science Citation Index, Thomson Scientific Publishers, 2006.

Table 2
Publication Rates for Deans and Directors of MSW Programs with a
DSW/PhD Component. Refereed Journal Articles Cited in the
Social Science Citation Index (SSSI)*

Number of Articles	No. of deans who published a total of:	% as total of all Deans/Directors
0	12	17.6%
1	7	10.3%
2	7	10.3%
3-5	13	19.1%
6-10	10	14.7%
11-15	6	8.8%
16-20	8	11.8%
21-44	1	1.5%
65-80	3	4.4%
81	1	1.5%
Total = 68 deans and directors		100.0%

* This includes BSW/MSW/PhD/DSW and MSW/PhD/DSW programs

Source: Table developed using the Social Science Citation Index, Thomson Scientific Publishers, 2006.

less than six; and 81 percent had fifteen or fewer articles. Only 19 percent of deans/directors in social work programs with a doctoral component had 16 or more refereed publications.

If tenure were partly based on 6 refereed articles, then almost 70 percent of all social work deans/directors would not have achieved tenure (some would not have even passed a third-year review) at the associate level, much less a promotion to tenured full professor. Although the number of deans/directors having six or fewer publications dropped to 57 percent for those in schools with a doctoral program, it remains strikingly high, especially since many administrative positions are in research-intensive universities where the minimum floor for tenure is significantly higher than six refereed publications. For example, if the minimum floor were raised to ten or more refereed publications, 78 percent of deans/directors in DSW/PhD programs would be denied tenure. When broken down, these low publication rates are even more troubling. All told, deans and directors published a total of 1,202 SSCI-cited articles. Roughly 35 percent (420) of those came from only six deans/directors. One dean alone accounted for almost 11 percent (130) of all SSCI-cited publications.

The implications of weak scholarship among deans and directors of schools of social work are not inconsequential. Like other organizations, institutions of higher education have a pecking order. Administrative stature in universities is a product of several skills: maintaining faculty productivity, attracting good students, securing grants and contracts, and representing the university to important stakeholders in the community. Scholarship advances most of these, while less scholarship is a handicap. Most colleges and universities have a high regard for research because it attracts dollars to the institution; however, research is also a basis for publications. Consequently, the dean or director who has secured a major grant achieves a measure of stature distinct from those who have not. Subsequent publications not only attest to the acumen of the administrator, but also provide a conduit to other grants and contracts. The dean or director who has been a competent scholar attains deference from the faculty by example; in addition, student research assistants benefit from the association with the project of the dean/director. Using SSCI publications as an indicator, perhaps only one-third of deans and directors would qualify as successful scholars.

While this structure is readily apparent in the more successful academic units on a campus, the obverse is equally true: the administrator who lacks research and scholarship has less authority vis-à-vishis peers in an institution. When push comes to shove, deans and directors defer to those with more stature, a particular problem when resources are scarce during a recession. Weak deans and directors are less able to advance an academic agenda especially when connections with foundations and government agencies are critical sources of external support. In this regard, although Title IV child welfare training funds augment the budgets of many schools of social work, they rarely are conduits to research grants. The SSCI publication rates of deans and directors of schools of social work suggest that half are weak scholars to a degree that it probably adversely affects the programs that they lead.

Organizationally, deans and directors who are weak scholars can shore-up their stature, although this has broader implications for a social work program. Some deans establish associate deanships to complement program directors and to lessen their workload, effectively battening their span of influence and increasing the school's administrative costs. Administrators tend to hire other administrators, positions which may or may not be legitimate based on the needs of the unit. Increased layers of bureaucracy can lead to wider salary gaps between administrators and faculty. The 2004 median salary for an associate dean was $91,841, but ranged as high as $138,985.[27] Elaboration of the administrative infrastructure creates a hierarchy that further distances faculty from the administration of a school.

Many deans and directors did not progress through normal academic ranks, but instead were given full professorships and tenure by provosts or deans based on their administrative appointment. Consequently, a number of social work administrators never underwent a peer review beyond the level of associate professor. The scholarship criterion under which a dean or director is hired is typically lower than for a regular full professor. This double standard may evoke resentment by research-active faculty who feel their academic credentials are significantly better than the dean or director under which they serve. Since deans/directors hold the purse strings and some are expected to publish, at least minimally, strong incentives exist to curry the favor of productive faculty for purposes of being listed as a second-author or co-principal investigator for a project to which he/she has diverted resources. This type of gratuitous back-scratching can lead to demoralized and cynical faculty members.

To what extent have schools of social work added administrative positions? Based on CSWE data for 41 graduate-only social work programs, 34 had associate or assistant deans or directors; 22 had PhD directors; 10 had MSW directors; 35 had field directors; nine had associate

Table 3
Annual Publications Expected*

Number of Publications Expected per Year	Research I Universities	Others
Less than 1	0 (0%)	8 (37%)
1	7 17%)	14 (47%)
2	23 (56%)	7 (23%)
3	9 (22%)	1 (3%)
More than 3	2 (5%)	0 (0%)
Total	41 (100%)	30 (100%)

* *Source:* 2007.10.08, Tenure Survey Report

field directors; ten had directors for admissions and minority recruitment; four had continuing education directors; and 10 had research directors.[28] According to Carlton Munson, an average of seven staff directly support the work of a dean. Munson found that 91 percent of deans had their own secretary; 57 percent of schools had associate deans (43 percent had assistant deans). Large schools employ support staff such as business managers, recruiters, advisors, development specialists, alumni liaisons and so forth. More recently, deans have embellished their administrations by adding multiple associate deans. At least two mid-level schools of social work (one with a faculty of 20 and the other with a faculty of 38) have followed this pattern with three associate deans.

The resources for top-heavy administrative structures in schools of social work are often derived from several sources: surcharges on student tuition, indirect charges against grants and contracts, and increasing reliance on adjunct faculty. The latter has been a trend in higher education in recent decades. Since 1987, the percent of full-time faculty has declined from 66 percent to 52 percent in 2005, while the percentage of part-time faculty has increased from 34 to 48 percent.[29]

Part-time instructors in social work education represented only 25.5 percent, comparatively, in 2006,[30] although these figures omit field instruction which is a large component of professional education in most social work curricula. Including field instructors would probably bring social work programs in line with other academic units with respect to that component of higher education taught by part-time instruction. While many part-time instructors teach as single-course adjuncts, that is not necessarily the case. "Part-timers work for the same institution for an average of 5.4 years and teach an average of almost two classes in each enrollment period," noted Vartan Gregorian.[31] Since part-time instructors are paid considerably less than full-time faculty, they serve an obvious advantage to administrators trying to cut program costs. Such administrators can quite plausibly argue that adjuncts augment instruction by tapping the expertise of experienced practitioners; however, their systematic use, especially when administrative positions are increased, raises fundamental questions about equity. Deans, associate deans, and program directors, enjoy a reduced teaching load, if they teach at all, yet their salaries are ordinarily significantly higher than full-time faculty. The gap in teaching caused by converting more faculty positions into administrative roles is compensated for employing more adjunct faculty, which probably reduces the quality of teaching and most certainly compromises the prospects of securing research grants.

The increasing reliance on part-time faculty raises profound questions for social work education. Enhancing administration may be justifiable when deans, associate deans, and the like are able to generate additional funding through grants and contracts; however, in the absence of such evidence, the school of social work reflects an academic class system in which academic administrators enjoy income and security far exceeding that of part-time faculty who are expendable by comparison. Equally problematic is the limited expectations of part-time faculty who are not expected to engage in the life of the school. As a result they tend not to be fully involved in governance, nor can they be expected to seek contracts, mount research projects, or mentor students. Indeed, one observer likened part-time and adjunct faculty who teach significant components of professional education to "guest workers," marginal teachers who effectively subsidize the salaries of the very administrators who hire them.[32]

The Social Agency Model

Under these conditions, social work education can easily devolve to an agency model of vocational education. In the absence of strong scholarship, deans and directors perceive themselves as executive directors; associate deans as program directors, faculty as professional staff, and students as clients. This transformation is reinforced by other considerations. When faculty lack strong research credentials and publish little, they are less likely to insist on academic leadership that is congruent with expectations typical of other professional schools. Because such a large component of social work education is in the form of internship credits, direct practice faculty already enjoy a significant influence in curricula, a pattern which is enhanced by the clinical nature of most social work programs and assured by the requirement that only MSWs can teach practice classes. Less capable students, as evident in their extremely low GRE scores, are unlikely to demand a more rigorous education. Instead, the low expectations of students evident in many social work programs help them manage concurrent obligations with family and employment. Even though there are provisions for students to intern in nontraditional agencies, these are rare. As a result, direct practice MSW supervision dominates, essentially replicating the status quo of professional education.

The traditional social agency model in social work education is marked by certain characteristics. For instance, appointments in a typical social agency are assumed to be permanent unless there are valid reasons to replace someone. Schools of social work that operate according to the social agency model occasionally have deans or directors who have appointments that span decades. Following the agency model, administrators have authority in all major decisions involving course assignments, evaluating faculty, coordinating projects, and the like. The school of social work that has adopted the social agency model features multiple and frequent faculty meetings, the proliferation of which wouldn't be tolerated by the faculty of other professional schools since they consume so much time. A logical consequence of so many meetings is that they interfere with activities standard for other professional schools, especially securing grants, mounting research projects and blocking out time for writing.

The financial rewards of directing a social work program are significant. Each year NADD conducts a nationwide study of the salaries of deans and directors.[33] Based on these findings, deans in some social work programs earn three or more times the salary of an assistant professor; twice the salary of an associate professor; and considerably more than a full professor, a differential that exists even when factoring in additional months of work. Large income differentials can lead to faculty resentment, especially when a dean/director exercises prerogatives of appointing and augmenting the salaries of subordinates. According to the 2005-2006 NADD report, the mean salary of 136 social work deans and directors (out of 164 members) was $118,494 while the median salary was $108,000. When disaggregated these numbers tell a different story. Deans and directors who headed public BSW/MSW/PhD (or DSW) programs earned $158,155 compared to $170,909 for those in private universities. Those in MSW/PhD/DSW programs in public institutions earned $143,359 a year compared to their cohorts in private institutions who earned $145,034. Beyond these two tiers the salaries drop off significantly with faculty in BSW/MSW programs earning roughly $95,000 a year.[34] By comparison, the 2004 median salary of full professors in joint graduate and undergraduate social work programs was $87,324; associate professors earned $63,528; and assistant professors earned $52,177.[35]

Once in place, the agency model is difficult to displace in social work education. There are several reasons why social work faculty might be receptive to the hierarchical, implicitly authoritarian nature of the traditional social agency. For one, the model is familiar to social work faculty who have spent time in an agency setting, often an expectation for an academic appointment. Second, the human relations orientation of social work—and the accompanying lack of reflection around the impact of unequal power and authority in social work practice of social work—is a factor that supports the social agency model. Third, students are easily converted into objects of social work intervention by a benevolent faculty, becoming clients who need social work services in the form of education and guidance. Time consuming curriculum issues takes on the characteristics of an intervention that requires endless hours of committee work, processing, and consulting, often about syllabi.

Accreditation serves to institutionalize the social agency model for social work education programs. CSWE's failure to identify specific standards which would bring social work education in line with other professional programs in higher education condones a regime of administration that is inferior to other modes of professional education. The social agency model, with its emphasis on process—moment-to-moment work—effectively lowers the expectations around research and scholarship that animates other academic units. To compensate for inferior research performance, social work faculty place a heavy emphasis on personal relationships, teaching, advising, service, and other concrete duties. Time spent in the office is seen as a measure of commitment and fealty toward the profession. In that sense, adopting the social agency model helps insulate social work faculty from expectations of the larger university community, while retaining a sense of connection to traditional norms in the practice arena more congruent with a social service agency.

Evidence of the social agency model can be inferred from research on the relative value attached to the conventional factors in promotion and tenure decisions: scholarship, teaching, and service. In a recent analysis, Robert Green found that 55.5 percent of the deans and directors of graduate programs that also awarded doctoral degrees valued scholarship above teaching which was valued above service; 36.2 percent of those managing MSW-only programs were likely to adhere to this pattern.[36] Although scholarship was valued above teaching and service, most graduate faculty reported that they actually placed it subordinate to teaching and service.[37] Unfortunately, the perceptions of undergraduate social work faculty have not been similarly evaluated; however, the likelihood is that they value teaching and service more than scholarship. Given the higher teaching loads of undergraduate faculty, they are probably even less able to squirrel away time for research than their colleagues in graduate programs, further eroding scholarship. Insofar as undergraduate programs have become more prevalent among accredited social work programs, the erosion of scholarship and elevation of service among social work educators as a whole is also likely.

Adopting a style of management more congruent with other professional disciplines may be problematic for a dean with limited scholarly credentials. A dean or director of social work who lacks scholarly productivity may expose him/herself to post-tenure review if he/she rotates to the faculty, providing a strong incentive for them to continue managing social work programs. Nor do most schools of social work have governance documents that explicitly permit a no-confidence vote for a dean or director. Since social work deans/directors can only be removed by a higher university administrator, rather than by a disgruntled faculty, the primary responsibility of a dean/director is toward the administrator who hired and supervises them, leading to a potential role conflict if the demands of higher-level administrators run counter to the best interests of a social work program. One example faced by many social work programs is the pressure to increase enrollments, secure external grants, and increase class sizes without a concomitant growth in faculty numbers. In other words, the faculty are expected to do more with less. When push comes to shove, the loyalties of many deans/directors lay with their provosts or deans rather than with the faculty they are supposed to represent, to say nothing of the larger objective of professional education they have pledged to advance. Confronted with funding reductions and faced with a highly tenured faculty, the temptation for deans/directors is to expand the corps of adjuncts for instruction. All too often deans and directors are essentially in middle management positions designed to ensure that the will of university administrators is implemented at the school or departmental level.

Since deans are replaced relatively often, there are opportunities to upgrade the administration of schools of social work. According to Carlton Munson, "Precise statistics are not available, but there has been a fairly high level of turnover in deanship positions in the last several decades. Heavy workloads, conflicting demands, inadequate resources, and limited support have been suggested as reasons for such turnover...."[38] NADD research indicated that the average dean or director has been in their current position for less than six years—the median time is four years.[39] Yet, overhauling the educational culture of a school of social work may not be forthright. Faculty serve as an essential component of any search committee for a dean, and their representatives enjoy some say so over the final candidates advanced to a provost for final selection. Not coincidentally, the power of the faculty to determine the dean is often counterbalanced by a committee chair typically from another academic discipline. In this way, central administrators are reassured that faculty won't feather their nest with a benign appointment. However, the committee chair often functions merely as facilitator for the process, thus forwarding the faculty's choice. In the end, finalists are unlikely to have diverged much from the preference of the faculty, and a highly tenured social work faculty with few research grants and publications is likely to nod approvingly in favor of candidates who will maintain the status quo. Mediocrity perpetuates itself.

Rapid program growth has further subverted leadership in social work education. The handful of accomplished deans and directors are hired by first-tier schools of social work, while less skilled administrators populate the ever expanding numbers of BSW and BSW-MSW programs. The increase in the number of smaller programs has weighted the membership of CSWE in their favor, subverting the prospect of more rigorous standards of administrative performance. As a result, the interaction of factors—complacent faculty, expansion in the number of accredited programs, and the inability of CSWE to elevate administrative performance—has created a perfect environment for driving down the quality of social work education.

The National Association of Deans and Directors

Instead of independently attempting to upgrade leadership in social work education, CSWE has collaborated with the National Association of Deans and Directors, which was formally organized in 1987 as a sequel to the National Conference of Deans and Directors of Schools of Social Work. CSWE not only houses and supervises a part-time position for NADD, but also houses the organization of Baccalaureate Program Directors (BPD). CSWE engages in the initial screening for the position and presumably gets a cut of NADD's dues to cover administrative costs (e.g., space and machines) and employee compensation. As a result of this close relationship, many deans/directors embed themselves in CSWE and NADD since these organizations afford them a social network, administrative visibility, and an inside track on future job opportunities. Some may also believe that active involvement with CSWE, and to a lesser degree NADD, provides some insurance against a negative reaccreditation study.

NADD evolved from a relatively informal organization that was open to deans or directors of graduate or combined graduate and undergraduate CSWE-accredited programs.[40] By 2006 NADD represented 186 member schools (plus two international ones) with each school paying $500 ($200 for international schools). NADD's budget was roughly $83,000 after subtracting the $10,000 it supposedly provided in yearly grants. The organization meets twice annually with meetings that tend to focus on the narrow interests of the membership. By comparison the Baccalaureate Program Directors (BPD) uses a broad-based conference approach that includes a call for papers.[41]

NADD's goals include: (1) educating the general public about the needs of social work education; (2) encouraging research that advances social work education; and (3) representing the interests of NADD members to CSWE. At best, NADD has failed to meet two of these three goals.[42] NADD's research objective has largely been limited to a Hartford Foundation funded position paper on geriatric social work education written by a doctoral student; and "Promoting Social Work Education for All Ages: A Guide for Deans and Directors."[43] NADD's success with other projects is even more doubtful, including its goal to "enhance the involvement of deans and directors to undertake legislative advocacy and other strategies that will ... promote progressive, responsible social policies."[44] Indeed, while NADDs 2006 conference focused on enhancing social work education's research infrastructure, the lack of interest in social and economic need was conspicuous.[45]

That NADD failed to improve the caliber of leadership was evident in the formation of the St. Louis Group in 2000. A founder of the Group was former Dean Ronald Feldman of Columbia University, who cited as a motivation,

> the relative impact of research-intensive schools upon the overall quality and direction of social work education actually has declined in the last two decades. To the extent they fail to play a determinate role in shaping social work education and improving social work practice, the profession's efforts to advance its knowledge base, enhance its expertise, and gain due legitimacy, credibility and public support are bound to falter and to adversely affect all of its constituent sectors.[46]

Feldman was not sanguine about existing organizations of social work educators, such as CSWE and NADD: "the leadership potential and future impact of research-intensive schools are increasingly being compromised and, even hindered by extant organizational and associational structures in social work."[47]

Edusclerosis

The social agency model of educational leadership and its *de facto* validation by CSWE and NADD have effectively subverted the prospects of institutional reform. This is ironic since Carlton Munson documented that the majority of academics who become deans and directors do so because they perceive opportunities for social change. They associate being an administrator with assuming a role that invites challenges in which they are willing to invest time and effort. Income and status are less motivating. Munson wrote that in 1994 and arguably times have changed.

In all likelihood the enthusiasm with which professors enter administration is dampened by the forces that snuff-out innovation in favor of institutional mediocrity. If the faculty are resistant to upgrading performance of a school of social work, the university provost may be similarly inclined so long as social work enrollments are adequate. All too often, social work programs have been accepted by university presidents and provosts, despite their inferior performance, because they are cash cows—they draw large numbers of students and are cheap to operate compared to the hard sciences that require expensive labs and equipment. That social work engages a disproportionate number of minority faculty and students is a decided plus for university administrators, since this is essential for addressing institutional diversity goals.Thus, a conspiracy of circumstances tends to erode the commitment of the social work dean or director who aspires to break free of the social agency model of social work education.

The dean or director who adjusts to the social agency model will, on the other hand, find an environment that, however suboptimal scholastically, is manageable politically. The strategic appointment of faculty as

Table 4
Reasons for Entering Academic Administration

Reason	% Reporting
Desire to influence change through leadership	55.8%
Interest in leadership role	32.7%
Desire for a challenge	30.8%
Desire for new stimulation	28.8%
Felt compelled by colleagues' nomination	23.1%
Desire for increased income	15.4%
Desire to increase skills and abilities	13.5%
Desire to implement specific goals	9.6%
Status, image and prestige	7.8%

Source: Carlton Munson, "A Survey of Deans of Schools of Social Work," Journal of Social Work Education (30)2 (Spring/Summer 1994), p. 158.

associate deans and program directors buys-off any incipient opposition because such positions ordinarily include salary bonuses and reduced teaching loads. An under-performing faculty is unlikely to object, even when an upward distribution of school resources required for augmenting the administration dictates a larger cohort of adjunct faculty. At professional meetings, the dean or director will find similar patterns extant at other schools of social work. Appointment and election to CSWE committees are often predicated on having signaled concurrence with the status quo, and this becomes essential for moving up the administrative food chain in social work education. The handful of deans and directors who have secured grants and maintained scholarship may have the inside track for open positions, but there will be ample opportunities for those comfortable with the social agency model. Indeed, a complacent faculty is likely to reject an accomplished candidate for leadership for fear that they may raise the performance bar in terms of research and publications. The dean or director who opts for the social agency model of leadership learns that there are ample opportunities for upward mobility through the discrete exercise of patronage.

In the absence of a sufficient cohort of scholarly deans and directors, rotational appointments could break the social agency model of educational administration and the patronage on which it is dependent. The adoption of a time-limited model of educational administration would have important consequences for social work education. For one, a time-limited appointment would reduce the stress on a search committee since candidates would not be viewed as the "permanent" head of a school. Disgruntled faculty would know a dean or director's term is time-limited, and would probably choose to wait for more amenable leadership than switch jobs. Knowing that their time is limited, faculty would also be less likely to expend energy in toppling an administrator they dislike. Another advantage to a time-limited deanship/directorship is that faculty would be assured that a candidate wants to join the faculty not only as a dean, but also as a colleague, thereby reducing "dean-hopping."

In most cases, a candidate's acceptance of a time-limited administrative post would signal an institutional commitment. Since a dean or director's position would be time-limited, any salary increments received during the administrative period would be eliminated once they return to the faculty. The salary of a former dean/director would be on par with similarly accomplished faculty members. An added benefit would be a reduction in the wide salary differential between administrators and faculty members. To make the position more attractive, perks could be added such as a paid yearlong sabbatical for each administrative stint. A dean/director who knows that return to an academic position is inevitable will likely strive to stay on top of their research. They will also be more likely to retain their identification as scholars and researchers rather than view themselves primarily as professional administrators. Retaining this identification will help narrow the distance between administrators and faculty. Lastly, deans/directors may be more earnest in attempts at consensus-building if they know they will eventually return to the faculty.

> Hebrew University's Paul Baerwald School of Social Work utilizes a model that differentiates between academic and administrative roles. In this model, the dean (a rotating position) is complemented by a non-academic associate dean who has decision-making power in the day-to-day administrative operations of the school. The associate dean remains in the position regardless of who occupies the deanship (thereby maintaining continuity), although he or she can be terminated for poor performance. In theory, this allows two things to occur: It frees the dean to pursue a larger vision, including leadership through research, publications and service; and it acknowledges the possible disconnect between good academic leadership and the skills for managing the day-to-day administrative details of running a social work school school. In a somewhat different form, this differentiation is used in health and mental health agencies in terms of a medical/clinical director complemented by an administrative or executive director. Behind the scenes, several schools of social work operate in a similar fashion, although it is often through a de facto staff or faculty member who functions as the unofficial administrative director. The Australian system is similar with the rotating appointment of Head of School complemented by a School Manager who influences the day-to-day operations of the school.
>
> This system would also be applicable to U.S. Schools of Social Work. For instance, a dean/director would be appointed or elected for a fixed three- to four-year term with the possibility of a shorter second term. The maximum time in the position would be capped at six years. Since the administrative appointment is time-limited, the next appointment is made before the end of the incumbent's term, which then gives the new dean/director a year to learn the job. This would provide the continuity absent when an administrative position is suddenly vacated.
>
> If a dean/director were hired externally, they would be treated like any other faculty member and would receive the rank and salary commensurate with their accomplishments. Candidates would be judged on their suitability for an administrative post and their potential contribution as a future faculty member. The second criteria would gain increased importance since a new dean/director would be expected to join the faculty in six years or less. Many European universities employ this model since their faculties tend to not view administration as a permanent career track.48 Instead, senior faculty members take turns at administration, even at the level of provost or chancellor. While university administrators would be ineligible to remain in their posts longer than the prescribed appointment period, they could move laterally or upward, although each administrative position would typically have term limits.

Social work education suffers from edusclerosis, a hardening of the intellectual arteries essential for transmitting the life-blood of knowledge in professional education. The weak scholarship of the majority of deans and directors—the leadership capacity of which is continually eroded by expansion in the number of accredited programs—fails to reach the critical mass necessary to achieve educational reform. Because institutions of higher education and accrediting authorities, such as CSWE, are self-governing, they are virtually immune from external influence. At best the leadership of social work programs affirms a status quo, at worst it subverts research and scholarship through patronage. Despite the inferior performance of most schools of social work, stakeholders, such as faculty and university officials, may validate the status quo even if it is suboptimal by standards of other professional schools so long as enrollments are sustained and diversity is achieved. Because of the paucity of deans and directors who have track records as researchers and scholars, there is no countervailing force demanding reform. Rather than serve as exemplars of social work education, the deans and directors of first-tier schools of social work, those who would normally become exemplars of leadership, have been held hostage by the rest.

References

1. Gene Maeroff, "The Media: Degrees of Coverage," in Richard Hersh and John Merrow, *Declining by Degrees* (New York: Palgrave MacMillan, 2005), p. 21.
2. Justin Kaplan, *Lincoln Steffens* (New York: Simon and Schuster, 1974), pp. 50-51.
3. William Safire, *Safire's New Political Dictionary* (New York: Random House, 1993), p. 559.
4. Max Weber, *On Capitalism, Bureaucracy and Religion* (New York: Harper Collins, 1983).
5. Ibid.
6. Hans Gerth and C. Wright Mills, *From Max Weber* (New York: Oxford University Press, 1974), p. 88.
7. Craig Calhoun, ed., *Dictionary of the Social Sciences* (New York: Oxford University Press, 2002), p. 305.
8. C. Wright Mills, *Sociology and Pragmatism* (New York: Oxford University Press, 1964), p. 51.
9. James Leiby, *A Hostory of Social Welfare and Social Work in the United States,* (New York: Columbia University Press, 1978), ch. 7.
10. Murray Levine and Adeline Levine, *A Social History of Helping Services*, (New York: Appleton-Century-Crofts, 1970.
11. Tom Wolfe, *I Am Charlotte Simmons* (New York: Farrar Straus and Giroux, 2004).
12. Allan Bloom, *The Closing of the American Mind*, (New York: Touchstone, 1987).

13. Roger Kimball, *Tenured Radicals* (Chicago: Ivan Dee, 1990), p. 218.

14. Dinesh D'Souza, *Illiberal Education* (New York: Free Press, 1991), pp. 242-44.

15. Russell Jacoby, *The Last Intellectuals*, (New York: Basic Books, 1987), p. 190.

16. Jacoby, *The Last Intellectuals*, p. 183.

17. David Kirp, "This Little Student Went to Market," in Richard Hersh and John Merrow, eds., *Declining by Degrees* (New York: Palgrave MacMillan, 2005), pp. 120-21.

18. Derek Bok, *Our Underachieving Colleges* (Princeton, NJ: Princeton University Press, 2006), p. 317.

19. Bok, *Our Underachieving Colleges*, p. 25.

20. Bok, *Our Underachieving Colleges,* pp. 323-28.

21. John Gandy, Jerry Randolph and Frank Raymond, *On Minding the Store: Research on the Social Work Deanship*. College of Social Work, University of South Carolina, 1979.

22. National Association of Deans and Directors of Schools of Social Work, 2005-2006 Academic Year Salary Study. NADD, CSWE Offices, Washington, DC.

23. Council on Social Work Education, *Statistics on Social Work Education in the United States, 2004* (Alexandria, VA: Author, 2007), p. 15.

24. Munson, "A Survey of Deans of Schools of Social Work"; and Jack Otis and Penelope Caragonne, "Factors in the Resignation of Graduate School of Social Work Deans: 1975-77," *Journal of Education for Social Work,* 15(2), pp. 59-64.

25. Ibid., p. 160.

26. "2005-2006 Academic Year Salary Survey," (National Association of Deans and Directors: Alexandria, VA, n.d.), p. 2

27. Ibid., p. 26.

28. Ibid., p. 17.

29. "Almanac Issue 2007-2008," *Chronicle of Higher Education* (August 31, 2007), p. 25.

30. "Statistics on Social Work Education, 2006," p. 7.

31. Vartan Gregorian, "Six Challenges to the American University," in Richard Hersh and John Merrow, eds., *Declining by Degrees* (New York: Palgrave MacMillan, 2005), p. 84.

32. David Kirp, p. 127.

33. Ibid.

34. Ibid.

35. Council on Social Work Education, *Statistics on Social Work Education in the United States, 2004*, p. 25.

36. Robert Green, "Tenure and Promotion Decisions at Graduate Schools and Departments: The Relative Importance of Teaching, Scholarship and Service ," (unpublished manuscript, 2008).

37. James Seaberg, "Faculty Reports of Workload: Results of a National Study," *Journal of Social Work Education*, 31, 7-19.

38. Munson, "A Survey of Deans of Schools of Social Work," 1994, p. 153.

39. National Association of Deans and Directors of Schools of Social Work, 2005-2006.

40. NADD, By-Laws of the National Association of Deans and Directors of Schools of Social Work, 1999. NADD. Retrieved November 16, 2005 from, http://www.naddssw.org/

41. Paul H. Stuart, "Reflections on the History of BPD," *BPD Update Online* (25)3, (Fall 2003). Retrieved March 1, 2007 from http://bpdupdateonline.bizland.com/fall2003/id19.html

42.   NADD, Strategic Plan, Three Year, 2002-2005. NADD. Retrieved November 16, 2006 from, http://www.naddssw.org.
43.   NADD website. Retrieved November 18, 2005, from http://www.naddssw.org.
44.   NADD By-Laws, Retrieved November 18, 2005, from http://www.naddssw.org.
45.   Ibid.
46.   Ron Feldman, "Back to the Future," (New York: Columbia University, n.d.), p. 7.
47.   Feldman, "Back to the Future," p. 8.
48.   Gary Becker and Richard Posner, The Becker-Posner Blog, March 5, 2005. Retrieved February 19, 2007 from www.becker-posner-blog.com/archives/2005/03/university_gove.html

6

The Doctoral Education Blues

In American higher education, the PhD has become the common denominator for academic appointments, the exception being the fine arts and practice positions in the subsidiary professions. The rationale for this has been that training under professors who have attained the pinnacle of scholarship is essential for the intellectual novice to be capable of contributing to the knowledge of a discipline. So credentialed, the doctoral-prepared scholar is not only able, but, indeed, is *expected* to add to a discipline's store of knowledge. According to the classical model, an aspiring professional seeks training from a professor who has cultivated a reputation as a scholar, becomes an acolyte, and once graduated, furthers and modifies the mentor's signature scholarship for the benefit of mankind. While there have been variations in this model, chiefly in the form of schools of thought, theoretical orientations, and research methodology, the model remains embedded in higher education in both the humanities and the sciences.

Although the doctorate has been a virtual requirement for positions in social work education in the last two decades, it has been an ambiguous degree. Historically, some schools awarded a DSW suggesting that it was a practice degree, comparable to law and medicine, while others followed the custom of the humanities and sciences, awarding the PhD on the basis of an original research contribution to a field's knowledge. To compound matters, social work doctoral programs have never been accredited, the result being wide variations in the skill set of social work doctorates. The result has been confusion about what the degree actually represents; ome doctoral-trained social workers have in effect acquired inflated practice degrees, while others have acquired sophisticated analytic and research skills.

CSWE has clouded the matter further by designating the master's degree as the terminal degree, which then serves as the qualifying credential for licensing. Very few social workers need to continue their educations beyond the master's level unless they plan to enter academia. Between 1985 and 2001 there was a 45 percent increase in the number of doctoral programs. Only five doctoral programs existed prior to 1950; seven were established in the 1950s; six in the 1960s; 16 in the 1970s, and 14 in the 1980s.[1] In 1985 there were 47 doctoral programs in social work; by 2006 that number grew to 69 with several in development.

Rapid Growth of Social Work Doctoral Programs

Despite the rapid growth in the number of doctoral programs from the 1980s to 1990s, doctoral student enrollment remained relatively constant from 1988 to 1999, hovering between 1,914 students in 1988 and 1,953 in 1999. By 2004 full- and part-time doctoral student enrollment had jumped to 2,817.[2] Despite this sharp increase, the number of doctoral degrees awarded failed to correspond to the larger student cohort or to the rapid growth in programs. In 1979-1980 there were 1,028 doctoral students and 213 degrees were awarded. In 2003-2004 that number rose to 2,817 students, yet only 313 doctoral degrees were awarded.[3] The 313 degrees awarded in 2003-2004 were less than the 332 doctorates con-ferred in 1987-1988.[4] Just seven schools (New York University, Columbia University, SUNY/Albany, University of Michigan, Catholic University, University of Georgia, and the University of South Carolina) accounted for 30 percent of all doctoral degrees in 2003.[5]

While the rise in doctoral programs does not closely correlate to the number of degrees produced, it does influence the size of the applicant pool and admissions rates. The mean acceptance rate in 2004 for all doctoral programs was 45 percent, an exceedingly high rate compared to other disciplines.[6] For example, psychology had a 17 percent acceptance rate in 2001.[7] When disaggregated, the data tell a dramatic story (see Table 1). Of the 56 doctoral programs reporting to CSWE in 2003-2004, 23 percent had an acceptance rate from 75 to100 percent; 39 percent ac-cepted from 51 to 74 percent of all applicants; and roughly 68 percent accepted 50 percent or more of doctoral applicants. Only 13 percent had an acceptance rate even approaching that of psychology (i.e., accepting less than 25 percent of applicants).[8] Equally striking is that in 2004 43 percent of doctoral programs had 15 or fewer applicants and 61 percent had 25 or less (see Table 1). The small applicant pool helps explain why admissions rates are so high, especially since many universities require at least five students to run a class.

Table 1
Doctoral Acceptance Rates 2004

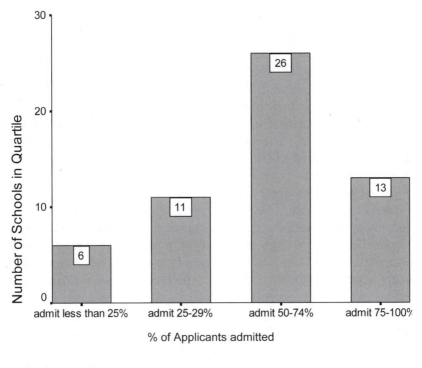

N= 56 schools
N= 1549 applicants

Source: Council on social Work Education, Statistics on Social Work Education in the United States" 2003(Alexandria, VA : 2007); and Todd Lennon, Statistics on Social Work Education in the United States: 2003 (Alexandria, VA: CSWE,2005)

The engine that most consistently drives faculty growth is the BSW/ MSW student body rather than the doctoral cohort. For instance, the 62 doctoral degree-granting social work programs reporting to CSWE in 2004 claimed a total faculty of 2,108; only 4.6 percent were assigned to the doctoral program for 50 percent or more of their time; 6.5 percent were assigned from 25-49 percent; and 13.5 percent from 1-24 percent. More than 75 percent of social work faculty had no involvement in the doctoral program whatsoever.[8] In contrast, the 47 doctoral degree-granting social work programs in 1985 had 759 faculty members, 12 percent of whom spent 50 percent or more of their time in doctoral education.[9]

Simply put, the small student enrollment (five to ten students a year) in many doctoral programs rarely generates enough semester credit hours to justify hiring additional faculty.

Doctoral education is both costly and labor-intensive. On the coursework side, doctoral programs can seem like moneymakers, especially in programs operating under capitation funding (i.e., funding based on the number of enrolled students). In that environment, programs can receive twice the university funding for doctoral students compared to MSW students, and four times more than for BSW students. Hence, a class of five doctoral students can theoretically generate as much revenue as ten or more MSW students or twenty undergraduates. But since most doctoral programs take in only a few students a year, the actual revenue generated is minimal compared to MSW programs.

Coursework is the wholesale side of the doctoral equation and its least expensive component. The highest costs occur in the retail end when doctoral students seek out dissertation chairs and committee members. The smaller the faculty, the more costly the program is in terms of faculty resources. In small faculties of fifteen or less, each faculty member will likely have to participate in several committees to meet the demand of even a small doctoral cohort. Out of the 67 doctoral programs in social work, 12 have less than 15 faculty members (see Table 2). However, since some faculty will undoubtedly refuse (or are unable) to chair or sit on dissertation committees, a small group of faculty typically takes on the major responsibility for doctoral education. This problem is especially acute in programs where no allowance is made—e.g., course relief, reductions in committee work and field duties—for faculty who sit on or chair dissertation committees. These programs contain little incentive for faculty involvement.

What accounts for the phenomenal growth of doctoral programs given the high cost and low returns? For one, having a doctoral program is prestigious since it demonstrates that a social work program has "arrived." In that sense, it is a status symbol. Having a doctoral degree is also a feather in the cap of a dean/director who gains higher status within their university and among their peers in social work education. As a director of a small social work program observed, "At NADD meetings, the deans of doctoral-granting schools mainly socialize with each other. If we had a doctorate they might take me more seriously." The same conclusion was reached by a CSWE staff member who confided that "NADD folks can be pretty snotty—or at least a clique of them can be—to the lesser directors of non-status schools." At least in theory, offering a doctorate enhances the status of a social work program. Doctoral programs also assist faculty recruitment since many job applicants will only consider positions in social work programs that contain a doctoral component.

Despite their rapid growth, doctoral programs are unable to meet the expanding personnel needs of social work education. In 2004, 711 doctoral students were accepted nationally but only 447 actually enrolled. If we assume a 50 percent dropout rate, which is normative for doctoral education, then about 223 will eventually graduate. However, since 36 percent of doctoral students are part-time, that may take a while. Among those 223 graduates at least a portion will not choose academia, some opting for agency work or private practice. At best, that leaves fewer than 200 graduates to fill vacancies in 453 BSW and 182 MSW programs. There is clearly a future need for more doctoral-trained faculty to meet the dramatic expansion of accredited social work programs and the graying of the faculty.[10] Between 1997 and 2002, 75 percent of BSW programs and 54 percent of MSW programs reported insufficient numbers of candidates with doctoral and professional degrees for academic positions they wished to fill.[11]

Fewer new doctorates results in a professorate dominated by older academics. Specifically, in 2004 almost 40 percent of social work faculties in MSW and BSW programs were 55 years or older; only 6 percent were younger than age 35.[12] Moreover, the rapid rise in the number of BSW and MSW programs means that an increase in the number of doctoral programs is not unwarranted; yet, supply of doctorates has not met demand for them.

Part-time enrollment status influences graduation rates and the length of time it takes to complete the degree. On one level, large numbers of part-time doctoral students are not necessarily problematic; in fact, it may be the preferred model in an applied discipline.[13] Moreover, part-time programs may assist the more than 50 percent of non doctoral-degreed faculty in BSW-only programs to earn a doctorate.[14] However, in many places high numbers of part-time students is a reflection of chronic under-funding that forces students into outside employment to pay for their education. It can also reflect the dearth of faculty with sufficient external funding to support doctoral students. Fully 56 percent of all doctoral students were part-time in 2004 and part-time students outnumbered full-time in 25 percent of doctoral programs.[15]

The high number of part-time doctoral students is problematic because of their relatively older age. In 2004 the mean age for doctoral students in social work was 37 for those taking courses and 40 for those who had completed coursework but not yet graduated. Of the 48 doctoral programs reporting on student age in 2004, seven reported a mean age of 50 for those who had completed coursework; in 35 percent of doctoral programs the mean age for students completing coursework was 48 years old.[16] Given the modest starting salaries in many social work programs, securing an entry level faculty position is not financially feasible for many older students responsible for family support, mortgages, repayment of student loans, and so forth. For example, the median salary in 2004 for an assistant professor teaching in a graduate program was $50,800, while an assistant professor in a baccalaureate-only program earned $43,200.[17] In most regions of the U.S. this is not sufficient as a sole source of income.

Uneven Quality of Social Work Doctorates

Concern about the quality of graduates is another problem arising from the rapid growth of doctoral programs in social work. Using the Carnegie Foundation's classification, only 62 percent of universities offering social work doctorates are classified as Doctoral Research Universities (Very High Research Activity) while another 22 percent are rated as Doctoral Research Universities (High Research Activity). The remaining are Master's (Large) and Baccalaureate institutions.[18] While the Carnegie rankings are open to criticism, higher ranked universities generally allocate more resources to research and doctoral education than lower-ranked institutions (see Table 2).

In the halcyon days of doctoral education, social work deans typically appointed their most distinguished faculty to head doctoral programs, and some schools still do. It was assumed that highly accomplished doctoral directors would provide a role model for aspiring graduate students. In addition, they were expected to provide the leadership and vision for social work education. In 2006, 24 doctoral programs (almost 35 percent) were headed by an associate professor rather than a full professor. One major school of social work appointed an assistant professor to head up their doctoral program (see Table 2). In some ways, this represents the extent to which doctoral education is valued in these schools. It also illustrates how some schools have demoted the doctoral directorship to an administrative appointment rather than one based mainly on providing intellectual and career leadership.

Some social work programs are so seriously under-resourced that they cannot adequately meet the demands of doctoral education. For example,

Table 2
Social Work Programs Offering Doctoral Degrees, 2005-2006

SCHOOL	# DOCTORAL LEVEL FACULTY	HEADED BY FULL PROFESSOR	CARNEGIE RANKING
	1= ;LESS THAN 15 2= MORE THAN 15	1= NOT HEADED BY FULL PROF 2= HEADED BY FULL PROF	1=RSEARCH U-VERY HIGH ACTIVITY 2= RESEARCH U-HIGH ACTIVITIY 3= DOCTORAL RESEARCH U 4= LARGE MASTER'S PROGRAM 5= MEDIUM MASTER'S PROGRAM 6=SMALL MASTER'S PROGRAM 7=BACCALAUREATE COLLEGES—ARTS & SCIENCES
SMITH COLLEGE	2	2	7
MARYWOOD U	2	1	6
CUNY HUNTER	2	2	6
SIMMONS	2	2	4
PORTLAND STATE U	2	1	3
ADELPHI	2	2	3
U OF WISCONSIN MILWAUKEE	2	2	2
U OF MARYLAND	2	2	2
U OF LOUISVILLE	2	2	2
U OF HOUSTON	2	2	2
U OF DENVER	2	2	2
U OF ALABAMA	2	2	2
LOYOLA U	2	1	2
INDIANA U	2	2	2
FORDHAM U	2	1	2
CATHOLIC U	2	1	2
BOSTON COLL	2	2	2
YESHIVA U	2	2	1
WAYNE STATE U	2	2	1
WASHINGTON U	2	2	1
VA COMMONWEALTH U	2	2	1
UC LOS ANGELES	2	2	1
UC BERKELEY	2	2	1
U TEXAS AUSTIN	2	2	1
U OF WISCONSIN MADISON	2	2	1
U OF WASHINGTON	2	1	1
U OF TENNESSEE	2	2	1
U OF SOUTHERN CALIFORNIA	2	2	1
U OF SOUTH FLORIDA	2	2	1
U OF SOUTH CAROLINA	2	1	1
U OF PITTSBURGH	2	2	1
U OF PENNSYLVANIA	2	2	1
U OF MINNESOTA	2	1	1
U OF MICHIGAN	2	2	1
U OF KENTUCKY	2	2	1
U OF KANSAS	2	2	1
U OF ILLINOIS URBANA	2	1	1

Table 2 (cont.)

SCHOOL	# DOCTORAL LEVEL FACULTY	HEADED BY FULL PROFESSOR	CARNEGIE RANKING
	1= ;LESS THAN 15 2= MORE THAN 15	1= NOT HEADED BY FULL PROF 2= HEADED BY FULL PROF	1=RSEARCH U-VERY HIGH ACTIVITY 2= RESEARCH U-HIGH ACTIVITIY 3= DOCTORAL RESEARCH U 4= LARGE MASTER'S PROGRAM 5= MEDIUM MASTER'S PROGRAM 6=SMALL MASTER'S PROGRAM 7=BACCALAUREATE COLLEGES—ARTS & SCIENCES
U OF ILLINOIS CHICAGO	2	1	1
U OF HAWAII	2	2	1
U OF GEORGIA	2	2	1
U OF CONNECTICUT	2	2	1
U N. CAROLINA CHAPEL HILL	2	2	1
SUNY STONY BROOK	2	2	1
SUNY BUFFALO	2	1	1
SUNY ALBANY	2	2	1
RUTGERS U	2	2	1
OHIO STATE U	2	1	1
NEW YORK U	2	2	1
MICHIGAN STATE U	2	2	1
FLORIDA STATE U	2	1	1
COLUMBIA U	2	2	1
CASE WESTERN	2	2	1
BRANDEIS U	2	2	1
BOSTON U	2	1	1
ARIZONA STATE	2	1	1
U OF CHICAGO	2	2	1
U TEXAS ARLINGTON	2	1	0
U OF UTAH	2	2	0
BRYN MAWR	1	2	7
VALDOSA U	1	2	4
NORFOLK STATE U	1	1	4
WIDENER U	1	2	3
BARRY U	1	2	3
JACKSON STATE U	1	1	2
HOWARD U	1	2	2
FLORIDA INTERNATIONAL U	1	2	2
CLARK ATLANTA U	1	1	2
U OF MISSOURI-COLUMBIA	1	1	1
U OF IOWA	1	1	1
LOUISIANA STATE U	1	1	1

some schools have three levels of programs (BSW, MSW, PhD) with only nine or ten faculty. One established school of social work operated its doctoral program with only one full professor on the faculty. Eight social work programs offer all three levels of degrees (BSW, MSW, PhD) with less than fifteen faculty members (see Table 2). In some instances, social work programs use doctoral education to justify hiring additional faculty. Once on board, these new faculty are often quickly shifted into resource-hungry BSW and MSW programs that generate the lion's share of revenues.

One criterion for measuring the quality of doctoral education is the publication rate of doctoral faculty. Publication rates are important since a major goal of doctoral education is to produce scholars able to maintain the intellectual vitality of the profession and keep social work competitive with other disciplines. A report by the National Institute of Mental Health (NIMH) Task Force on Social Work Research found that—with the exception of the top tier of schools composed of 10–12 faculties—the majority of the faculties of schools of social work with doctoral programs had not demonstrated sufficient scholarly leadership in the 1980s.[19] About 50 percent of all graduate schools with doctoral programs were assigned to the lowest tier of research development and productivity.[20] Findings from earlier studies revealed that half of all graduates of doctoral programs between 1960 and 1980 had not published a single article in the professional literature.[21]

A later study by Green, Baskind, and Bellin confirmed the disturbing findings of the earlier Task Force report.[22] In a longitudinal study of doctoral faculty publication rates in social work journals, they found that only 12 out of 61 doctoral faculties were responsible for 43 percent of all articles published in approximately 5,700 journal articles abstracted in the *Social Sciences Citation Index* in the 1990s. They also found that the mean number of articles published in the 1990s by the 61 doctoral faculties were 72.23 (or 7.2 articles a year) and ranged from a low of three to a high of 259. Five doctoral faculties failed to publish even two articles a year; and five doctoral faculties failed to publish 20 articles over the course of the decade. Twenty-three doctoral faculties (38 percent) averaged fewer than five publications a year. On a positive note, Green et al., found that doctoral faculty publication rates had risen in the 1990s.[23] Newer research by Robert Green and Frank Baskind found a persistently strong correlation between faculty publication rates and the *U.S. News & World Report* (USNWR) ranking of social work programs.[24] Conversely, using a slightly different criterion, Ronald Feldman found a weak correlation between a school's USNWR ranking and its scholarly productivity.[25]

Green and Baskind found that the top ten social work programs accounted for more than one-third of all the articles published.[26] Moreover, refereed articles from top-ranked Columbia University exceeded the sum of all articles published by the ten lowest ranked faculties. Even more striking, almost 20 doctoral programs—many that began in the last 15 to 20 years—did not even make it on the list. Nor was any school of social work in the process of developing a doctoral program on Green and Baskind's list. If most of the doctoral programs in the 1980s and 1990s emerged from second tier programs and universities, then the new crop of doctoral programs represent third or fourth tier programs in universities of comparable stature.

In 2007 Academic Analytics included social work doctoral programs for the first time in its ranking of 7,294 doctoral programs at 354 institutions. The primary factors employed in ranking doctoral programs included (1) publications (books and journal articles as well as citations), (2) federal research funding received, and (3) awards and prizes. Because the methodology used by Academic Analytics originated from evaluating doctoral programs in the physical sciences, its application to social work is questionable. (The 2007 Academic Analytics rankings of social work programs can be found at the end of this chapter.) Regardless, the Academic Analytics project has an important lesson for scholars evaluating the quality of social work programs: multiple factors can be used to rank social work programs. If social work scholars fail to craft a method more congruent with its unique attributes, the task will probably be left to analysts from other disciplines.

One reason that many schools of social work have such poor publication rates is the low value they put on research and scholarship. Seaberg examined faculty workload in a national probability sample and found that faculty perceived research and writing as add-ons to their teaching and service work. A majority reported that they were expected to engage in research *after* they completed their teaching and service responsibilities.[27] Seipel found that uniform standards for crediting faculty publications had not been established at many schools, making rewards for scholarship absent or ambiguous.[28]

The Task Force and the Green, et al. studies confirmed a highly entrenched pattern of stratification in social work education.[29] In effect, a tiered system exists whereby a small minority of doctoral programs occupies the top tier while a relatively large number (almost 40 percent) occupies the lowest tier in terms of publications. This finding raises questions about whether doctoral students who receive degrees from lower-ranked programs are sufficiently prepared to carry out the basic research responsibilities necessary in social work education, no less achieve tenure in a major university. Moreover, the danger exists that the proliferation of doctoral programs in under-resourced social work programs will deflate the value of the degree, furthering the caste-like system of faculty hiring (i.e., top-ranked schools hire doctoral graduates from other top-ranked schools). It may also create a large cadre of newly-minted doctorates with significantly diminished prospects for tenure at highly ranked institutions. Diminishing employment prospects for Ph.Ds in the liberal arts and sciences due to the recession have been exacerbated as retirement-age faculty hold onto their jobs in order to compensate for the loss of value in their retirement plans.[30] The same dynamic may also attenuate employment possibilities for recently graduated doctorates in social work.

Lowering Admission Standards

Given the stagnant applicant pool and increasing competition from new programs, many doctoral programs—including some of the more established ones—are scrambling for students. Some programs are experimenting with online doctoral education to increase their applicant pools. To get the necessary headcount, GRE scores are frequently discarded in the frantic need to fill classes. One social work program admitted doctoral applicants with combined GRE scores of less than 400. Only a few years earlier, a combined GRE score of 1,000 was considered the minimum for admission into many MSW programs, no less doctoral education. By comparison, many—if not most—psychology programs require a minimum combined GRE score of 1,250 or above.

Ironically, it is sometimes easier to gain admission to a school of social work's PhD program than its MSW program, especially in years with a scant doctoral applicant pool. Since most new doctoral programs are small, there is often a close equivalence between university-mandated minimal class size and new cohort admissions. As noted earlier, some institutions will not let classes "make" with less than five students. Maintaining the doctoral program means accepting marginal candidates in years when the applicant pool is small Conversely, admissions standards may rise slightly in years with larger applicant pools. This pattern of acceptance creates both ethical and quality problems.

Concurrent with the decline in admissions standards, many doctoral programs are forced to rethink comprehensive examinations and lower dissertation expectations. High failure rates have led some programs to discard comprehensive examinations altogether in favor of softer integrative papers or other forms of evaluation that reduce the possibility of failure. A survey by Michie Hesselbrock found that 43 percent of doctoral programs now give take-home comprehensive examinations. Still other schools have so reduced the expectation for dissertations that they resemble inflated term papers.[31] In many cases, the glut of doctoral programs and the subsequent competition has not led to increased quality, but a dumbing down of the social work doctoral degree. The contradiction that this poses in relation to doctorates awarded in other disciplines is as striking as it is inexcusable.

The Social Work Paradox

Erosion in the quality of social work doctorates contrasts with the increasing demand for faculty given the burgeoning number of accredited social work programs. "On the one hand, rapidly growing numbers of education programs and practitioners typically are presumed to reflect thriving or success on the part of a profession and its educational sector," noted Ronald Feldman, former Dean of Columbia University's School of Social Work. "But, paradoxically, that very growth in our profession has substantially and incrementally outstripped the capacity to staff educational programs with research-competent social work faculty. As a result, advances in the overall quality and impact of social work education have decelerated rather than accelerated over time."[32] The growth of social work programs that accompanied industrialization and the expansion of the American welfare state provided the ideal conditions for enhancing the stature of social work education, yet the obverse may well have happened.

Factors compromising social work's capacity to cultivate a first-class professorate included the absence of standards for institutions awarding social work doctorates, academics' enthusiasm for research methods that were alternatives to, or outwardly hostile toward, empiricism, and the lack of scholarship requirements for faculty of BSW and MSW programs. Instead of becoming a co-equal producer of applied social science on which it had become dependent for its knowledge base, social work evolved a problematic collection of journals which published less than satisfactory research. As Karen Sowers and Catherine Dulmus observed

It is embarrassing that only four social work journals meet credible benchmarks to even be considered for inclusion in the SSCI. This is reflective of the overall quality of the scholarship being produced in a plethora of social work journals. It appears that many of these journals may indeed exist solely as publication outlets so we can meet the requirements for tenure and promotion rather than to disseminate new and important knowledge. All too often social work educators publish discreet and unrelated manuscripts, many which push around existing knowledge but do not produce substantive new knowledge.[33]

Unable to generate knowledge that would be publishable in journals of the applied social sciences, social work developed a subsidiary network of outlets through which its faculty could publish the manuscripts essential for promotion and tenure. Rather than adding to the luster of professional education by publishing in mainstream social science journals, social workers devised a faux literature primarily to meet the career needs of its academics.

Yet, the accreditation of social work programs continued apace, regardless of the absence of an adequate supply of sufficiently skilled faculty necessary to achieve objectives of professional education. Feldman charted the consequences:

> In short, the rapid proliferation of social work education has not been accompanied by corresponding growth in the number of doctoral graduates required to staff them and advance the knowledge base of social work education and practice. To the contrary, the educational sector finds itself confronting a steadily widening and seemingly irreversible gap between demand and supply for doctoral-trained educators. This threatens the overall quality of social work education and, in turn, social work practice. From virtually every perspective, this double-barreled trend will adversely affect the expertise, legitimacy, public acceptance, and future well-being of social work.[34]

Despite the growth of BSW and MSW programs, the academic value of a social work doctorate came into question, and the number of doctoral students not only reached a plateau in total enrollment but actually fell behind the demand for faculty in accredited programs. Baccalaureate Program Directors (BPD) meetings were rife with complaints about the difficulty of recruiting enough doctoral-degreed faculty. The 453 BSW programs encompassed more than 5,000 faculty and 40,000 students, thereby eclipsing the student and faculty bodies in the top-ranked research-intensive social work programs. Apart from prestige-related issues, there were other reasons why doctoral graduates from top universities were reluctant to teach in BSW-only programs, including heavy course loads, multiple course preparations, extensive field visits, high expectations around community service, and frequent departmental meetings. In addition, salaries in BSW-only and small MSW programs were lower than in social work programs offering a doctorate.[35] Consequently, small BSW/MSW programs often became unattractive to doctoral graduates eager to develop a research agenda and a name in the field.

Mediocrity in Social Work Education

The economics of an academic career in social work are problematic, effectively dissuading a sufficient number of prospective applicants from applying to doctoral programs. In 2005, the median salary of a Masters level social worker was $47,689[36] compared to the median salary of an assistant professor at $48,835.[37] A social worker with these income attributes would probably question pursuing an academic career. If she had committed to a doctoral program full-time and completed her studies in four years (an optimistic scenario since only 24.9 percent of doctoral graduates finish within that period), and adjusting for a nine-month work-year that allowed her to work summers, she would not have recovered the opportunity costs until the midway into the tenth year as an academic. The total debt burden of six to eight years of graduate education necessary to earn a doctorate piled on top of that needed for an undergraduate degree would make many question the prudence of a career in higher education. "The poverty-stricken graduate student is a cliché`," concluded Melanie Benson, "but the debt-ridden professor is a humiliating aberration."[38]

Yet a consideration peculiar to the academy influences that decision; namely job security. Because the tenure-with-promotion decision is typically made sometime during her sixth year as an assistant professor, the newly minted doctor of social work will be prudent to use all her free time conducting research and drafting manuscripts for publication. Assuming she dedicates all her free time during the first six years of academic employment to develop the scholarship necessary for promotion-with-tenure (an important consideration if she is ever to recover the income lost while she earned her doctorate) and, post-promotion is able to augment her nine- month faculty salary with additional income, she does not recover her opportunity costs until mid-way through her twelfth year as a professor. Under the best of scenarios, her doctorate does not begin to eclipse her previous income trajectory as a social worker until well after she has been promoted and tenured, more than a decade after finishing her doctoral studies. If she fails to attain tenure, she is faced with dilemma: start over at another academic institution, and possibly, a new community, or return to a conventional practice setting. However, it is often difficult to return to the conventional practice world at high enough levels of compensation after having been out of circulation for a decade, compounded by the loss of traditional professional practitioner networks, since new doctoral graduates often need to relocate to pursue an academic position. An additional challenge arises from the confusion caused by the common practice in the field of considering the MSW to be the terminal degree; a new Ph.D. can be seen as an inexperienced beginner who hasn't followed the usual apprenticeship path, and is at the same time over qualified for line level practice positions. Even if she has achieved some practice seniority prior to moving into academia, the faculty member who has been denied tenure may no longer be seen as credible in the practice community, so has the further dilemma of reducing her income until she can build up a portfolio, or moving on to another institution and taking the chance that she will achieve tenure there. Any of the possible eventualities dramatically increases the time necessary to recover the opportunity costs of her doctorate.

Under these circumstances, it is not surprising that doctoral graduates from research-intensive institutions would consider alternatives to traditional academic employment. Many will opt out of social work education altogether in preference for commercial research companies, such as Mathematica Policy Research, Abt Associates, the Manpower Demonstration Research Corporation, or Maximus. Others may choose private practice or high-level government or NGO positions. Obviously, social work education is the poorer when its best researchers leave the academy for greener pastures elsewhere.

Bringing doctoral education in social work more in line with the income requirements of new doctorates while supplying sufficient numbers for professional programs is unlikely. CSWE has no regulatory authority over doctoral education, and no credible voice is calling for it to intervene. On the contrary, CSWE's track record in BSW and MSW education hardly inspires confidence in its ability to inject accountability into doctoral education. Although the Group for the Advancement of Doctoral Education (GADE)—an independent and voluntary association of doctoral programs—has made some cursory advances in "Guidelines for Quality in Social Work Doctoral Programs," their recommendations are too broad to have any real impact on new or existing programs.[39] Besides, without regulatory and enforcement powers, GADE cannot establish (or enforce) even minimal standards for doctoral education. When social work programs with few faculty, weak students, too many levels of programs, and virtually no track record in publications or research grants are able to offer doctorates, one can only conclude that GADE is either asleep at the switch or is too ineffectual to establish real standards. While doctoral programs are supposedly regulated by their universities, even that oversight is frequently absent as small programs can fly under the radar screen once approved.

Conclusion

Since the academic marketplace does not operate in a similar fashion to the commercial market, there is little reason to believe it will weed out poor quality doctoral programs. Quality and price points have only limited impact on social work education, and are often superseded by considerations such as geographical proximity, especially for students with familial responsibilities. One way to control the runaway growth of doctoral programs is to employ a form of accreditation, but who would execute such accreditation is open to conjecture. Any accreditation of doctoral programs should include several basic criteria including the establishment of a minimum number of faculty members based on the number of social work programs and the size of the overall student body. For example, a rule of thumb might be that a social work program wanting to develop a doctorate while also offering the MSW and BSW degrees should have at least twenty full-time faculty members to ensure a viable and minimally-resourced doctoral program. MSW-only programs should have no fewer than 15 faculty members.

Without concomitant growth in the doctoral applicant pool, increased competition from newer programs has essentially resulted in cutting the applicant pie into thinner slices. To stay afloat, many if not most, social work programs are lowering their admissions criteria. The resulting competition for doctoral students is creating lower admissions standards, not better programs. At the end of the day, social work education is better served by fewer and higher quality doctoral programs than by pursuing a strategy of market saturation similar to MSW programs.

Inadequate salaries for new doctorates militate against attracting the best and brightest candidates for the professorate. New and existing MSW and BSW programs will have little choice but to employ graduates from under-resourced and under-performing doctoral programs, and as their numbers increase, these graduates will have a greater role in social work education. Their impact will increase as graduates of weak programs are appointed to decision-making positions in academic social work, such as serving as site visitors, journal editors and reviewers, and CSWE board members, the implications of which are explored in other chapters. Rather than represent the apogee of scholarship, the doctorate in social work has come to symbolize its antithesis—the irregular quality of doctoral programs reinforce the view of social work as an academically light discipline that translates into mediocre social work practice and education.

Table 3
Doctoral Social Work Program Rankings*

Rank	School	Faculty Scholarly Productivity Index
1	University of California-Berkeley	1.99
2	University of Pennsylvania	1.63
3	Washington University-St. Louis	1.54
4	Florida State University	1.53
5	State University of New York-Albany	1.29
	Columbia University	1.29
7	University of Michigan	1.20
8	Boston University	1.19
9	University of North Carolina-Chapel Hill	1.15
10	University of Wisconsin-Madison	1.11
11	New York University	1.09
12	Florida International University	1.08
13	Case Western Reserve University	1.06
14	University of Iowa	0.92
	University of Washington-Seattle	0.92
16	University of Illinois-Chicago	0.88
17	University of Kansas	0.62
18	University of Maryland-Baltimore	0.60
19	Bryn Mawr College	0.59
20	University of Illinois-Urbana-Chambaign	0.48
21	Catholic University of America	0.42
22	University of Pittsburgh	0.41
23	Portland State University	0.40
24	University of Minnesota-Twin Cities	0.38
25	University of California-Los Angeles	0.34
26	University of Southern California	0.23
27	University of Missouri-Columbia	0.19
28	City University of New York (Hunter College)	0.15
29	University of Tennessee	0.13
30	University of Kentucky	0.05
31	Loyola University-Chicago	0.02
32	Arizona State University	-0.12
33	University of Georgia	-0.17
	Wayne State University	-0.17
35	University of Texas-Austin	-0.20
36	Yeshiva	-0.23
	University of Alabama	-0.23
38	State University of New York-Buffalo	-0.26

Table 3 (cont.)

39	Rutgers University	-0.36
40	University of South Carolina	-0.39
41	University of Denver	-0.43
42	Louisiana State University	-0.45
43	Indiana University	-0.50
44	Marywood University	-0.52
45	University of Louisville	-0.54
46	State University of New York-Stony Brook	-0.73
47	Norfolk State University	-0.74
48	Virginia Commonwealth University	-0.81
49	Tulane University	-0.91
50	Boston College	-0.97
51	University of Houston	-1.03
	Barry University	-1.03
53	Howard University	-1.08
54	University of Texas-Arlington	-1.16
55	Loma Linda University	-1.23
56	Ohio State University	-1.24
	University of Utah	-1.24
58	University of Hawaii	-1.27
59	Simmons College	-1.28
60	Michigan State University	-1.40
61	University of South Florida	-1.43
62	Smith College	-1.47
63	University of Connecticut	-1.66
64	Institute for Clinical Social Work	-1.83
65	Clark Atlanta University	-1.86

*By evaluating the faculties of each doctoral program, Academic Analytics computed a z-score with zero representing the national mean of faculty productivity. For details on the methodology to construct the ranking, visit the Academic Analytics Web site: www.academicanalytics.com.

The Academic Analytics ranking, the most comprehensive available to date, validates the place of the top schools of social work, although their positions are quite different from the rankings by reputation or journal publications. Florida State, a third-tier institution in other rankings appears among the top tier. Additions to the second tier include New York University, Case Western Reserve, and Florida International. All of these programs have z-scores of at least 1.00. Remarkably, several programs that had appeared higher vis-à-vis their reputations, plummet. The University of Washington, the University of Southern California, UCLA, Pittsburgh, and Bryn Mawr have z-scores below 1:00 suggestive of average performance; the University of Texas at Arlington and Smith College actually have negative scores, well below the mean for schools with doctoral programs.

Table 3 (cont.)

Several months after releasing the first ranking of social work doctoral programs, Academic Analytics released another ranking; the top ten programs changed somewhat from the first list:

Ranking	Institution	Productivity Index
1	Berkeley	2.16
2	Michigan	1.98
3	U. of Washington	1.54
4	Florida International	1.53
5	New York U.	1.37
6	Boston U.	1.26
7	Case Western Reserve	1.15
8	U. of Wisconsin-Madison	1.13
9	Rutgers	1.07
10	U. of Pennsylvania	1.03

Source: http://chronicle.com/stats/producitivity, retrieved November 13, 2007.

References

1. Robert Green, Frank Baskind, and Michael Bellin, "Results of the Doctoral Faculty Publication Project: Journal Article Productivity and its Correlates in the 1990s," *Journal of Social Work Education, 38* (2002), pp. 135-152.
2. Council on Social Work Education, *Statistics on Social Work Education in the United States, 2004* (Alexandria, VA: Council on Social Work Education, 2007).
3. David Biegel, M. C. "Terry" Hokenstad, Mark Singer, and Shenyang Guo, "One School's Experience in Reconceptualizing Part-time Doctoral Education in Social Work," *Journal of Social Work Education* (42)2 (Spring/Summer 2006), pp. 231-247; Council on Social Work Education, *Statistics on Social Work Education in the United States, 2004,* p. 48.
4. Council on Social Work Education, *Statistics on Social Work Education in the United States:* 2004, p. 48.
5. Council on Social Work Education, *Statistics on Social Work Education in the United States, 2004.*, p. 120-122.
6. Ibid.
7. American Psychological Association Research Office, "2000 Graduate Study in Psychology. Application, Acceptance and Enrollment Characteristics of U.S. Graduate Departments of Psychology," 2002. Retrieved May 30, 2002 from http://research.apa.org/ gs00tab11.pdf.
8. Council on Social Work Education, *Statistics on Social Work Education in the United States, 2004.* Alexandria, VA: Author, 2006, p. 6.
9. Todd Lennon, *Statistics on Social Work Education in the United States: 1999,* Council on Social Work Education: Alexandria, VA, 2001; Rubin, *Statistics on Social Work Education in the United States: 1985*; and Council on Social Work

Education, *Statistics on Social Work Education in the United States: 2004,* p. 18.

10. Jeanne Anastas, "Employment Opportunities in Social Work Education: A Study of Jobs for Doctoral Graduates," *Journal of Social Work Education* (42)2 (Spring/Summer 2006), pp. 195-209.

11. Zastrow, Charles and Judith Bremner, "Social Work Education Responds to the Shortage of Persons with Both a Doctorate and a Professional Social Work Degree," *Journal of Social Work Education,* 40, 2 (Spring/Summer 2004), p 353.

12. Council on Social Work Education, *Statistics on Social Work Education in the United States: 2004,* p. 7.

13. Beigel, et al, 2006, op cit.

14. Biegel, et al, 2006, op cit; Anastas, 2006, op cit.

15. Lennon 2001, op cit.

16. Council on Social Work Education, *Statistics on Social Work Education in the United States: 2004,* p. 112.

17. Ibid., p. 24.

18. Carnegie Foundation, Rankings of Universities: From Highest to Lowest Ranking, 2005. Retrieved October 11, 2006, from http://www.carnegiefoundation.org/classifications/index.asp?key=782

19. Task Force on Social Work Research, *Building Social Work Knowledge for Effective Services and Policies: A Plan for Research Development.* Austin: University of Texas at Austin, School of Social Work, 1981.

20. Ibid.

21. Ibid; Robert Green, Elizabeth Hutchinson, and Bibhuti Sar, "The Research Productivity of Social Work Doctoral Graduates," *Social Service Review, 66* (1992), 441-466.

22. Green, Baskind, and Bellin, op cit.

23. Green, Baskind, and Bellin, 2002, op cit.

24. Robert Green and Frank Baskind, "The Second Decade of the Faculty Publication Project: Journal Article Publications and the Importance of Faculty Scholarship," *Journal of Social Work Education,* forthcoming 2007.

25. Ronald Feldman, "Reputations, Rankings, and Realities of Social Work Schools: Challenges for Future Research," *Journal of Social Work Education* (42)2 (Spring/Summer, 2006), pp. 483-505.

26. Green and Baskind, 2007, op cit.

27. James R. Seaberg, "Faculty Reports of Workload: Results of a National Study," *Journal of Social Work Education, 31* (1998), pp. 7-19.

28. Michael Seipel, "Assessing Publication for Tenure," *Journal of Social Work Education* (2003) 39, pp. 79-88.

29. The Task Force on Social Work Research, op cit; and Green, Baskind, and Bellin, 2002, op cit.

30. David Spergel, "Nation Needs Recovery Plan for Science Faculty Jobs," *Science News* (February 28, 2009), p. 32.

31. . Michie Hesselbrock, Patterns of Doctoral Education: Preliminary Results of a GADE Survey. Presented at the 24th Annual Conference of the Association of Baccalaureate Social Work Program Directors, Los Angeles, CA, October 2006.

32. Ronald Feldman, "Back to the Future with the St. Louis Group," (New York: Columbia University, n.d.), p. 11.

33. Karen Sowers and Catherine Dulmus, "Social Work Education: Status Quo or Change?" *Research on Social Work Education,* 19, 1 (January 2009), pp. 114-15.

34.   Feldman, *Back to the Future*, pp. 11-12.

35.   Council on Social Work Education, *Statistics on Social Work Education in the United States: 2004,* p. 24.

36.   "Assuring the Sufficiency of a Frontline Workforce," (Washington, DC: National Association of Social Workers, 2005), p. 11.

37.   "2005-2006 National Faculty Salary Survey by Discipline and Rank in Four-Year Colleges and Universities," College and University Professional Association for Human Resources, 2008).

38.   Melanie Benson, "At What Cost?" *The Chronicle Review* (December 4, 2009), p. B11.

39.   Jeane Anastas, Denise Bronson, Wendy Crook, Howard Doueck, Rena D. Harold, Fariyal Ross-Sheriff, David Tucker and Rowena Wilson, "Guidelines for Quality in Social Work Doctoral Programs (Revised 2003)." Retrieved October 11, 2006, from http://web.uconn.edu/gade.

7

The Pink Collar Ghetto

In a labor market, wages vary based on the supply and demand for workers, although this conventional understanding must be adjusted for educational requirements and for the cost of professional training. Ordinarily, an oversupply of workers will depress wages. For a half-century schools of social work have been accredited by CSWE. The leaders of American social work have held as an article of faith that social programs and the jobs necessary to run them would continue to expand as the nation's welfare state grew. Yet, that supposition is questionable. For example, between 1990 and 2000, a decade mostly under the administration of a Democratic president, federal expenditures for the Department of Health and Human Services increased from $175.5 billion to $382.6 billion, more than doubling. A corresponding increase in federal employment might have been expected, but that did not happen. In fact, the number of jobs at HHS actually fell from 123,959 to 62,605, a drop of 49.5 percent.[1] In other words, while federal social programs continued to expand, federal jobs at HHS contracted.

Social work as an occupation has been difficult to categorize, adding to the difficulty of understanding the human services labor market. "Social work is a diverse profession, unique among the human service professions in that the term *social worker* is defined so broadly in different organizations and settings" notes NASW's Center for Workforce Studies, "the lack of a standard definition has left the social work profession without reliable data upon which to base future projections about the supply of, and demand for, social work professionals."[2] Yet, the proliferation of professional activity in all fields contradicts the perceived wisdom that social work's ambiguity defies labor market analysis. A review of occupations conducted by the Bureau of Labor Statistics reveals that other occupations have evolved to a considerable extent, concomitant with social work.

The Social Work Labor Market

Despite the unbridled expansion of social work programs, only re-cently have labor market considerations factored into discussions about the number of professionals that graduate. In 2004, NASW established the Center for Workforce Studies in order to analyze the social work labor force. Notably absent as an institutional sponsor of the Center was CSWE, which bears ultimate responsibility for the expanding number of social work education programs. The Center's initial survey of social workers, *Assuring the Sufficiency of a Frontline Workforce: A National Study of Licensed Social Workers*, was limited as a labor market analysis. Despite a survey of a random sample of 10,000 licensed social workers drawn from lists of state licensing boards, the Center's methodology was flawed in several respects. It excluded Delaware and Hawaii because the lists of licensed social workers were not available. Because BSWs are not licensed in many states—California, Connecticut, Delaware, Florida, Georgia, Hawaii, Montana, New Hampshire, New York, Oregon, Penn-sylvania, Rhode Island, Tennessee, Vermont, Virginia, Washington[3]—they were excluded from the analysis, effectively skewing the results in favor of graduate practitioners. By employing a methodology that conflated undergraduate and graduate training, the study was unable to differenti-ate the experiences of BSWs, MSWs, and those with doctorates around work settings, client characteristics, and income. Ultimately, 79 percent of survey respondents were MSWs, 12 percent were BSWs, 2 percent held doctorates, and 8 percent did not have social work degrees. Moreover, fewer than half of those sampled, 49.4 percent, responded.[4] Finally, the study failed to generate any projections about future labor market trends for social workers.

Aggregating the disparate training of social workers, the Center's sur-vey reported their median salary at $47,640,[5] not significantly different from incomes reported by the Bureau of Labor Statistics (BLS).

The BLS data are noteworthy in several respects. While, the salaries of social workers approximate that reported by NASW's Center for Work-force Studies, those of related professions are significantly higher. Teach-ers earn about 10 percent more than social workers, while the income of nurses is about 20 percent higher. The salaries of social workers only begin to approximate those of front-line teachers and nurses once social workers become managers. More surprising are those occupations that have prospered with less education, eclipsing the income of social work-ers. With only an associates or baccalaureate degree, a dental hygienist's

Table 1
Median Annual Salaries of Selected Occupations, May 2007

Occupation	Salary
Social Workers	$47,170
School, Child, and Family Social Workers	41,920
Mental Health and Substance Abuse Workers	39,380
School Social Workers	51,690
Substance Abuse and Behavior Counselors	37,830
Elementary Special Education Teachers	51,230
Elementary Teachers	50,040
Secondary Education Teachers	52,040
Registered Nurses	62,480
Physicians Assistants	77,800
Dental Hygienists	64,910
Social and Community Service Managers	59,070
Counseling Psychologists	68,150

Source: Bureau of Labor Statistics, downloaded March 12, 2009

salary exceeds that of a social worker with a graduate degree. With the equivalent of a graduate degree in clinical health practice, a physician's assistant boasts a salary well above comparably educated social workers. Women are predominant in all of these occupations.

The issue of gender pay equity has become prominent in labor market analysis as it has in social work. NASW's Center for Workforce Studies reports a salary differential of 14 percent favoring male social workers, although it is not clear if this may be due to women being more likely to take time out of their careers for dependent care purposes.[6] A more recent analysis of Census and BLS data by Hannah Fairfield shows that female social workers have achieved parity with male social workers. In Fairfield's analysis, two groups of women earn more than their male coworkers, postal clerks and special education teachers, and both earn significantly more than social workers. Elementary and secondary teachers as well as registered nurses also earn much more than social workers, although women in these occupations earn 90 percent of men's wages.[7] Fairfield's analysis validates the vestiges of gender discrimination in the workplace, but it also raises questions for typically female occupations. Female social workers may have achieved gender parity with men with respect to equity in pay, yet their incomes are significantly less than other jobs traditionally held by women, even postal clerks.

Costs of Professional Education

The prudent student will gauge post-graduate earning in relation to the cost of higher education, and increasingly, the gap between the two has widened. Tuition and fees at four-year public colleges have been rising dramatically, averaging $5,836 in 2006-07 (at four-year private colleges they averaged $22,218). While high, tuition and fees constitute only part of the costs of attending college. In 2006-2007, the average tuition, fees, and room and board charges for in-state students in public institutions was $12,796, and $30,367 for private colleges and universities. When education-related expenses are added, including books, transportation, and sundry items, tuition and fees constitute only 36 percent of the budget for in-state residential students at public four-year institutions and only 67 percent of the total budget for full-time students enrolled in four-year private colleges and universities.[8]

From 2001 to 2006, tuition and fees for public colleges rose 35 percent after adjusting for inflation. Despite a 3.7 percent increase in student aid in 2005-06, total federal grant aid failed to keep pace with inflation. While the value of Pell Grants was augmented in the 2009 economic stimulus package, from 2005-2006 the average Pell Grant per recipient fell by $120, which meant that more students were forced to rely on loans. To compensate for higher enrollment costs and fewer grants, college students borrowed $17.3 billion in 2005-06.[9] Yet, the high costs of education are justified for most college graduates because they are soon eclipsed by wages once they begin work. In 2005 women between the ages of 25 to 34 holding bachelors degrees earned 70 percent more than those with only high school diplomas; for men the difference was 63 percent. The average yearly earnings premium for a four-year college degree for full-time workers in the 25- to 34-age group was almost $14,000.[10]

For almost two-thirds of full-time students, the costs of tuition and fees are partly subsidized by grant aid. Millions of students also benefit from federal tax credits and deductions for college tuition, and in 2005-06, post-secondary students received a total of $134.8 billion in student aid from federal and state governments, colleges, and other private sources. About 44 percent of this aid was in the form of grants while 51 percent was through various loans. The remainder was made up by subsidies awarded through the income tax system and work-study. Undergraduate students receive significantly more grant aid than graduate students.[11]

Revenue reductions by state and local governments for higher education are strongly correlated to rapidly rising tuition costs at public colleges. In that sense, states are shifting more of the fiscal burden for higher education onto consumers. Since grants have not kept pace, students are forced to assume more debt to pay for their degrees, and two-thirds of all four-year college graduates in 2004 left school with student debt compared to less than one-third in 1993. On average, baccalaureate graduates leave college with almost $20,000 in student loans and almost 60 percent of master's students owe roughly $27,000. When undergraduate debt is added, many graduates with a master's degree owe almost $40,000 in student loans.

Because students from lower income families are more dependent on student loans and other financial assistance than their higher income cohorts, they face significant challenges in attending college. For example, tax benefits favor middle- and upper-income families over lower-income families: Only 22 percent of the benefit of the tuition tax deduction goes to taxpayers with yearly incomes below $50,000; 41 percent goes to those with annual incomes between $100,000 and $160,000.[12] (Some of this difference is attributable to the higher enrollment rates of children from higher-income homes.) The differential impact of tax policy, fewer grants, and more student debt, means that many students from low-income families experience the effects of loan debt on career choice more than those from upper-income families. In turn, these students are also more stressed by high loans than students from higher income groups.[13]

Nevertheless, student loan debt affects most income groups, and according to the Department of Education, nearly 40 percent of recent college graduates make unmanageable monthly loan payments.[14] In addition, student debt also contributes to rising bankruptcy rates among young adults, a group with the second highest rate of bankruptcy. According to a Demos study, young adults are more likely to file bankruptcy than baby boomers were at the same age.[15] This trend exists despite changes in the federal bankruptcy law making student loans almost impossible to discharge in bankruptcy hearings.[16]

Off-loading the fiscal burden of higher education from government onto consumers influences career choice by driving college students into higher-paid areas like business, computer science, engineering, bio-medical science, and others. At first glance, this fits with the conservative view about what constitutes a "productive career choice" but it is also congruent with occupational ambitions of young women who have left behind traditional female jobs. It also fits in with Jacob Hacker's contention that the conservative "ownership society" pushes people—under the guise of personal freedom—to assume more of the risks associated with their choices, including education.[17] Conversely, serious ramifications for U.S. global competitiveness emerge when college attendance rates fall behind those of other developed nations as education becomes unaffordable for more prospective students.

The Debt Burden for Social Work Students

The likelihood of high loan debt invariably discourages some students from entering lower-paying careers like social work and teaching. This choice of careers can occur on the front end (the choice of a major) or on the back end (finding a job in something other than the student's major). Economists Sandy Baum and Saul Schwarz developed a benchmark for estimating the debt burden of student loans.[18] They maintain that recent graduates with very low salaries—about half of the median U.S. income for individuals—cannot repay their student loans while simultaneously meeting their other needs. Baum and Schwarz's framework takes into account that recent graduates with low incomes experience greater financial hardships at lower debt levels than do their higher earning peers. To the extent that social work students fall below the threshold established by Baum and Schwarz, professional education is less a route to upward mobility and more an invitation to penury. Rather than serve to accelerate the upward mobility of professional women, low social work salaries reinforce the pink collar ghetto.

The loan debt incurred by BSW and MSW graduates is similar to the debt incurred by students in other disciplines. A joint 2004 CSWE-NASW study on student loan debt found that 79 percent of BSW and 68 percent of MSW graduates had student loans. The average BSW loan was $18,609 and for MSW graduates it was $26,777. (Significantly, the debt for MSW graduates did not factor in undergraduate loans.) When disaggregated, this debt takes on a different characteristic. Undergraduate student loan debt in private schools ranged from $10,000 to a whopping $76,000 for a BSW degree. Many student loans in private universities were clustered in the $30,000 range. Similarly, student debt for an MSW degree ranged from $10,000 to $63,140.[19]

If an undergraduate were repaying a $20,000 student loan at a 6.8 percent interest rate for 10 years, they would be paying $230 a month, or around 15 percent of their after-tax income. (We differ with Baum and Schwartz's contention that repayment of 20 percent of gross income over 150 percent of the poverty line is reasonable.[20]) Hence, a recent BSW graduate living frugally, and earning $26,000 a year, will likely spend almost all of her income on basic necessities such as housing, food, transportation, health care, utilities, clothing, and so forth, leaving little remaining for student loan repayment. In contrast, a recent college graduate earning $60,000 a year with a $40,000 student loan (at the same terms) will pay $460 a month. The difference is that a frugal higher income graduate will have more disposable income after paying for necessities, thus making repayment easier.

Many debt-laden college graduates are averse to accruing even more debt in graduate school. While this fear is partly ameliorated when a potential graduate student chooses a high-income career in computer science, law, or business administration, it will undoubtedly deter some from entering lower-paying but important careers, such as social work and teaching. A study by the Public Interest Research Group (PIRG) documented the impact of student loan debt on public servants by examining the average starting salaries of teachers and social workers nationally, and by state. PIRG researchers then estimated the percentage of these former students who would carry unmanageable (payments with a burdensome impact on a borrower that hinders their ability to afford basic necessities) loan debt.[21] Factoring in high debt levels, the Congressionally fixed interest rate of 6.8 percent for federal student loans, and low starting salaries, the PIRG study found that 23 percent of undergraduates from four-year public colleges had too much debt to manageably repay their student loans as a starting teacher. Faring even worse, 37 percent of public four-year university graduates could not repay their debt as a starting social worker. Graduates of private four-year colleges face even greater debt burdens. While 38 percent of private four-year college students face an unmanageable debt burden as a starting teacher; 55 percent of private college graduates face serious repayment challenges as a starting social worker (see Table 2).

According to the NACE fall 2005 survey of starting job offers, the average annual starting salary for a social worker (presumably undergraduate) was $27,163.[22] At that salary, a first year social worker could only manage a $140 monthly loan debt payment, equivalent to repaying a $12,153 loan. According to the NPSAS data in Table 1, 37 percent of public four-year college and 55 percent of private four-year college graduates have accrued more than that in undergraduate loan debt.

Although the above data applies to undergraduates, the same income-to-debt imbalance holds true for MSW graduates. While there is a prob-

Table 2
Percentage of College Graduates from Four-Year Institutions with Unmanageable Debt on a Starting Teacher or Social Worker Salary

Profession	Percentage of public 4-year students with debt exceeding manageable levels if they entered this profession (U.S. Average)	Percentage of private 4-year students with debt exceeding manageable levels if they entered this profession (U.S. Average)
Teacher	23.2	38.1
Social Worker	37.3	54.8

Sources: NCES, "2004 National Postsecondary Student Aid Study (NPSAS)," Washington, DC; American Federation of Teachers, "Survey and Analysis of Teacher Salary Trends," Washington, DC; and National Association of Colleges and Employers (NACE), "fall 2005 Salary Survey," Washington, DC.

lem securing reliable data on MSW-level social work salaries, the 2001 salary study by NASW found the median salary for MSW's with two to four years' experience was $35,600. For those with 25 years or more experience the median salary jumped to $60,000.[23] Using $38,000 as a liberal starting salary in 2007, and assuming a full-time MSW student borrowed $26,777 over their two years of study, their loan repayment, excluding undergraduate debt, would total $308 a month. If their net monthly take-home pay were $2,100, they would spend about 15 percent of it on student loan repayment, leaving only $1,792 to cover their remaining expenses. In addition, if they also held an undergraduate debt of $19,000, their total indebtedness would soar to $45,777 and their monthly payment would rise to $526, or more than 25 percent of their net income, leaving just $1,574 to cover other expenses. If a student repays their loan over ten years, they will have paid $17,440 in interest on a combined loan cost of $63,000.

Sandy Baum and Marie O'Malley maintain that difficulty in repaying a student loan is particularly high when debt-to-income ratios exceeds 17 percent (the median debt-to-income ratio for all borrowers is only 8 percent) of gross income.[24] MSW graduates with 25 percent of their income earmarked for student loan repayment fit into Baum and O'Malley's hardship category. This income deficiency is further aggravated if the new graduate is the single head of a family.

While rapidly rising salaries in some professions partly mitigate the burden of student loan debt, a survey by the John A. Hartford Foundation found that between 1992 and 1999 the annual inflation-adjusted wage growth for all degreed social workers was a meager 0.8 percent. For MSW-degreed social workers, the annual wage growth was about one percent, indicating only a modest effect of advanced education on wage growth.[25] (There is little reason to believe that the slow wage growth of social workers was reversed in the late 1990s let alone following the recession beginning in 2008.) While college graduates who have been repaying loans for at least three years experience lower debt payment-to-income ratios as their income grows, veteran payers ironically report feeling more burdened than those in repayment for less than three years. Despite the decrease in student debt burdens relative to income, factors such as higher levels of consumption and increased family obligations may contribute to the perceived difficulty experienced by veteran pay-ers.[26] The long-term debt burden will have an even greater effect on most social workers whose wage growth is slower than in other professions. In fact, when social work salaries are adjusted for inflation based on the Consumer Price Index (CPI), there is a declining trend between 1976 and 2004 as wages fell below the rate of inflation.[27]

The widening gulf between salary and educational costs is especially pronounced in MSW programs in private colleges and universities. For example, tuition and fees at Columbia University for a full-time MSW student in 2007 were $64,154 for the full two years. In the same year, tu-ition and fees at New York University were $55,398 while the University of Denver's tuition and fees were $95,754 for the MSW. The University of Chicago's tuition and fees for the MSW totaled $61,876. These costs exclude books and living expenses. While Columbia University, the Uni-versity of Chicago and other private universities claim that more than 90 percent of their students receive scholarships, grants or stipends, much of the educational costs are covered by student loans. For example, the aver-age loan debt of MSW students at the University of Denver was $42,485 in 2004.[28] In contrast, annual MSW-level salaries in Denver were around $40,000. If getting an MSW at a less expensive public university is a ques-tionable investment, earning that degree at an expensive private university is even dicier. Unlike professions such as law, business and medicine, the prestige of the university that offers an MSW degree apparently has little, if any, impact on a graduate's subsequent salary. More pointedly, there is no empirical evidence that the income derived from social work educa-tion at more prestigious private universities is superior to public schools.

University administrators have not made the case that the prestige of their university adds additional value to the MSW degree. Indeed, the standardization mandated by CSWE accreditation negates the ability of schools to develop asignature pedagogy in relation to labor market demands.

In large measure, the inherent costs of a social work degree are more pronounced on the MSW than at the BSW level. Specifically, since a BSW is an undergraduate degree, a graduate can easily—and presumably some do—choose an alternative career if they become disenchanted with social work. With the exception of specialized undergraduate degrees in accounting, engineering, computer science, and so forth, a bachelor's degree in liberal arts or the social sciences is thought of more or less as a general undergraduate degree. Consequently, a BSW graduate would likely not be seriously hampered when competing against a history, sociology, anthropology or communications major in the non-social service job marketplace. On the other hand, a master's degree connotes a firm commitment to a specific professional field. Graduates frequently stay in the field in which they earned their master's degree, and these degrees don't translate well into other areas of the job market. For instance, an MSW graduate would have difficulty competing against an MBA for a corporate managerial position. Nor would they successfully compete against a candidate with a master's degree in human resources for a position in that field. Since the MSW degree doesn't translate well into the non-social service job market, a graduate who walks away from a social work career has little to show for the time, money and effort they invested in the degree.

Trying to Make It on a Social Work Salary

Understandably, NASW, CSWE, and social work educators are bullish about the growth in social work jobs.[29] According to the Bureau of Labor Statistics (BLS), there were 595,000 social work jobs in 2006. The BLS predicts that jobs in the social work field will grow faster than the national average, increasing by 22 percent until 2016. BLS also predicts more competition for these jobs in cities. However, a major problem in BLS projections is how social work and social work jobs are defined. Specifically, BLS maintains that "A bachelor's degree in social work (BSW) degree is the most common minimum requirement to qualify for a job as a social worker; however, majors in psychology, sociology, and related fields may qualify for some entry-level jobs."[30] In the BLS world, the appellation of "social worker" is given to anyone who calls themselves a social worker or who is listed by state, country or federal authorities as occupying a social work position, regardless of their academic training. While the number of social work jobs is predicted to increase in the future, the question remains as to what kinds of jobs they will be and at what salary,

As noted above, social work salaries lag behind those of other traditionally female professions. The salary gap also widens when social work is compared to other graduate professions. Graduates from the third (lowest) tier of Master's of Business Administration programs ranked by *BusinessWeek* earned more than $75,000 a year in 2001, almost double that of social workers.[31] In effect, salaries of social workers are closer to those of blue-collar workers than to other professional groups with similar (or below) levels of education and training (see Table 3).

Although masters-level social work salaries are very low compared to other professions, bachelors-level salaries are even lower. Based on Illinois' *Top Occupations by Annual Openings,* the average beginning social worker in Illinois earned $19,680 in 2001, roughly comparable to a beginning painter, paper-hanger, or roofer.[32] Moreover, the average $27,163 for a beginning level social worker reported by NACE in fall 2005 was almost $10,000 below the U.S. median wage.[33] The low salary for social workers is even more striking given that only 30 percent of the U.S. workforce are college graduates.[34]

The salary structure for bachelor's social workers is especially bleak for single heads of families. For example, a single mother with two children (and no other means of support) who takes an entry-level baccalaureate position at $25,000 a year would net roughly $1,500 a month after deductions for taxes and health insurance. Repaying an average student loan debt of $20,000 ($230 a month) would reduce her net monthly income to $1,270 which is insufficient to manage rent, transportation and food costs. Moreover, her $25,000 yearly gross income would be only $7,830 above the 2007 federal poverty threshold of $17,170 for a family of three. Put another way, this BSW graduate's income would be at 146 percent of the federal poverty line and more than $10,263 below the 2006 Earned Income Tax Credit cutoff ($35,263) for a family with two children.[35] Her children would qualify for the State Child Health Insurance Program (S-Chip), set at 150 percent of the federal poverty line. In states, such as Minnesota, where eligibility guidelines are at 150 percent of the poverty line, this graduate would also qualify for Medicaid. This same BSW graduate with two children would be eligible for $27 worth

Table 3
Incomes in Various Sectors of Social Work Practice May 2007

Child, Family, and School Social Workers
Elementary and secondary schools	$48,360
Local government	43,500
State government	39,000
Individual and family services	32,680
Other residential care facilities	32,590

Medical and Public Health
General medical and surgical hospitals	$48,420
Home health care services	44,470
Local government	41,590
Nursing care facilities	38,550
Individual and family services	35,510

Mental Health and Substance Abuse
Local government	$39,550
Psychiatric and substance abuse hospitals	39,240
Individual and family services	34,920
Outpatient care centers	34,290
Residential mental retardation, mental health and substance abuse facilities	30,590

All Other
Local government	$46,330
State government	45,070
Individual and family services	35,010

Source: U.S. Department of Labor, Bureau of Labor Statistics, "Social Workers," Occupational Outlook Handbook, Washington, DC, 2007. Retrieved March 13, 2009, from http://www.bls.gov/oco/ocos060.htm

of Food Stamps.[36] Simply put, a newly-minted BSW graduate would earn poverty-level wages after four years of paying tuition and fees, spending roughly 500 hours in unpaid internships, and incurring indebtedness on multiple student loans. Arguably, BSW education fosters social services by creating its own customers. Regardless of the social work degree, low salaries combined with the concentration of women in the field (81 percent of social workers are female) qualifies the profession as a pink collar ghetto.

The Added Costs of a Social Work Career

The social work profession has all the trappings of a legitimate well-respected profession—professional organizations, annual conferences, state licensing, supervision, malpractice insurance, subspecialties, and so forth—except for its inadequate salaries. The cost of a social work career does not end with graduation. Post-graduation costs involve licensing and license renewal fees, preparation costs for the licensing exam, supervision expenses, malpractice insurance, NASW membership dues, subspecialty organization dues, Continuing Education Unit (CEU) credits, supplemental certifications, and annual conference registration fees, to name a few. These costs can add hundreds or thousands of dollars to the costs of practicing social work and exacerbate already low salaries (see Table 3).

In many states employment prospects are enhanced by having a clinical license, regardless of the field of specialization while in school. The process of obtaining and maintaining this license is costly. Most states require about 3,000 hours of Board (i.e., state licensing board) approved supervised employment over a minimum two-year period, and demonstration of having been supervised by a licensed social worker during this period. While some agencies provide the required supervision for free, others have no approved supervisor on staff or charge for it. The social worker who lacks free supervision must contract for these services outside the agency, and group supervision fees can range from $25 an hour upward. One-to-one supervision will cost considerably more. All told, supervision fees alone can cost a new social worker upward of $2,500, which is an additional burden on top of student loans.

Face-to-face supervision does not ensure that a social worker will pass the LCSW examination, and many opt to take exam preparation courses which can cost from $35 to $310. In fact, a robust business has developed in the test preparation area. The ASWB (Association of Social Work Boards), which gives the social work exams, offers a practice version of the clinical licensing examination, the masters licensing examination, and the bachelors licensing examination. Access to any of the full-length practice tests costs a non-refundable $75. For only $125 a social worker can buy *The Complete Guide to Social Work* which promises to "contain everything you need to become a licensed social worker."[37] A more upscale License Review lectures (home study program for all masters' exams) costs $315.[38] This is on top of the $178 it costs to take the exam and the average $140 yearly fee for the social work license. Taken together, the full range of licensing-related fees can approach $3,000 or more.

The costs of maintaining a social work career continue even after acquiring a license. For instance, all licensing authorities require CEUs for license renewal. These CEUs must be offered through approved providers and can be earned by participating in institutes, seminars, workshops, conferences, independent study programs or related college academic or continuing education courses. These training activities range in price from inexpensive $25 courses to full-blown conferences costing hundreds of dollars. Like social work licensing, CEUs have become big business requiring more on-going payments from social workers.

Many social work graduates choose to join NASW (the organization has about 150,000 members) which costs another $190 a year plus $87 to $160 a year for optional malpractice insurance. Becoming a Qualified Clinical Social Worker (QCSW) costs $100, an ACSW $140, plus another $35 to join a speciality practice section in health; mental health; private practice; school social work; social and economic justice and peace; aging; alcohol, tobacco and other drugs; child welfare; and children, adolescents and young adults. General membership in the Clinical Social Work Association costs another $125. If a social worker chose to attend the 2007 annual NASW he or she might spend $180 plus additional fees for any CEU's. Depending on additional certifications and professional organizations the social worker may join, costs may be even higher than those hypothesized in Table 4.

Table 4
Hypothetical Post-Graduate One-Time and Yearly Costs for an MSW-Level Social Worker

One-Time Professional Costs

Application Fee for License-eligible hours	$ 91
Licensed Clinical Social Worker Application Fee	$ 178
Licensed Clinical Social Worker Exam Fee	$ 175
Course preparation LCSW exam	$ 400
License-eligible Supervision for LCSW	$2,500
Total	**$3,344**

Hypothetical Yearly Costs for Being a Social Worker

Social Work License (LCSW)Renewal Fees	$180.00
Malpractice Insurance	$100.00
NASW Membership Dues	$190.00
NASW Subspecialty Organization Dues	$ 35.00
CEU	$600.00
NASW Conference Fees	$180.00
Clinical Association of Social Workers Fees	$125.00
Total	**$1,410**

Increasing Social Work Salaries

There are several ways to address the problem of low social work salaries aggravated by high student loan debt. Congress understood the potential impact of loan debt on teacher recruitment and retention when it passed the Taxpayer-Teacher Act of 2004, ending an excessive subsidy to private lenders. The savings were then used to increase loan forgiveness for math, science and language teachers with five years of tenure in low-income schools.[39] While this legislation rewarded teachers for service under difficult conditions, it did not address the larger problem of how to recruit more college graduates into a low-paying career in which they begin making large loan payments only two months into their first year of teaching.

As evident in this 2004 plea, NASW promoted loan forgiveness for social workers in child welfare, schools and other practice areas:

> Even greater financial difficulty awaits social workers following graduation. Some social workers finish their education with bachelor's degrees in social work (BSW), but the vast majority go on to complete master's degrees (MSW).... After four, five, six, or more years of education, social workers are offered positions in both the public and private sectors that often fail to adequately reward them for their educational attainment, professional licenses, and credentials.... Social work salaries continue to be among the lowest for professionals in general and for those with master's level educations in particular. In 2001, 22 percent of social workers earned under $30,000; 20 percent earned between $30,000 and $39,999; 18 percent earned between $40,000 and $49,999. The median salary for social workers with two to four years' experience was $35,600.[40]

As of this writing, the details of loan forgiveness included in the 2009 economic stimulus plan have yet to be written; however, given the working conditions and high turnover in public social services, it is unlikely to benefit a large number of staff or be sufficient to reverse the abandonment of the public sector by social workers. NASW also pushed social work graduates into the Perkins Loan Forgiveness Program (also available for teachers, nurses and law enforcement officials), which provides loan relief and cancellation to those who work in public or private non-profit agencies that provide services to high-risk children and families from low-income communities. In addition, NASW promoted the National Health Service Corp—a Federal Program which applies to trained health professionals, including clinical social workers, who work with underserved populations. NASW is also lobbying for state-level loan forgiveness.[41]

Similar strategies can address unmanageable student debt, including adjusting need-based grants upward to reflect higher college costs. Until

2009, the maximum federal Pell grant (designed to help students with lower incomes) was $4,310 in 2007-2008, less than adequate to cover the soaring costs of undergraduate education. At the same time, state colleges and universities are trying to raise their rankings by attracting the best and brightest students. To accomplish this goal, universities often replace needs-based aid with merit-based grants and scholarships.

As college costs rise higher than federal loan limits, students and parents turned to unregulated private loans to fill the gap, which all too frequently led to a debt trap for students and parents. The largely unregulated private loan market needs to be more highly regulated, and student loans should have fair and clear interest rates as well as other basic consumer protections. Lastly, there needs to be incentives to control the rise in tuition and fees. A PIRG study proposed that state governments and colleges that kept tuition costs low should receive extensive financial incentives which further enable them to maximize enrollment at an affordable cost to students.[42]

Although important, loan forgiveness and other attempts to curb college costs are no substitute for a livable wage that allows social workers to enjoy a middle class lifestyle, such as homeownership, purchasing a newer reliable vehicle, and being able to afford vacations. Loan forgiveness will help ease the burden of unmanageable debt, but it will not compensate for the otherwise low social work salaries. Nor will loan forgiveness make social work a more attractive career for potential students concerned with financial stability. As such, NASW and CSWE's time would be better spent lobbying for higher social work salaries than pleading poverty for social work graduates. Simply put, loan forgiveness is little compensation for the 44 percent of social workers who earn less than $40,000 a year and the 62 percent who earn less than $50,000 a year.[43]

Unionization is a strategy that has led to wage increases in professions like teaching and nursing. About 75 percent of teachers are unionized either through the National Education Association (NEA) or the American Federation of Teachers (AFT). The NEA is the largest union in the U.S. with 2.5 million members while the AFT claims 1 million. In comparison, roughly 24 percent of social workers (204,000) are unionized, most of whom (89 percent) are in the public sector with about half employed by local government.[44] The higher number of unionized teachers helps explain why the AFT teacher salary survey for 2004-05 found the average teacher salary was $47,602, higher than for social workers but still low compared to other professions with similar education and training.[45] Studies by Caroline Hoxley and U.S. Census Bureau data suggests that unionized teachers earned 5.1 percent more than non-unionized teach-ers.[46]

While only 10 percent of nurses are unionized, a study by the Insti-tute for Women's Policy Research found that unions raise nurses' pay and improve staffing ratios. Unionized nurses enjoy a 13 percent wage boost over non-union members, and nurses' salaries are higher in cities with a strong union presence—for both union and non-union members. Nurse/patient ratios are also 18 percent lower in the most unionized cities compared to cities with low levels of nurse unionization. In short, this study found that a collective voice through unionization raises nurse pay and improves patient care.[47] Across occupations, the Economic Policy Institute calculates that union membership accounted for a 10.5 percent wage boost for women.[48] While unionization would likely not bring social work salaries up to those of nurses, it would make them comparable to elementary school teachers. Yet, social workers are employed in relatively small and highly dispersed units, across the public, commercial, and not-for-profit sectors, making them harder to unionize, which may explain why unions do not play a major role in social work labor markets.[49]

Another way to influence social work salaries is to carve out a niche, a set of skills, or a field of practice that is unique to social work. In large measure, social work has tried to hold its territory by vigorously promot-ing statewide licensure. By 2004 there were more than 300,000 social workers licensed to practice in all states and the District of Columbia. These licensed social workers represented about 38 percent of all self-identified social workers in the United States.[50] While licensing may help to legitimize a profession, it did not dramatically influence salaries nor did it preclude social agencies from recruiting job candidates from outside social work. Increasingly, positions that were once exclusively earmarked for social workers are now open to disciplines such as licensed profes-sional counselors, marriage and family therapists, applied sociologists, masters-level psychologists, and nurses. As state and local government seek to stretch revenues in the face of the recession, they will employ labor market strategies that reduce social work incomes, such as hiring freezes, involuntary lay-offs, and filling staff openings with less educated and less expensive replacements.

Ironically, the interchangeability of social work with other human service disciplines is evident in job postings on NASW's own Web site: "Bachelor's degree in Social Work or similar professional qualifications"; "LMFT [Licensed Marriage and Family Therapist], LICSW [Licensed Clinical Social Worker], LP [Licensed Psychologist] required;" "Valid state clinical license in social work, marriage and family therapy, or professional counselor license;" "Master's degree in one of the social sciences—must possess valid license as a LCSW [Licensed Clinical Social Worker], LPC [Licensed Professional Counselor], or LMFT;" and "Possess a master of arts or science degree in social work, psychology, nursing, occupational therapy, or related field." The encroachment by other disciplines is occurring in social work's backyard and under the very nose of its main professional organization.

The erosion of social work's occupational territory is predictable since the profession cannot lay claim to a unique set of skills or practice areas. Even in the child welfare field, what social workers do can be replicated by other human service (or even non-human service) disciplines. Florida State University researcher Robin Perry examined whether the educational background of child welfare workers in Florida had an impact on performance evaluations of their work. Perry used a random sample of child protective investigators and child protective service workers with university degrees in social work, psychology, sociology, criminology, education, business, and other fields. The research found that ratings of social workers' skills and competence did not statistically differ from workers with other educational backgrounds; the educational background of child welfare workers was a poor predictor of their performance.[51]

If social work is to claim or reclaim a particular occupational domain, it must credibly develop a high level of skills and expertise in that area. It must also demonstrate its effectiveness. Without empirical evidence of effectiveness, the preferential hiring of one discipline over another is largely subjective with rational social agencies often opting for the least expensive employee. It is here that the trends in education negatively affects the field; the dearth of theory and research reflected in its academic programs leaves social work vulnerable to charges of ineffectiveness. It is hard to raise the skill bar in a milieu of open enrollment, grade inflation, and the myriad other problems that plague social work education. Bringing this controversy into the open is unlikely so long as NASW conducts workforce surveys that artificially inflate the salary profile of social workers and while CSWE is engaged in arcane discussions around esoteric curriculum issues. To raise wages and reclaim its professional domain, social work could reinvent itself by claiming a field or fields of practice where it can make a unique and substantial contribution that other professions cannot match. This redefinition would require a concerted national dialogue among social work educators, practitioners and others.

Salaries can be driven upward by regulating the rapid growth in social work programs. This would assume almost *a priori* that the law of supply and demand applies to social work as it does to other professions. However, this supposition may be spurious since the relative flatness of social work salaries is based on the funding structure for social services rather than the normal marketplace laws of supply and demand.[52] In other words, the expansion of social services is not simply based on demand; to the contrary, social service budgets are generally conceived within a limited framework of competition for state and federal funding and partly allocated according to the effectiveness of key lobbying groups. This process is often disconnected from the needs of consumers. For instance, despite long waiting lists, a limited number of Section 8 housing waivers are issued each year irrespective of the need. Non- and for-profit social service agencies are not exempt from the similar fiscal constraints faced by public social services since their funding is often tied to public funding streams. Additionally, some of the same forces driving problems in the the educational arena have become infused in the practice of social work.

In a free market scenario, supply and demand account for fluctuations in the wages of occupational categories. A labor shortage of computer

Text Box 1
Deflating Social Work Salaries—Collusion Social Service Agencies and Funders

Mountain County, encompassing a large urban area as well as several impoverished rural enclaves, engaged a consultant to assist with developing a program concept and contracting process for programs aimed at providing support for vulnerable families. The consultant suggested that quality of staff and retention would be enhanced by building adequate compensation into the contracts. County staff took this to heart and included a requirement within the Request for Proposals that salaries meet minimum standards, benefits be offered, and a career ladder be established.

The non-profit social service agencies bidding on the contract revolted, arguing that paying staff hired on this contract at the higher level would require them to increase compensation and benefits for other staff within their organizations. Rather than use the minimum standard to develop an equitable "floor" for all staff, these administrators, focused on their understanding of a business model of providing services for the least amount possible.

One can argue that this response by the administrators demonstrates a low level of administrative and budgeting skill, along with a devaluing of the work and those doing it. In the end, Mountain County relented, permitting contractors to pay staff low wages and offer little or no benefits.

systems analysts or nurses normally results in higher wages for these professions. In the absence of demand for highly skilled technicians or assertive collective bargaining, social service funding is generally disconnected from market, consumer or wage demands; instead, public budgets allocate restricted funds to serve a client population regardless of the need. In the process, the wages of frontline workers become inelastic since the supply of labor has little influence on wages.[53] This is especially true for state monopolies—such as public welfare—where quality is rarely a crucial factor in the market dynamic and where a low-income recipient cannot shop elsewhere if they are unhappy with public services.

As Peter Kindle points out, social work wages are primarily a function of the will of the public sector to provide funding rather than a response to the market demand for services. Clearly, public attitudes regarding services for vulnerable populations have a strong effect on how much social work is valued and remunerated. With the conservative, negative view toward those in need that has held sway in the U.S. from 1980 to 2009, market forces alone would exert a negative pressure on social work salaries. Add to this ideological disputes and social work's failure to prove itself as an effective field of endeavor, and it is no surprise that the public is unlikely to value those who are working with devalued populations. Because social service provision is driven largely by budgetary constraints, worker quality and job experience comes second to budgetary exigencies. Hence, little incentive exists to create a wage structure designed to attract and retain qualified personnel. Nor is there much incentive to significantly raise wages to retain qualified personnel. During a period of stagnant or declining funding for public social services, the wage inelasticity characterizing social work salaries becomes even more problematic. The nature of social service funding means that a reduction in the supply side of social workers will not necessarily drive up wages; instead, cheaper workers will replace more expensive workers through the downward declassification of social work positions. Hence, restricting the number of social work programs—and thereby tightening the labor market—may have only a minimal impact on wages and the overall supply of social workers. While there are good reasons to stem the number of social work graduates, driving up their wages may not be one of them.

The value of social work wages is quickly eroding as the effects of inflation whittle away already low incomes. Concurrently, the nagging chasm between stagnant social work salaries and escalating college costs is growing wider each year for many students, thereby wearing away the economic viability of a social work degree. While psychic income and job satisfaction are of intrinsic value, they don't pay bills or reduce student debt. Unless social work salaries dramatically rise (or the costs of a college education plummet—an unlikely scenario), the financial burden incurred in obtaining a social work degree will make it untenable for all but a relatively small group of well-off students who either have independent wealth or an affluent partner/spouse to compensate for substandard wages, or the hopelessly altruistic who insist on doing good works in spite of inadequate economic rewards. In an odd twist, social work may inadvertently revert back to its early, pre-feminist roots, where it was a calling for upper-class men and women with a social conscience rather than being an economically viable profession.

The silence of academics on this issue is remarkable. Given social work's inferior wages, an emerging question for professional educators is whether offering a BSW or MSW degree in today's labor market is ethical, especially given the range of career choices available to potential students. Most social work educators fail to appreciate or adequately explain to students the long-term financial ramifications of high levels of loan debt coupled with low wages. Rarely are students forewarned about the potential financial hardships awaiting them. While social work educators spend a great deal of time discussing ethics, they evince a studious, perhaps self-serving, avoidance of examining the ethical implications of their complicity in training students for jobs with substandard income. A contradiction of colossal proportion is that while the social work curriculum is bursting with content on oppression, gender inequality and poverty, most educators turn a blind eye to how the profession abets the economic exploitation of their graduates, most of whom are women.

It is no small irony that while professional organization like NASW and CSWE espouse social justice, empowerment and self-determination, they seem more comfortable casting the profession as a hardship case requiring loan forgiveness than championing efforts at unionization that can potentially raise salaries and foster empowerment. One can only surmise that professional social work organizations are more content begging for handouts than demanding wage equality. During the very period when women's organizations, such as the National Organization for Women and the Institute for Women's Policy Research, have made a clarion call for pay equity, social work seems determined to dodge the issue. The irony here is that a profession that cannot advocate for its own self-respect and justice is not likely to be effective in doing so for its clients.

References

1. U.S. Department of Commerce, *Statistical Abstract of the United States, 2006* (Washington, DC: USGPO, 2006), pp. 318,331.
2. "Assuring the Sufficiency of a Frontline Workforce: A National Study of Licensed Social Workers," (Washington, DC: National Association of Social Workers, 2006), p. 5
3. "Social Work Regulation," (Culpeper, VA: Association of Social Work Boards, n.d.).
4. "Assuring the Sufficiency of a Frontline Workforce," pp. 5-6.
5. "Assuring the Sufficiency of a Frontline Workforce," p. 29.
6. "Assuring the Sufficiency of a Frontline Workforce," p. 29.
7. Hannah Fairfiels, "Why Is Her Paycheck Smaller?" *New York Times* (March 1, 2009), p. BU4.
8. College Board, Annual Survey of Colleges, 2006-07, October 24, 2006. Retrieved April 9, 2007, from http://www.collegeboard.com/press/releases/150634.html
9. Ibid.
10. Ibid.
11. Ibid.
12. College Board, Annual Survey of Colleges, 2006-07.
13. See Sandy Baum and Marie O'Malley, College on Credit: How Borrowers Perceive their Education Debt, Results of the 2002 National Student Loan Survey, National Student Loan Survey, Final Report, February 6, 2003, Washington, DC, Nellie Mae Corporation; and Tracey King and Ellynne Bannon, The State PIRGs, The Burden of Borrowing: A Report on the Rising Rates of Student Loan Debt, March 2002. Retrieved April 7, 2007, from http://www.pirg.org/highered/BurdenofBorrowing. pdf.
14. National Center for Education Statistics (NCES), National Postsecondary Student Aid Study (NPSAS), 1993 & 2004 Undergraduates, Data Analysis System (DAS), Washington, DC.
15. Demos, Generation Broke: Crushing Debt Burden Takes Toll On Generation X, October 21, 2004. Demos, New York.
16. See Howard Karger, *Shortchanged: Life and Debt in the Fringe Economy* (San Francisco, CA: Berrett-Koehler, 2005).
17. Jacob Hacker, *The Great Risk Shift: The Assault on American Jobs, Families, Health Care, and Retirement--And How You Can Fight Back* (New York: Oxford University Press, 2006).
18. Sandy Baum and Saul Schwartz, How Much Debt is Too Much? Defining Benchmarks for Manageable Student Debt, Project on Student Debt and the College Board, November 2005. Retrieved April 6, 2007, from http://projectonstudentdebt. org/files/pub/Debt_is_Too_Much_November_10.pdf
19. Council on Social Work Education (CSWE) and NASW, Loan Debt Data: Social Work Students, CSWE, Sliver Springs, MD, May 27, 2005.
20. Baum and Schwartz, How Much Debt is Too Much?
21. State PIRGs, Paying Back, Not Giving Back: Student Debt's Negative Impact on Public Service Career Opportunities, State PIRGs' Higher Education Project, April 2006. Retrieved April 6, 2007, from www.pirg.org/highered.
22. National Association of Collegiate Employers (NACE), Salary Survey, Fall 2005.
23. See NASW, Practice Research Network, Social Work Income, PRN: 2:1, 2003. Retrieved April 16, 2007, from http://www.socialworkers.org/naswprn/surveyTwo/

Datagram1.pdf. The 2001 NASW salary study may be skewed since it is based on a random sample of 2000 NASW members which may not reflect social workers in general. Specifically, many social workers opt not to join NASW. Other estimates can be found in Jeann Linsley, Social Work Salaries: Keeping Up w/the Times? Social Work Job Bank Career Center. Retrieved April 5, 2007, from http://www. socialworkjobbank.com/careercenter/article.php?id=003.

24. Baum and O'Malley, College on Credit.
25. Jeann Linsley, Social Work Salaries: Keeping Up with the Times?
26. Baum and O'Malley, College on Credit.
27. Peter Kindle, Wage Inelasticity in the Social Work Labor Market: Implications for BSW Programs. PowerPoint presentation, Graduate School of Social Work, University of Houston, 2006.
28. NASW, Government Relations Update: Selected Loan Debt of Social Work Students By State, April 22, 2004. Retrieved April 26, 2007, from, http://www. socialworkers.org/advocacy/updates/2004/042204.asp
29. Leon Ginsberg, "The Future of Social Work as a Profession," *Advances in Social Work*, 6, 1 (Spring 2005).
30. U.S. Department of Labor, Bureau of Labor Statistics, Social Workers, *Occupational Outlook Handbook,* Washington, DC, 2006. Retrieved April 19, 2007, from http://www.bls.gov/oco/ocos060.htm
31. "B Schools: Facts and Figures," *Business Week* (April 18, 2002). Retrieved May 27, 2003 from http:// bwnt.businessweek.com/faqsnfigs/ index.asp?sg=5&cat=9.
32. Wages were converted from hourly to yearly for the purposes of comparison. Data compiled from State of Illinois using 2002 data.
33. Social Security Administration, National Average Wage Index, Updated October 18, 2006. Retrieved April 23, 2006, from http://www.ssa.gov/OACT/COLA/AWI. html.
34. U.S. Department of Labor, Employment Situation Summary, April 6, 2007. Retrieved April 23, 2007, from http://www.bls.gov/news.release/empsit.nr0.htm.
35. Internal Revenue Service, Do You Qualify for the Earned Income Tax Credit? FS-2006-15, January 2006, IRS, Washington, DC.
36. Project Bread, Can I Get Food Stamps?, East Boston, MA. Retrieved April 20, 2007, from http://www.gettingfoodstamps.org/qualify.htm.
37. Social Work Guide, http://www.socialworkguide.com/order.asp.
38. Social Work Examination Services, Inc. http://www.swes.net/products.html
39. Committee on Education and the Workforce, Taxpayer-Teacher Protection Act *(H.R. 5186),* 108th Congress, accessed April 2, 2006 at www.house.gov/ed_workforce/issues/108th/education/highereducation/5186billsummary.htm
40. National Association of Social Workers (NASW), Government Relations Update: Loan Forgiveness for Social Workers, June 9, 2004. Retrieved April 20, 2007, from https://www.socialworkers.org/advocacy/updates/2004/060904.asp
41. National Association of Social Workers, Loan Forgiveness, 2007. Retrieved April 23, 2007, from https://www.socialworkers.org/advocacy/issues/loanForgiveness. asp
42. State PIRGs, Paying Back, Not Giving Back: Student Debt's Negative Impact on Public Service Career Opportunities.
43. Social Security Administration, National Average Wage Index.
44. See Michael Barth, The Labor Market for Social Workers: a First Look , John A. Hartford Foundation, New York, February, 2001; and the Institute for Women's Policy Research, Solving the Nursing Shortage through Higher Wages, Institute for Women's Policy Research, Washington, DC, 2006.

45.   American Federation of Teachers, AFT Salary Survey: Teachers Need 30 Percent Raise, Teacher Pay Insufficient To Meet Rising Debt, Housing Costs in Many Areas. Press Release, March 29, 2007. Retrieved April 24, 2007, from http://www. aft.org/presscenter/releases/2007/032907.htm.

46.   See Caroline M, Hoxby, "The Toll of Teacher's Unions," *Economist* (342) 33, 1996, pp. 33-34 (1996); and Joe Stone, "Collective Bargaining and Public Schools," in Tom Loveless (Ed.), *Conflicting Missions? Teachers Unions and Educational Reform* 47, 2000, Brookings, pp. 47-67.

47.   Institute for Women's Policy Research, Solving the Nursing Shortage through Higher Wages.

48.   Lawrence Mishel, Jared Bernstein, and Sylvia Allegretto, *The State of Working America, 2006/2007* (Washington, DC: Economic Policy Institute, 2007), p. 183.

49.   Jacob Fisher, *The Response of Social Work to the Depression* (New York: Schenkman Books, 1980).

50.   NASW, *Assuring the Sufficiency of a Frontline Workforce.*

51.   Robin Perry, "Do Social Workers Make Better Child Welfare Workers Than Non–Social Workers?" *Research on Social Work Practice* (16)4(2006), pp. 392-405.

52.   Much of the content of this section is owed to Peter Kindle's ideas regarding the inelasticity of social work wages. Personal conversation with Peter Kindle, Graduate College of Social Work, University of Houston, April 2006.

53.   Michael Anthony Lewis & Karl Widerquist, *Economics for Social Workers: The Application of Economic Theory to Social Policy and the Human Services* (New York: Columbia University Press, 2001).

8

Empirical Amnesia

Classical empiricism, embodied in the scientific method, served as the epistemological foundation for the developing field of social work. From the beginning, a tension between theory and practice emerged; objective research was seen as a way to test theory and practice, and to identify both concepts and methods that were efficacious. Early social workers set about identifying social issues and their causes, and utilizing data to develop programs and advocate for social policies. The assumption was that by systematically studying social phenomena and their causes, social workers could convince rational decision makers to initiate ameliorative and preventive policies.[1] Social workers of the Progressive Era saw themselves as the initiators and users of a research agenda focused on social change. Two important assumptions were that social phenomena could be systematically measured and understood, and that the recipients of the data would respond rationally.

Empiricism—An Early Commitment

The empiricist focus of early social workers was evident in their research organizations and journals which published articles designed to make the case for social progress. The American Social Science Association, established in 1865, influenced the Conference of Charities, and evolved into the National Conference on Charities and Corrections in 1874, furthering "scientific charity."[2] In 1891 the New York Charity Organization Society began to publish *Charities Review*; in 1896 the Chicago Settlements introduced *The Commons*. In 1905 these merged as *Charities and the Commons,* a periodical which morphed into *The Survey,* edited by Paul Kellogg and funded by the Russell Sage Foundation.[3] This was congruent with the Progressives' belief in social engineering: progress required accurate indicators of human misfortune.

Early pioneers like Jane Addams and Mary Richmond emphasized the importance of systematic data collection as a strategy to remedying social ills. "Both COS and Hull House staff members developed and promoted neighborhood-based research."[4] The empirical approach would be adopted by Progressives who advocated on behalf of the poor. "Most of the leaders of the [National Conference on Charities] accepted the implications of a scientific approach to social work problems. They acted on the tacit assumption that human ills—sickness, insanity, crime, poverty—could be subjected to study and methods of treatment, and that a theory of prevention could be formulated as well," observed a social welfare historian, later, "This attitude raised these problems out of the realm of mysticism and into that of science."[5]

Addams made dual contributions to social research. As director of the National Conference on Charities and Corrections, she appointed Paul Kellogg to develop data for its labor agenda, which included the minimum wage, child labor, and social insurance.[6] A social worker, Kellogg had overseen the Pittsburgh Survey conducted from 1907 to 1908, the first systematic analysis of social problems in the U.S. Subsequently published in a research periodical, the *Survey,* the study incorporated data on an impressive array of factors: "wages, hours, conditions of labor, housing, schooling, health, taxation, fire and police protection, recreation [and] land values."[7] Accordingly, data collection was essential for Addams' reform initiatives. Her close connection to the University of Chicago and their methods led her to systematize efforts to collect data such as the famous Hull House Maps which documented problems and needed services. She had this to say about her efforts to protect exploited workers.

> ... of all the aspects of social misery nothing is so heart-breaking as unemployment, and it was inevitable that we should see much of it in a neighborhood where low rents attracted the poorly paid workers and many newly arrived immigrants who were first employed in gangs upon railroad extensions and similar undertakings. The sturdy peasants eager for work were either the victims of the padrone who fleeced them unmercifully, both in securing a place to work and then in supplying them with food, or they became the mere sport of unscrupulous employment agencies. Hull-House made an investigation both of the padrone and of the agencies in our immediate vicinity, and the outcome confirming what we already suspected, we eagerly threw ourselves into a movement to procure free employment bureaus under state control until a law authorizing such bureaus and giving the officials intrusted [sic] with their management power to regulate private employment agencies, passed the Illinois Legislature in 1899.[8]

But Addams did not view Hull House in isolation; she understood it as contributing to an incipient moral and philosophical discussion in learned circles. In sponsoring lectures by John Dewey, Hull House became instrumental in the evolution of American pragmatism. Prior to the establishment of Hull House, Dewey had argued that a democratic social science, the collection of data for the benefit of common people, was essential for an individual to participate fully in a modern, industrial community.[9] Dewey's experience at Hull House and later Lillian Wald's Henry Street Settlement, thus, provided the grist for his experiments in social progress. Under Dewey's intellectual guidance, pragmatism would provide the philosophical justification for the social programs of the American welfare state.[10]

Mary Richmond also viewed data as essential for establishing and improving social casework. She looked to the law as a model for determining facts. Directing the Baltimore and Philadelphia Charity Organization Societies provided Richmond the basis for her thinking about professionalizing social casework. Her 1897 paper, "The Need of a Training School in Applied Philanthropy," generated wide interest and served as the pretext for the New York Charity Organization Society's establishment of the first school of social work by way of a "six-week summer training program."[11] As a result of her vast experience, Richmond became an advocate for scientific interventions. Toward that end, she authored *Social Diagnosis,* an exhaustive taxonomy of the problems that caseworkers encountered in their work, and later *What Is Social Case Work?*, elaborating the skill and knowledge base of casework. Fundamentally, social casework depended on social evidence: "any and all facts as the person or family history which, taken together, indicate the nature of a given client's difficulties and the means for their solution."[12] In 1909 Richmond assumed the directorship of the Field Department of the Russell Sage Foundation, a philanthropy which was a pivotal supporter of the survey movement and continues to be a leader in social science research

Individual vs. Social Focus

Historical epochs have cycled between conservative and liberal phases, and social work, which is highly contextual, shifted its attention accordingly. Thus, during the Progressive Era, social workers tended to focus on social programs, social change, and social justice, whereas during subsequent conservative periods, the unit of attention focused on the individual and how he or she fared.[13] During the 1920s, as prosperity and consumption accelerated, social work began to focus on human behavior and helping individuals to adjust to and function within the existing social order. Instead of producing data related to social injustice, or attempting to change the social order, social work began to seek legitimacy in the application of psychological theories that would explain and promote social adjustment. Whereas during the Progressive Era the focus was upon changing society to meet the needs of vulnerable individuals, the new psycho-dynamic focus encouraged social workers to look at how the individual could change to better fit into his or her social reality. Sigmund Freud's psychoanalytic theory was seized upon because it helped social workers think about why both clients and policy makers would not always respond rationally. Psychoanalytic theory allowed social workers to think about unconscious motivations and the complex underlying dynamics of a given behavior; thus, a client's repetition of problematic behavior, or a policy maker's distortion or refusal to believe data could be explained.

As the prosperity of the 1920s descended into the bleakness of the Depression, social work again applied itself to issues of social justice and many social workers embraced Marxist ideologies. Karl Marx contended that capitalists' exploitation of the proletariat was abetted by traditional institutions, such as the family and religion. Marxists held that in order to advance social justice it was necessary to understand the oppressive uses of power to enslave workers and the poor. Marxist theory reverberated through the academy and labor unions in America, attracting the allegiance of thinkers who became experts in Marxism. Understanding the nuances of the philosophical dialectic and the class struggle were critical, Marxists knew, since only those steeped in historical determinism could understand the actual machinations by which money and politics colluded to manipulate society. Marxists considered the very social welfare institutions that supported the social work enterprise to be corrupt confederates of capitalism, and thus, some social workers became self-critical of their own culpability in the oppression of vulnerable populations. For their part, the masses were largely ignorant of their oppression, according to Marxists, victims of their false consciousness.

The community practice/casework split in social work widened as proponents of different theories of human behavior transformed their theories into ideologies. Within each branch (the social change versus the individual adjustment schools of thought) various theoretical splinter groups emerged. As the theories multiplied, more and more semi-religious conflicts emerged in social work, pitting one practice ideology against another. Freudian and other psychodynamic theories as well as Marxism questioned key epistemological assumptions that had existed during the more pragmatic Progressive Era. Freud's theories, especially when applied as ideology, not only called into question the ability to really *know* through conventional empirical research, but also promoted skepticism towards authority and unstated assumptions as well as judgments about human behavior. Since none of these assumptions could be empirically tested, debates were won by the contender with the best reasoning, or the best grasp of theoretical minutia. Similarly, Marxist critiques of capitalist society led many proponents to question the motives and uses of data by researchers who were seen as apologists and perpetuators of oppressive capitalist systems.

Producers or Consumers of Research?

Social work as a profession failed to chart a clear course through the battles among the theories and the critiques of traditional epistemology. In 1935, with the passage of the Social Security act, the American Welfare State was tentatively established, offering social work important opportunities to exploit research into poverty and other social ills. Not only were social workers the architects of major portions of the Social Security Act, but they moved on to direct many of its primary programs; yet, the profession's research capability lagged. It was not until 1946, that the National Council on Social Work Education was established, an organization succeeded by the Council on Social Work Education (CSWE) in 1952; but, the reports commissioned by these organizations, Hollis-Taylor (1951) and Boehm (1959), did little to elevate research in professional education. The goal expressed in these reports was "*understanding* rather than *doing* research."[14] This approach to research reflected social work's withdrawal to a backseat role in engineering social change: rather than drive the topics of research, social workers would utilize research initiated by others.

The 1962 Curriculum Policy Statement (CPS) went further, demoting research in professional education:[15] CSWE's designation of social workers as consumers placed the field in a passive, as opposed to active role. Social work withdrew into ideological battles and concerned itself very little with the empirical basis for its positions. As noted in Chapter 2, affirmation of the apprenticeship model of professional training, compounded by the profession's embrace of psychoanalytic theory, had three implications: (1) "practice wisdom" was elevated to the level of proven knowledge; (2) the ability of empirical research to adequately understand the complex and unconscious factors associated with social work practice was discounted; and (3) social workers could argue that what they did not only could not be measured, but was an "art" that could only be learned at the master's knee . Subsequently, the 1969 CPS omitted research as a method altogether. A decade later, social work had lost its capacity to define a unique knowledge base:

> Because of the shortage of research-trained social work instructors, teachers continued to be imported from other disciplines. Few schools had systematic research programs, and few faculty members were involved in ongoing research studies. Methodology was borrowed from sociology or from experimental psychology; other forms of investigations, such as historical and qualitative methods, were rarely taught.[16]

The failure to actively engage in research meant that social work moved from the forefront of social change and social policy debates to a more reactive position, content with the belief that the art of social work was unknowable through traditional research methods. A report on research in social work education during the early 1980s revealed that not only were the vast majority of graduate programs training students as consumers of research but that most showed "no evidence of attempts to demonstrate the usefulness of research to social work practice or its relevance."[17] A 1988 attempt to strengthen the CPS with respect to research failed. To this day, accreditation standards for graduate social work programs continue to be so weak that they do not require MSW programs to offer a research thesis as an option for research-capable students. In most MSW programs, students would not be allowed to complete a research thesis even if they had the ability to do so.

Alternative Epistemologies

Social work's inability to use data to identify and resolve important social issues was further weakened by the popularization of alternative epistemologies. In different ways, existentialism, hermeneutics, decon-struction, and critical theory, challenged the use of empirical methods for understanding not only human behavior but social affairs as well. Social work education's engagement with alternative epistemologies has led to a polarization between the empirical conception that reality is "out there" and can be known through objective observations, and an alternative conception that views "reality as relative to social interaction and the social context rather than as completely objective and 'out there' waiting to be discovered."[18]

"Throughout its history, social work practice has been guided by a number of different fictions," announced two proponents of alternative epistemologies in 1989, "Because the profession has not yet fully examined them, these fictions are in danger of becoming myths, passed on to the successive generations of social workers with a resulting rigidity of practice."[19] Because the logical empiricist approach to social work has "interfered with the natural development of the client's narrative," they argued, other epistemologies warranted equal time.[20] Deconstruction was one such candidate since it

> questioned all existing structures because they excluded alternative views expressed through the pressures of constant change from those (such as women and others lacking power) at the boundaries. This fiction emerged from clinical and linguistic traditions and was prevalent in French feminist and radical psychoanalytic circles. It was a conflict theory that assaulted the dominance of white males or any others in the dominant positions and was based on a dialectic between the subject and the signifier.[21]

The constructivist insistence on personal interaction in a dynamic milieu effectively negated the empirical basis of social research. Because conventional language and roles were likely to be contaminated with oppressive connotations, constructivists preferred a more authentic interplay through reflexivity and dialogical interaction. In constructivism, the roles of teacher and therapist merged: "From this perspective, teaching resembles clinical practice." The implications for social work pedagogy were radical.

Like the therapist using a social constructivist approach in clinical practice, the teacher using a social constructivist perspective should become an expert in asking questions from a position of "not-knowing" … rather than aiming to discover the "truth," the social constructivist teacher takes a position of curiosity out of the belief that there are many possible explanations for the phenomena under discussion, from which one will be discovered as fitting the situation.[22]

The transformation of education from a cognitive activity to one that was therapeutic fit hand-in-glove with the increasingly ascendance of clinical social work. The old pedagogy was one in which the professor instructed students about artificial concepts such as deviance and mental illness, while constructivism broke down the dualism of instructor-student, rejected oppressive problem classifications, and offered co-learners the opportunity to evaluate themselves on their own terms. The other benefit to the new epistemology was that it offered a justification for those social work students suffering from math anxiety to avoid traditional research courses.[23] It is worth noting that the Educational Testing Service reported that applicants to graduate social work programs score dead last in relation to all other graduate disciplines in their quantitative scores.[24]

The Promotion of Anti-Empirical Methods

The new pedagogy not only contended that social work was an un-knowable *art*, but also repudiated the conventional "bean counting" mentality that had formed the context of social work. Subsequently, many research-averse social workers sought out these alternative episte-mologies, such as postmodernism. Postmodernism holds that established institutions and professions exert social control by adhering to procedures that exclude more authentic voices. Because postmodernists view estab-lished conventions as instruments of power, it follows that the plight of the oppressed can be elevated by disregarding established rules. From this standpoint professional ethics are but a means for disempowering clients. Just as marginalized groups had been subjugated by powerful institutions, postmodernists contend that social workers must throw off the yoke of oppression in whatever form: empirical research or profes-sional ethics included.

Several academics, formed a working group that promoted the under-standing of multiple realities and challenged the oppressive hegemony of the traditional empirical models.[25-28] Members of this group were able to exert influence social work education, and, by extension, practice and research, by virtue of their roles as journal editors, us-ing *Social Work* as a platform to promote an anti-positivist agenda for the profession.[29-34]

Text Box 1
Epistemological Purgatory

One editor who adhered to postmodernism concluded that "the privileging of the methods of science and unitary knowledges have led to the subjugation of previously established erudite knowledge and of local, popular, indigenous knowledge located at the margins of society."[35] Proposing that knowledge was power, the editor called for an "insurrection of subjugated knowledge." How was social work to avoid be-ing implicated in the oppression of victimized populations? "First, in research and practice we must abandon the role of expert, we must abandon the notion that we are objective observers and our clients are passive subjects to be described and defined," instead, "We must enter into a collaborative search for meaning with our clients and listen to their voices, their narratives, and their constructions of reality."[36]

Before becoming editor of *Social* Work, another proponent of postmodernism had earlier signaled his antipathy toward empiricism. In a 1992 Point/Counterpoint, "Should Empirically-Based Practice Be Taught in BSW and MSW Programs?" his verdict was a resounding, No! "By oversubscribing to the empirical model, we risk valuing effectiveness questions over moral ones, goal achievement over goal wor-thiness, and empirical data over personal, lived experience," he argued. "Research and evaluation should be participatory, emancipatory, and social change-oriented and, moreover, conducted within the context of social work values."[37] In his last issue as editor of the journal, he critiqued empiricism: "Interest in alternative forms of writing coincides with the emergence of the postmodern critique of Western enlightenment thinking," he proposed, "Previously unassailable notions such as progress, objectivity, and rationality have all been subject to critique—'unpacked' and reassembled as historical and cultural expressions."[38] This issue of *Social Work* bordered on the bizarre.

The lead article was "Hidden Voices," an essay that would have startled feminists for its traditional imagery. "Identifying social work as a woman's profession evokes the mental image of thousands of women toiling in the vineyards of want and need, dutifully or generously reaching out to those whom society has consigned to the social fringes," she began, "The image, if too sentimental, is also all too true. Social work has been a woman's profession."[39] Social work is a "hidden profession," because, "as an extension of family caretaking," its work is under-appreciated.[40] "Caretaking," she observed, "is a necessary but thankless job."[41] Duly noting that both Mary Richmond and Bertha Capen Reynolds had held empiricism in high regard, the author summarily dismissed this as an accommodation to "dominant culture."

> In the ensuing years the profession has moved more vigorously to authenticate its approach to practice by aligning with the dominant voice epitomized by the scientific enterprise. In contrast to the ordinary concerns of human relationships, social improvement and community well-being, the methodology of scientific research requires parsing and dissecting discrete elements. Emotions are replaced with studied disinterest; complexity is resolved by narrowing the point of study; mystery evaporates in the face of calibrated instruments and precise numbers.[42]

In place of the second (male) voice that social work had adopted, the author proposed a first (female) voice. "The profession's first voice is found most fully in what we have come to call *practice wisdom*, the accumulation of knowledge that is flavored with the richness and intricacies of years of collective practice experience," she argued.[43]

The author's invocation of a caretaking role for social work was revisionist history. Most of the pioneers of social work were, in fact, women, and they sought to professionalize their work. In response to Flexner's "report," they redoubled their efforts to amplify empirical methods in social work because they were the hallmark of social improvement during the Progressive Era. Thus, the rejection of the voice of these women is all the more troubling since it fails to recognize the truly heroic nature of their work: many of these pioneers' accomplishments preceded their attaining the right to vote! Not only did the author dismiss early heroines of social work, but she diminished the considerable accomplishments of contemporary women whose work diverges from caretaking: Congresswomen, such as Barbara Mikulski, Barbara Lee, and Debbie Stabenow, as well as researchers, such as Jane Waldfogel, LaDonna Pavetti, and Michelle Derr.

In another article, two authors cited Foucault's critique of the social sciences, and contended that "the body" was an under-valued phenomenon in social work practice.

Ignoring a century of medical science, the authors blithely asserted that"Knowledge of the body, which is inherently personal, immediate, and messy, falls outside the dominant understanding of acceptable knowledge."[44]

If liberating "the body" means dispensing with a century of scientifically-based knowledge based on anatomy, physiology, and biology, then that is the sacrifice necessary to advance the postmodern agenda. Through "micro-practices" administered by professionals, "bodies are cared for, controlled, and constructed according to dominant cultural paradigms and institutional expectations."[45] That the bodies of humans might be cured of ravaging disease and communities rid of unsanitary conditions accounting for increased longevity, both attributable to science, fail to warrant mention at all.

Another pair of social work scholars introduced Mikhail Bakhtin, an obscure Russian philosopher, to the profession. "The social work profession is deeply rooted in the Enlightenment of the 18th century and its modernist frames of reference. The Enlightenment attitude advanced the idea that there was a single code for knowing: scientific inquiry and empirical investigation." This, they argue, is history. "With its origins in the artistic, culture of spontaneity and improvisation of the 1950s an intellectual discourse, postmodernism, has been at work challenging and disrupting many of the certainties and dichotomies of modernity," the academics observed:

Postmodernism celebrates multiplicity, diversity, contingency, fragmentation, and ruptures and accepts cheerfully that we live in perpetual incompleteness and permanent unresolve. Postmodernism promotes the notion of radical pluralism, many ways of knowing and many truths. Science is knocked off its pedestal as the one true way to truth and simply seen as one of the many stories we tell about the self, the world, and reality.[46]

With this as prolog, the scholars describe Bakhtin's dialogical relationship between knowledge and practice, which provides continuity in daily affairs, and "carnival," the inversion of power relations. "Carnival," the spontaneous eruptions that mock established authority, provides a dramatic catharsis: liberation from the oppressive banality of everyday life.

Validated by support from the editors of *Social Work* and the *Journal of Social Work Education*, postmodernism gained a place as a credible intellectual stance, both in clinical and macro practice. A survey of philosophies studied in social work doctoral programs revealed that alternative epistemologies had made significant in-roads. While all doctoral programs in the survey examined logical positivism in great depth, doctoral students also studied critiques of logical positivism, alternative epistemologies like constructivism, heuristics, and postmodernism were included in the doctoral curriculum. In the aggregate, anti-positivist philosophies may well have reached parity with positivism in doctoral education. The researchers surmised that increasing philosophical content on positivism was associated with content on constructivism and postmodernism.[47] They concluded that this contributed to a dynamic synergy in doctoral studies, a conclusion that was applauded by advocates of alternative epistemologies who, like adherents of Creation Science who lobbied for equal time when science classes study Darwinism, had long argued for equal billing, but was received bitterly by traditional empiricists who equated this with further diluting social work's research legacy. As constructivism and postmodernism have ascended, empirically-based methods have become less prominent in social work education. A study of empirically supported interventions in MSW programs, revealed that most of the program directors who responded to the survey reported that such methods were *not* taught.[48]

Social work's epistemological schizophrenia appealed to students with perverse consequences. The empirical consensus of the Progressive Era had been undercut by CSWE's demotion of research in the graduate curriculum, presuming that MSWs would be consumers, but not producers of knowledge. In the thrall of postmodernism, many younger scholars rejected the scientific method outright, preferring ad hoc approaches to epistemology. This orientation, largely derivative of French philosophy, lacked the conceptual clarity and methodological requirements essential for replication. Ironically, the rejection of the scientific method occurred at the same time conservative and centrist politicians were demanding demonstrations of the effectiveness of investments in social welfare programs. But, postmodernism resonated with the liberationist theme of philosophical romanticism, evident in social work's concern for social justice, historically associated with political radicalism. As two British philosophers would observe, the result was intellectually intoxicating: "radical thought can go anywhere and tackle anything." To its adherents postmodernism has been the portal through which authenticated experience would flow into true knowledge. Since knowledge is power, the process of obtaining knowledge, became by definition, ideological:

> rethinking is inherently and necessarily political, not factual or technical; that it is a matter of morals, of values, of justice, rather than one of statistics; of ought rather than is. This implies both that anyone and everyone is qualified to engage in it, and that no one is qualified to gainsay its insights on the basis of expertise or technical knowledge.[49]

Postmodern Ascendance

Contrary to its adherents, the end-state of postmodernist epistemology in social work has not been to establish equal footing with the traditional positivist paradigm. Proponents of alternative epistemologies have sought to eject scientific methods from the professional project altogether: "the world will become oppression-free once science and 'Western ways of knowing' have been expelled from the garden."[50] Supporters of alternative paradigms proposed that social work could create a post-colonial, non-oppressive practice only by purging itself of patriarchal, elitist, dehumanizing scientism.

Significantly, postmodernism served to validate the scholarly persona of its practitioners by legitimating the perceptions of the oppressed groups to which they belonged or with which they identified. "Postmodernists," observed Harry Frankfurt,

> rebelliously and self-righteously deny that truth has any genuinely objective reality at all. They therefore go on to deny that truth is worthy of any obligatory deference or respect. Indeed, they emphatically dismiss a presumption that is not only utterly fundamental to responsible inquiry and thought, but that would seem to be—on the face of it—entirely innocuous: the presumption that "what the facts are" is a useful notion, or that it is, at the very least, a notion with intelligible meaning. As for the entitlements to deference and to respect that we ordinarily assign to fact and to truth, the postmodernists' view is that in the end the assignment of those entitlements is just up for grabs.[51]

Ultimately, postmodernists were anti-empirical in their objectives. Frankfurt located postmodernism among "various forms of skepticism which deny that we can have any reliable access to an objective reality, and which therefore reject the possibility of knowing how things truly are."[52] Evading commonsensical notions of truth has psychological implications:

> "antirealist" doctrines undermine confidence in the value of disinterested efforts to determine what is true and what is false, and even in the intelligibility of the notion of objective inquiry. One response to this loss of confidence has been a retreat from the discipline required by dedication to the ideal of *correctness* to a quite different sort of discipline, which is imposed by pursuit of an alternative ideal of *sincerity.* Rather than seeking primarily to arrive at accurate representations of a common world, the individual turns toward trying to provide honest representations of himself. Convinced that reality has no inherent nature, which he might hope to identify as the truth about things, he devotes himself to being true to his own nature. It is as though he decides that since it makes no sense to try to be true to the facts, he must therefore try to be true to himself.[53]

Under the guise of alternative epistemologies, social work began credentialing scholars who had little credibility except to their own narrow reference groups. Given the diversity of American society, the reality of cultural variation is certainly undeniable, as is the apparent seduction of becoming a scholar who represents a marginal population. A problem arises, however, when the scholar eschews conventional research methods for constructivism and postmodernism. In rejecting empirical methods as vestiges of Western imperialism, alternative epistemologies cannot validate concepts, verify outcomes, or report data; its product is, instead, conversation. To be sure, there are many virtues to authentic communication, but the systematic development of knowledge is not among them. The result is rife with irony: commercial research firms saturate the culture marketing various products—financial services, beauty lotions, political candidates—employing state-of-the-art empirical methods, including experiments, focus groups, and surveys. Increasingly, marginal groups are being served and exploited by such commerce; yet, lacking the ability to generate countervailing research, social work's scholars can do little but inveigh against the ruthless predations of capitalist, patriarchal institutions. CSWE has been complicit in the promotion of anti-empirical epistemology. In 2007 CSWE published *Social Work Dialogues: Transforming the Canon of Inquiry*, which included "a variety of topics using social constructionist and other perspectives associated with postmodern thought."[54]

Reviving Empiricism

In 1988 the disconnect between the volume of services provided by social workers and the integrity of their knowledge was so great that the Director of the National Institute of Mental Health (NIMH) agreed to support a Task Force on Social Work Research. Chaired by David Austin, the Task Force reported in 1991 that social work was not preparing sufficient numbers of researchers to generate knowledge needed by the profession. Independent of the Commission's report, researchers who surveyed social work doctoral programs found that only half emphasized research scholarship. If the future leaders within the academy were neglecting research, those preparing for practice fared little better; MSW programs continued to view graduate students as passive consumers of research. Despite the importance of research, "a number of schools simply lack research cultures sufficiently diverse to support training for research scholarships. Few faculty members cultivate their substantive interests by pursuing a series of extramural funded research projects," observed researchers, "Thus schools are unable to provide students with fiscal incentives, such as research assistantships, for information participation in research learning experiences."[55]

Subsequently, NIMH established the Social Work Research Development Center (SWRDC) initiative, offering social work programs willing to outline a substantive research agenda up to $5 million for five years. For the burgeoning number of doctoral social work programs and the MSW programs which emphasized clinical practice, this might have been an opportunity to seize the gold ring; but, social work's response was unimpressive. During the first 10 years (1993-2003) of the NIMH development centers initiative, only eight social work research centers were funded at social work graduate schools. In light of the few social work schools who applied successfully to be grantees, it is not surprising that on November 1, 2004, NIMH changed the program and offered it to all disciplines.

Social work was even less visible within the training centers funded by the National Institute of Drug Abuse (NIDA). Through its pre- and post-doctoral training programs, NIDA funds research centers at 38 of the nation's premier universities. While the training is interdisciplinary, specific areas of research are identified: pharmacology, neurobiology, immunology, psychiatry, psychology, epidemiology, medicine, physiology, public health, microbiology, biochemistry, toxicology, anatomy, biophysics, and others representing cross-disciplinary research. Social work's minimal presence is striking, particularly in light of substance abuse being associated with a variety of social and psychological circumstances with which social work has claimed some mastery. In fact, social work is identified as a distinct discipline in only one program, the University of Washington's Nurse Research Training Program. Among departments, the George Warren Brown School of Social Work at Washington University is the only school of social work boasting a separate grant.[56] Undoubtedly, social workers are among the interdisciplinary teams mounted through NIDA training projects, yet their presence will be overshadowed by other disciplines which will be defining the training project.

The small presence of social work in the NIMH and NIDA training programs validates the concerns of educators about the low quality of social work research and bodes poorly about the profession's prospects vis-à-vis more research capable disciplines. A century after having been at the nexus of social research, integrally involved in efforts to grapple with some of the most intractable problems in America, social work could not muster ten professional programs capable of mounting a serious research agenda.

A Social Work Research Infrastructure

In 1993 a number of organizations with a vested interest in research established the Institute for Advancement of Social Work Research (IASWR). Following the success of the American Nursing Association in establishing the National Center for Nursing Research, which was funded at $100 million in 2001,[57] IASWR lobbied for passage of the National

Center for Social Work Research Act. A dozen years after IASWR's creation, the prospect of a National Center for Social Work Research was remote: NIMH was consolidating rather than expanding the number of its research centers. As evident in the NIDA training grants, discipline-specific support was giving way to interdisciplinary projects.[58] As conceived, a National Center for Social Work Research was a set-aside program, an ongoing earmark appropriation specifically for social work research. The recession of 2008-2009, makes it unlikely that Congress will establish a research center for social work; even though several initiatives have been undertaken to jump-start the economy, few have a direct bearing on social work education.

In retrospect it is tempting to speculate about the prospects of a National Center for Social Work Research had CSWE affirmed the centrality of research in knowledge development during the 1950s, had MSWs been expected to be producers of knowledge instead of consumers, had doctoral programs become engines of empiricism during the 1960s, and had social work programs exploited fully the SWRDC opportunity. Had all those occurred, social work would, in all likelihood, have been as competitive as other disciplines in securing NIDA training funds and never have needed a set-aside for its own development.

Some social work researchers attempted preserve a focus on research within the field and academy. The Society for Social Work Research (SSWR) was created in 1994 by a group of social work researchers who were disillusioned about the demise of the Council on Social Work Research within NASW. The journal, *Research on Social Work Practice*, which had been started in 1991, served to disseminate the empiricist agenda of SSWR. Within ten years of its inception, SSWR boasted 2,000 members.[59] Along the same lines, in 1999 eighty social scientists met at University College London to consider ways to systematize research evidence. A year later the Campbell Collaboration was formally established for the purpose of providing a forum for collecting "high quality evidence on 'what works'" Through its internet library the Campbell Collaboration posts the status of research trials in education, criminology, and social welfare; by 2006 the Collaboration had registered over 90 ongoing research projects in several countries.[60]

By the turn of the new century, administrators in universities with strong research programs became alarmed about the profession's inability to formulate a credible research agenda. In January 2000 twenty-nine deans and directors met in St. Louis and began an informal set of meetings under the aegis of The St. Louis Group. Initially consisting of private research universities, such as the University of Chicago, Columbia University, the University of Pennsylvania, Washington University, and the University of Southern California, representatives sought more rigorous accreditation requirements while redoubling the emphasis on research. A primary concern was the "*growing*—rather than a diminishing—gap" not only in the number of doctoral prepared social workers, but also in "the number of educators who generate research-based knowledge for social work and the practitioners who seek such knowledge."[61] The chronic struggle to advance serious empirical scholarship was being jeopardized by the rapid expansion of CSWE-accredited programs which competed for a static supply of doctoral-trained academics. Unplanned program growth also jeopardized the St. Louis Group. As the Group expanded to represent the ever-increasing number of doctoral programs in social work, its effectiveness was compromised. Eventually, deliberations of The St. Louis Group began to resemble those of CSWE, the very organization whose mediocrity had provoked the Group's creation.[62]

Belatedly, Evidenced Based Practice (EBP) rallied social work researchers around the need to demonstrate efficacy through mainstream research methods.[63] Eileen Gambrill has argued valiantly in favor of EBP, noting that, in its absence, social work education consists of little more than "professional propaganda."[64] By basing its credibility on "authority" of the professional community to demonstrate its efficacy, while eliding "evidentiary" sources, social work has devolved into a self-affirming coterie of well-credentialed practitioners. Instead of establishing proficiency and accountability through state-of-the-art research, Gambrill states that social work has contrived a "recipe for bamboozlement":

(a)   a fine sounding (but unimplemented) code of ethics,

(b)   lots of discussion of ethical issues but little investigation of related behaviors (e.g. percentage of instances in which clients are fully informed),

(c)   reliance on methods of investigation that obscure rather than reveal what is happening (e.g. what social workers do and to what effect),

(d)   advocacy of a relativistic view that all ways of knowing are equal,

(e)   reliance on the authority of an elite in the vacuum created by (c) and (d),

(f)   propagandistic strategies designed to maintain the status quo (e.g. distortion of disliked views, censorship of counterevidence to preferred views),

(f)   hyperbole (e.g.) inflated claims in place of an honest description of services and their outcomes.[65]

The consequences of social work's neglect of evidence as a basis of practice are pernicious in two respects, according to Gambrill. First, professional education is inferior, essentially "propaganda." Second, a professional elite condemns criticism of social work education since it disrupts the social bonds—the glue—that hold professional training together. The result is that much of professional education "is spend trying to create an illusion that social work is doing the work it says it does rather than clearly describing what is done to what effect, and closing gaps between what is claimed and what is achieved."[66]

In addition to clinical practice, EBP raises fundamental questions about social work's orientation toward advocacy. The profession's promotion of client empowerment and social justice, for example, amount to little more than rhetorical flourishes intended "to maintain and expand our turf in relation to competing professions."[67] A society that is increasingly diverse, in which economic opportunities are diverging, and in which service provision in understood by justifying numbers of service providers to clientele, is one in which measurement is essential to the viability of the professional project. Denigrating empiricism, under these circumstances, is simply self-defeating.

EBP is an important trend because it promises to move social work back in line with other professions, such as psychology and medicine,[68-69] the very groups that used empiricism to establish their professional credibility. At the same time, EBP repudiates the narratives advanced by proponents of constructivism and postmodernism because they are unique and resist systemitization. Despite its import, EBP has yet to be widely embraced by academics or practitioners. The implications of this are critical insofar as social work's research capability continues to be compromised in direct proportion to the resources consumed by anti-empirical epistemologies.

The fall-out from the EBP versus postmodern epistemology debate represents an intellectual schizophrenia that has seriously handicapped social work as a profession. In institutions where social work had been securely established, such as hospitals and child welfare agencies, it has been losing ground because it has been unable to demonstrate its efficacy. The neglect of an empirical orientation and the use of postmodernism to justify solipsistic, identity-based analyses effectively impede social work's ability to compete with other disciplines as the information age unfolds. A century after its inception, social work is incapable of generating the most basic knowledge about its traditional concerns, compromising its prospects of shaping the future of human services. Most poignantly, social work is unable to credibly account for the effects of its activities.[70]

While other professions dedicated to social welfare, such as nursing and public health, are committed to developing a distinct knowledge base derived from empirical research, social work remains dependent on other disciplines. Direct social work practice, to the extent its methods are more than folk wisdom, has become little more than applied psychology. A widely used text, *Theories of Direct Social Work Practice,* surveyed theories that social workers employ, all of which were psychological. Contending that social work's clients have "the right to effective treatment," Laura Myers and Bruce Thyer inventoried empirically validated treatments, all of which originated with psychology.[71] Absent validated clinical methods of its own, social work has been reduced to the status of imitator, by adopting the *Diagnostic and Statistical Manual* of the American Psychiatric Association, or spectator, in offering little more than "a social work perspective" on direct practice, utilizing methods developed by other professional fields.

As a specialization, social administration is so poorly developed that it is hard to find or replicate data on what it costs to deliver services. In an era of scarce resources, public officials have to reconcile demand for services with available revenues; unable to demonstrate what it costs to deliver services, social work is vulnerable to competition from others who have done their homework. Among disciplines, public and business administration have been keen to develop such data; organizations operating under commercial auspices are more competitive than nonprofit agencies because of their superior data capability. Thus, social workers' complaints about privatization have the tone of ideological rants as opposed to reasoned critiques based on evidence. Absent essential data, social administrators simply lack the ability to show what their agencies and programs do. Most damning is their inability to systematically deploy and replicate innovations.[72]

Conclusion

A century after social work's emergence as an applied social science during the Progressive Era, its ability to generate knowledge and actionable evidence about practice has been seriously compromised. A convergence of factors have served to stall the profession's ability to measure its impact and effectiveness or to develop a meaningful literature on theory and practice: faculty poorly prepared in contemporary research methods, graduate students trained not to produce knowledge, doctoral programs teaching alternative epistemologies, and the failure of academic leaders to reestablish the scientific method as central to a modern profession's development of knowledge.

Anti-empirical methods have moved to the fore of social work education, increasingly shaping the intellects of the profession's future scholars. Beginning with junior faculty at second- and third-tier schools of social work, constructivism and postmodernism eventually infiltrated editorial decision-making of the profession's flagship journals. In less than two decades, opponents of empiricism have successfully challenged empirical epistemology of social work. But beyond the scintillation of the exotic, postmodernism and constructivism offer little: provocative conversations, perhaps, but no validated concepts, no replicable method, no outcome data. The tragedy is that, just as social work's mission is poignantly relevant due to a severe recession and a political context ripe for revisiting the social welfare contract, social work lacks the capacity to generate valid information about issues of critical importance to Americans. In this failure by omission, social work education looms large.

References

1. Katharine Kendall, *Social Work Education* (Alexandria, VA: Council on Social Work Education, 2000): chapter 4.
2. Bruce Thyer, "The Quest of Evidence-based Practice," a paper presented at the International Conference, *What Works—Modernizing the Knowledge-Base of Social Work,* sponsored by the Centre for Social Service Studies at the University of Bielefeld, Germany, November 10-12, 2005, pp. 5-6.
3. James Leiby, *A History of Social Welfare and Social Work in the United States* (New York: Columbia University Press, 1978): 120.
4. Donald Brieland, "The Hull House Tradition and the Contemporary Social Worker," *Social Work*, 35, 2 (March 1980): 135.
5. Frank Bruno, *Trends in Social Work* (New York: Columbia University Press, 1964): 26-27.
6. Edward Berkowitz and Kim McQuaid, *Creating the Welfare State* (New York: Praeger, 1980): 28-29.
7. Quoted in June Axinn and Herman Levin, *Social Welfare: A History of the American Response to Need*, 2nd ed. (New York: Harper & Row, 1982), pp. 146-47.
8. Jane Addams, *Twenty Years at Hull-House* (Cutchogue, NY: Buccaneer Books, 1994): 130.
9. Robert Westbrook, *John Dewey and American Democracy* (Ithaca, NY: Cornell University Press, 1991): 54.
10. David Stoesz, *Quixote's Ghost* (New York: Oxford University Press, 2005).
11. Walter Trattner, *From Poor Law to Welfare State* (New York: Free Press, 1974): 199.
12. Roy Lubove, *The Professional Altruist* (New York: Atheneum, 1965): 47.

13. Murray Levine and Adeline Levine, *A Social History of Helping Services* (New York: Appleton, Century & Crofts, 1970).
14. Original emphasis, Katherine Dunlap, "A History of Research in Social Work Education: 1915-1991," *Journal of Social Work Education,* 29, 3 (Fall): 296..
15. Dunlap: 296.
16. Dunlap: 297.
17. Quoted in Dunlap: 298.
18. Mo-Yee Lee and Gilbert Greene, "A Social Constructivist Framework for Integrating Cross-Cultural Issues in Teaching Clinical Social Work," *Journal of Social Work Education*, 35, 1 (Winter): 25.
19. Ruth Dean and Barbara Fenby, "Exploring Epistemologies," *Journal of Social Work Education*, 25, 1 (Winter): 47.
20. Dean and Fenby: 52.
21. Dean and Fenby: 51.
22. Lee and Greene: 26.
23. David Royce and Elizabeth Rompf, "Math Anxiety," *Journal of Social Work Education*, 28, 3 (Fall): 270-78.
24. See Table.
25. Dennis Saleebey, "Building a Knowledge Base," *Famlies in Society*, 80, 6 (1999): 659.
26. Quoted in Saleebey, "Building a Knowledge Base," p.657.
27. Saleebey, "Building a Knowledge Base," p. 661.
28. Saleebey, "Building a Knowledge Base," p. 661.
29. Ann Hartman, "Words Create Worlds," *Social Work*, 36, 4 (July 1991): 275.
30. Hartman, "Words Create Worlds," p. 276.
31. Ann Hartman, "In Search of Subjugated Knowledge, *Social Work*, 37, 6 (November 1992): 483.
32. Stanley Witkin, "Should Empirically-Based Practice Be Taught in BSW and MSW Programs? No!" *Journal of Social Work Education,* 28, 3 (Fall): 267.
33. Stanley Witkin, "Ethics-R-Us," *Social Work*, 45, 3 (May): 198-99.
34. Witkin, "Ethics-R-Us,": 199.
35. Ann Hartman, "In Search of Subjugated Knowledge," *Social Work* 37, 6 (November 1992): 483.
36. Hartman, "In Search of Subjugated Knowledge," p. 484.
37. Stanley Witkin, "Should Empirically Based Practice Be Taught in BSW and MSW Programs? No*! Journal of Social Work Education*, 28, 3 (Fall): 267.
38. Stanley Witkin, "Writing Social Work,"*Social Work*, 45, 5 (October): 390.
39. Ann Weick, "Hidden Voices*," Social Work*, 45,5 (October): 395-96.
40. Weick: 397.
41. Weick: 398.
42. Weick: 400.
43. Weick: 400.
44. Kathleen Taugenberg and Susan Kemp, "Embodied Practice*," Social Work*, 47,1 (January): 11.
45. Taugenberg and Kemp: 14.
46. Allan Irving and Tom Young, "Paradigm for Pluralism*," Social Work*, 47, 1 (January): 19-20.
47. Jeane Anastas and Elaine Congress, "Philosophical Issues in Doctoral Education in Social Work," *Journal of Social Work Education*, 35, 1 (Winter):143-44.
48. Jane Woody, Henry D'Souza, and Rebecca Dartman, "Do Master's in Social Work Programs Teach Empirically Supported Interventions?" *Research on Social Work Practice,* vol 16, no. 5 (September 2006), p. 475.

49. Benson and Stangroom: 45.
50. Benson and Stangroom: 129.
51. Harry Frankfurt, *On Truth* (New York: Knopf, 2006): 20-21.
52. Harry Frankfurt, *On Bullshit* (Princeton, NJ: Princeton University Press, 2005): 64.
53. Frankfurt, *On Bullshit*: 64-66.
54. CSWE e-newletter, downloaded April 19, 2007.
55. Mark Fraser, Jeffrey Jenson, and Robert Lewis, "Research Training in Social Work," *Journal of Social Work Education*, 29, 1 (Winter 1993): 57.
56. Based on an analysis of NIDA training programs downloaded January 31, 2009 from http://www.drugabuse.gov/researchtraining/TrainingSites.html
57. Sue Hoechstetter, "Key Strategist Shares Thoughts on Legislative Advocacy," *Social Work Education Reporter,* 49,1 (Winter): 40.
58. Joan Zlotnick and Barbara Solt, "The Institute for the Advancement of Social Work Research," *Research on Social Work Practice*, 16, 5 (September 2006): 535.
59. Thyer, "The Quest of Evidence-based Practice," p. 7.
60. http://www.compbellcollaboration.org/about.asp. Downloaded October 18, 2006.
61. Ronald Feldman, "The Human Resource Crisis in Social Work Education," *Journal of Social Work Education*, 35, 3 (Spring/Summer): 178.
62. Ron Feldman, "Back to the Future with the St. Louis Group," (New York: Columbia University School of Social Work, n.d.).
63. Eileen Gambrill, "Evidence-Based Practice," *Journal of Social Work Education*, 39, 1 (Winter):3-23.
64. Eileen Gambrill, "Evaluating the Quality of Social Work Education," *Journal of Social Work Education*, 37, 3 (Fall 2001).
65. Eileen Gambrill, "Social Work: An Authority-Based Profession," *Research on Social Work Practice*, vol. 11, no 2 March 2001, p. 170.
66. Gambrill, "Social Work: An Authority-Based Profession, pp. 169, 168.
67. Eileen Gambrill, "Educational Policy and Accreditation Standards," *Journal of Social Work Education,* 37, (Spring/Summer 2001).
68. Eileen Gambrill, "Evidence-based practice: An Alternative to Authority-based Practice", *Families in Society* 80(4): 341-350(1999)
69. David Pollio,"The Art of Evidence-Based Practice", *Research on Social Work Practice* 16(2): 224-232(2006)
70. William Epstein, *Psychotherapy as Religion* (Reno, NV: University of Nevada Press, 2006).
71. Laura Myers and B ruce Thyer, "Should Social Work Clients Have the Right to Effective Treatment?" *Social Work*, 42, 7 (May 1997).
72. Carrilio, Terry, Packard, Thomas, and Clapp, John (2003) >Nothing In-Nothing Out: Barriers to Data Based Program Planning=, *Administration in Social Work* 27(4): 61-75; Carrilio, Terry (2005) >Management Information Systems: Why Are They Underutilized in the Social Services?= , *Administration in Social Work.* 29(2): 43-61.

9

The *Council on Social Work Education* and the *National Association of Social Workers*: A Concerned Critique

Bruce Thyer

My career as a social worker began in my late teens, when I was hired as a "cottage parent," providing care and supervision to 60 adults with severe and profound developmental disabilities who lived in a dormitory at a large state residential institution located near my hometown of Fort Myers, Florida. I worked the night shift, 11 pm - 7 am, monitored the residents, dealt with their needs as necessary, recorded the occurrence of (not infrequent) seizures, helped the residents get up in the morning, distributed clothing and assisted those who needed to get dressed. Living conditions for the residents were Spartan, as was the diet. If memory serves the amount budgeted for food each day was 87 cents per resident, a Dickensian sum even 30 years ago. There were occasional messes to clean up, fights to interrupt, and during the quiet of the night I could pursue my studies as a community college student.

Leaving that early position, I served in the U.S. Army as an enlisted drug and alcohol abuse counselor, worked as an aide on a psychiatric ward, used the G.I. Bill benefits to earn my MSW at the University of Georgia (joining the NASW in 1978), and then my Ph.D. in social work and psychology from the University of Michigan (joining the CSWE in 1980). I worked as a clinical social worker throughout my doctoral studies and for several years thereafter, prior to obtaining my first full time academic position. I became a "Certified Social Worker" in the state of Michigan in 1980 (there was no licensure then available in Michigan), an LCSW in Florida in 1985, and an LCSW in Georgia in 1993. While a

175

doctoral student I began attending the annual conferences of NASW and CSWE, presented at these meetings, papers, avidly read their journals, and, in the fullness of time, began to contribute to their journals via writing articles. I shared then, as now, the profound sense of social mission both NASW and CSWE exemplify, seeing both entities as valuable institutions to improve our field and society as a whole. My membership was mutually reinforcing. With my annual payment of membership dues, conference presentations, and publications, I was strengthening the organizations and perhaps the profession. My involvement in both groups could be seen by some as a mark of my socialization into the field, of active intellectual and professional engagement.

This personal narrative places my subsequent remarks about CSWE and NASW into context. I am not some disaffected outsider, grumbling over imagined slights or smarting over perceived insults. I have greatly benefited from my memberships and I have regularly encouraged my students and colleagues to join these two groups. I have met many delightful and respected colleagues through my membership, I have had some success in getting my work published in their journals, and have enjoyed the annual conferences. Nevertheless, my affection for my two disciplinary homes has not blinded me to some conspicuous problems in their operations, governance, and member services. I would like to review a few of these problems and to present some possible solutions.

Governance—CSWE

The following story is absolutely true. It may make you angry. It does me. In the late 1990s I was contacted by a colleague on CSWE's National Nominating Committee who asked me if I would like to serve on CSWE's Board of Directors (BOD). I said sure, but that I doubted I could get elected. My colleague responded by saying that would not be a problem, since they would match me on the slate with a person who was relatively unknown. To my discredit I consented to this perversion of democracy, submitted my nomination, and in due course appeared on the ballot, matched against someone that I, at least, had never heard of. I was duly elected to the BOD as a Graduate Faculty Representative, credibly served my three year term and was then rotated off.

What is wrong with this picture? Could this be called a fair election, governed by genuinely democratic processes? Of course not. How could this distorted process come about? Well, the answer is complicated. At the time I am writing this chapter, the governance of CSWE ostensibly resides with a 29 member Board of Directors, consisting of the elected officers of CSWE plus 20 other members, six program directors (three undergraduate and three graduate), six faculty (23 undergraduate and three graduate), one practice representative, two non-social work educators appointed by the President, and 5 Chairs of various CSWE Commissions (*ex officio* and non-voting). The officers of CSWE consist of the President, Vice President, Secretary, Treasurer and a President-Elect. An Executive Committee consists of CSWE officers, the Chair of the Commission on Accreditation (*ex officio*), and three other members elected by the entire BOD.

The Chairs and members of the various Commissions (i.e., Accreditation, Curriculum and Educational Innovation, Diversity and Economic Justice, Global Social Work Education, Professional Development) are all appointed by the President, with "consultation" from the BOD. The Commissions are of various sizes, ranging from 10-25 members. Another crucial role is that of Executive Director of CSWE, an individual appointed by the BOD, who in turn appoints all other professional personnel and clerical staff within CSWE.

All nationally elected positions are chosen on the basis of a "double slated" ballot, with two persons chosen for each elective opening by the members of the National Nominating Committee (NNC), and it is this practice which enabled me to be virtually guaranteed "election" to membership on the BOD. The NNC consists of 13 elected members serving rotating three year terms and the NCC is an incredibly influential group, with the power to arbitrarily decide who shall or shall not appear on the ballot. I personally benefited from my friendly relationship with one such member, who not only arranged my placement on the ballot but also my election. My own experience in being elected via manipulating the composition of the slate of nominees is by no means a rare practice. This is not right, even if it is a common practice. There are other problems with the election processes.

The NCC members themselves, noble and well-meaning persons every one, are themselves constrained by CSWE's Affirmative Action Policy and Plan, which states that "The Council on Social Work Education shall not discriminate on the basis of race, color, religion, creed, gender, ethnic or national origin, sexual orientation, disability, or age" (CSWE, 2000, p. 1). This of course is a laudable standard and avoids lawsuits. No doubt all CSWE members (including myself), support such non-discriminatory practices. But the plan goes further, including the following elements:

- "The Council on Social Work Education commits itself to an affirmative action policy that permeates the entire organization and reflects the diversity of its membership. The Affirmative Action Policy shall apply to all areas and activities of the Council on Social Work Education as reflected in the composition of staff, *elected* (italics added) and appointed voluntary positions and vendors. The Council shall make specific, continuous efforts to ensure diversity in all areas, with particular attention to the inclusion of persons from under-represented groups."

- "The Affirmative Action Policy shall be implemented by means of the Affirmative Action Plan for the purpose of *ensuring* (italics added) diversity in all Council areas and activities with particular attention to the inclusion of persons from under-represented groups. For purposes of the Affirmative Action Policy, under-represented groups include but are not limited to women, transgender, African American/Other black (non-Hispanic), American Indian/Native American/Alaskan Native, Asian American, Pacific Islander, Mexican American, Puerto Rican, Other Latino(a)/Hispanic, persons with disabilities, and gay, lesbian and bisexual persons."

- "The Affirmative Action Policy shall apply to all *elected* (italics added) and appointed positions in the Council."

- "The Nominating Committee shall develop and maintain specific procedures designed to *ensure* the *election* (italics added) of persons from historically under-represented groups on *slated and in elected bodie*s (italics added), including the Board of Directors and its Executive Committee, the Nominating Committee, and other elected positions." (all of the above bulleted points are direct quotations from CSWE, 2000)

When affirmation action penetrates to the level of composing ballots and in deciding who can run for office, it runs up against a fundamental tenet of democracy, which holds to the principle of one-person, one-vote, meaning that all electors are treated equally, not just in voting but in all arenas of enfranchisement, including the right to run for elective office. It requires strong and compelling arguments to violate these ideals, e.g., adjusting (not compensating) for prior discrimination. Can such arguments legitimately be made to justify these practices? According to the *NASW Social Work Dictionary* (Barker, 2003, p. 11), affirmative action is defined as "Steps taken by an organization to remedy imbalances in the employment of people of color and women, promotions and other opportunities." Does either NASW or CSWE have a history of "imbalance" in this regard? Certainly not during the quarter century I was a member. If anything, their efforts to bend over backward have produced the opposite result.

These policies militate against genuinely democratic governance within CSWE, and, I strongly suspect, without apparent need or justification. Affirmative action plans are usually justified as essential to redress past wrongs, such as discrimination, committed against some minority group. For example, universities with a history of refusing to admit African American students or to hire African American faculty could be legally required to develop an Affirmative Action plan to redress these past and perhaps current wrongs. I submit that it is obvious both CSWE and NASW lack a history of discrimination against members of various minority groups. Do the leaders of our associations really suspect that in a free election its members would not vote to elect the best qualified individual running for office, choosing instead, for example, to elect an under-qualified white male in lieu of a better qualified African American woman? Yet that seems to be the underlying premise justifying the strong affirmative action practices as they pertain to elected office. In effect, the leadership of CSWE says that we cannot trust the membership to vote in a non-discriminatory manner and therefore we must force the election of members from the various groups we designate as under-represented, by preparing ballots that commonly pair individuals from similar backgrounds, and also ensure a minimal level of representation from groups that have never been under-represented within CSWE or NASW (e.g., women). The astute reader will notice the conspicuous absence of males from the list of under-represented groups in the CSWE's list. This is despite the fact that males are a distinct minority in the memberships of NASW and CSWE. If you are familiar with the ballots prepared by the Nominating Committees from CSWE and NASW you will agree I have described their practices accurately.

While I benefited from the undue patronage of a member of CSWE's Nominating Committee, via my personal relationship, slipping in between the cracks as it were, of the affirmative action policies in being elected to the CSWE BOD, that does not make it right. I had a different experience with a NASW chapter which composed its ballots in a manner consistent with a similarly non-democratic, misanthropic and unnecessary affirmative action policy.

Governance—NASW

My state chapter of NASW issued a call for nominations for state-wide elected office. Wanting to be a good member, I nominated myself. In due course I received the following email message from the person in charge of nominations:

> Bruce, NASW national office dictates that our board composition parallel our member-
> ship. Unfortunately we cannot run a male for Board-Member-at-Large. The maximum
> number of males are on the board already…. We are a largely female organization.

I protested this exclusion, pointing out that I had been a member for over 20 years, I paid my dues like any other member, and deserved equivalent treatment in being afforded the opportunity to appear on the election ballot. I then got the following email in reply:

> I am sorry you feel this way. It is certainly understandable. Perhaps I did not fully
> explain. Two of the units are running males. It is a given that one male from each will
> be elected. Two males have been nominated for president. It is also certain, provided
> that both run, that a male will be elected president. Given our gender makeup as a
> state, there are three slots on the board for males. That is why we have to run females
> against all other slots. (The above two statements are direct quotes from the emails
> but I will refrain from providing full citations to these personal communications in
> order to avoid embarrassing their sender).

This standard of comprising ballots based upon the composition of the membership appears to be a very flexible one, invoked in favor of certain groups (women and minorities of color), and then the same principle is applied to exclude others (e.g., whites and males). For example, according to Ginsberg (1995) in 1994 the NASW membership consisted of whites (87%), African Americans (6.2%), Hispanics (2.9%), as well as some other groups with lesser percentages. If the composition of the membership determines the composition of the slate (as it appears to in the instance of gender), then should not race also dictate that no more than 7% of the elective offices be held by African Americans? The absurdity and unfairness of this latter position is clearly evident with respect to race. Why should it be invoked in the case of gender? It is equally unfair and absurd.

The practice of gerrymandering election ballots in the name of affirmative action is not needed in my opinion, and indeed I believe it to be highly destructive. The members of CSWE and NASW are highly educated persons with a clear dedication to the high moral standards, values and ethics that have historically characterized the profession. Their commitment to social justice cannot be questioned. Is it really necessary to continue the anti-democratic practice of including/excluding persons from running for office on the basis of gender, race or other characteristics? These practices taint the legitimacy of those from officially designated under-represented groups who do appear on the ballot and enjoy elective office, and also discriminate against those members who would like to make a more active contribution to organizational governance. Both results are demoralizing and perhaps contribute to the dwindling membership of the NASW and the flat-line of individual CSWE memberships despite the substantial growth of social work educational programs. What can be done?

I belong to some other organizations that employ a more democratic process to comprise ballots. When there is a forthcoming opening for an elective office, all members are notified of this opening and a call for nominations is issued. Self-nominations and nominations by others are welcome. In due course the nomination process is closed. At that point the Nomination Committee tabulates the top 2-4 or more members with the most nominations, and these persons are placed on the ballot. The process is completely neutral with respect to diversity or affirmative action considerations and devoid of patronage. Your appearance on the ballot is dependent upon your ability to get fellow-members to nominate you. The more members who nominate you, the more likely it is that you will appear on the ballot. Strict policies prohibit one from using institutional or organizational email accounts, distribution lists, telephonic, or postal services—doing so disqualifies you from running. While not without its own flaws, this more democratic process does away with the hideous and awkward contortions that characterize the efforts of NASW and CSWE to comply with its own affirmative action policies, and also attenuates the role of patronage and personal relationships that mar the existing system.

Affirmative action policies within NASW and CSWE should be maintained of course. They should work to ensure that ALL members are afforded equivalent treatment with respect to opportunity to run for elective office. At present they do not. They actively discriminate against males and whites, and unfairly promote the participation in organizational governance of other groups, groups with no-evident history of past discrimination at the hands of these organizations. Some have contended that that these policies promote mediocrity in organizational leadership. They certainly do not accomplish what they are supposed to achieve. Witness the fact that fewer than 7% of NASW members are African American—hardly a glowing testament to the effectiveness of its existing affirmative action policies! The existence of the entirely separate membership group called the *National Association of Black Social Workers,* with its own journal, conference, etc. is further testament of the failure of NASW to advocate effectively on behalf of African American social workers. NASW really needs a strong affirmative action program to *recruit and retain* more African Americans and other visible minorities among its membership, This is a far more pressing need for organizational health than striving for an unnecessary and antidemocratic "balance" in ballots.

This critique is offered in the spirit of wishing the organizations to which I belonged for so long to become better, more inclusive groups. The memberships of NASW and CSWE are stagnating or shrinking. The organizations are scrambling around for solutions. The Society for Social Work and Research affords a good example of an alternative structure. SSWR has NO affirmative action policy, or even a statement on the issue. Yet during its 13 year history the Presidency of SSWR has been held by a majority of women, and one African American. Fairness and equal treatment of members are the default assumptions of this thriving organization, all without the contrivances associated with creating the ballots of NASW and CSWE.

Journal Operations

CSWE produces one professional periodical, the *Journal of Social Work Education* (JSWE, received by all members), while NASW produces four, *Social Work, Social Work Research, Health and Social Work, Children and Schools*. Another journal is *Social Work Abstracts* which does not publish articles, only abstracts, so it will not be included in this section. *Social Work* goes to all NASW members and the other three NASW journals go to a couple of thousand subscribers each. Despite the vast opportunity to make a substantial profit from its journal operations, NASW found it necessary a few years ago to reduce the numbers of issues per year of *Social Work* from six to four. This was said to be a cost cutting move. Another recent (2009) cost-cutting move was to provide *Social Work* to NASW members as an emailed journal, rather than a mailed print periodical. Members' dues were not reduced following this move. Meanwhile the lag time from acceptance into print remained very long for this journal, and was even exacerbated by the reduced numbers of issues available in which to publish accepted papers! Also, there was no corresponding reduction in membership dues to take into account this reduction in the number journal issues received by the members.

The journals produced by these two organizations have other troubles. Table 1 depicts the impact scores of these and a few other social work journals, as well as some other indices of journal quality. A journal's impact factor based on the numbers of times articles appearing in it are in journals during the two years following an article's initial appearance in print. The more times a journal's articles are cited, the greater the supposed contribution that journal is said to be making to the intellectual discourse of a given field. Higher impact scores are better. Members of NASW and CSWE, given the immense resources these organizations possess, should expect that their in-house periodicals would be the highest quality journals, and to be making the greatest impact in the field. Sadly this is not the case.

As can be seen in the section of Table 1, NASW and CSWE journals are rated lower than several other independent journals. In fact, of 28 journals appearing in the 2006 JCR ranking of impact factors, NASW's flagship journal, *Social Work,* was only rated 11th (in the interests of disclosure, I am the editor of one of these more highly ranked journals, *Research on Social Work Practice).* Apparently the NASW journal *Children and Schools* is not even rated by the Institute for Scientific Information, the publisher of the Journal Citation Reports (JCR), which produces these impact factors. This is a damning indictment, not so much against this journal, but against NASW's organizational ineptitude that has failed to get this important periodical included in the JCR listing. Being listed in the JCR is seen as an important benchmark of a journal's credibility. If it is not listed, some promotion and tenure committees greatly discount the value of articles appearing in such "invisible" journals.

Other indicators are also grim. In a survey of faculty perceptions of overall journal quality, Sellers, Smith, Mathiesen and Perry (2006) found *Social Work* and *Health and Social Work* to not even make it into the top quartile of journals evaluated. CSWE's *Journal of Social Work Education* appears in the third quartile (see second portion of Table 1). In surveys of authors whose work was published in various social work journals, Thyer and Myers (2003) and Barker and Thyer (2005) asked the authors to evaluate their experiences with the submission and review processes of various journals. One such question asked them to rate the overall quality of the review process, using an "A" (highest) to F (lowest) grading scheme. Again the journals supported by NASW and CSWE did not fare well, being consistently ranked lower than the *Social Service Review* and *Research on Social Work Practice.* In fact, in Thyer and Myers (2003), *Social Work* was graded by the published authors as sixteenth (very low) out of some 20 listed journals, and twentieth out of 22 journals in the replication by Barker and Thyer (2005). The corresponding rankings for the *Journal of Social Work Education* were seventeenth in both studies, again a shockingly low rating for presumptively flagship periodicals. In contrast the flagship journals of the American Psychological Association, the American Medical Associa-

Table 1
Selected Quality Indicators of Major Social Work Journals.
**2006 Impact Factor Scores of NASW, CSWE and other
Selected Social Work Journals***

Journal Title	Impact Factor	Publisher
Social Service Review	.896	University of Chicago Press
Research on Social Work Practice	.789	Sage Publications
Health and Social Work	.787	NASW Press
Social Work	.779	NASW Press
Children & Schools	*n/a*	NASW Press
Journal of Social Work Education	.773	CSWE

Faculty Perceptions of Overall Journal Quality**

First Quartile Ranking	Mean Appraisal (7 = Outstanding)	
Social Service Review	5.99	University of Chicago Press
Social Work Research	5.52	NASW Press
Research on Social Work Practice	5.35	Sage Publications
Second Quartile Ranking		
Social Work	4.90	NASW Press
Health and Social Work	4.85	NASW Press
Third Quartile Ranking		
Journal of Social Work Education	4.69	CSWE

Authors' Ratings of Overall Quality of the Review Process

Journal Title	Ratings		
	(4 = a grade of "A," or Highest, 1 = a grade of "F")		
Research on Social Work Practice	3.83***	3.74****	Sage Publications
Social Service Review	3.56	3.43	University of Chicago
Social Work Research	3.17	3.08	NASW Press
Health and Social Work	2.95	2.80	NASW Press
Social Work	2.88	2.67	NASW Press
Journal of Social Work Education	2.80	2.94	CSWE

*from 2006 *Journal Citation Reports*
**from Sellers, Smith, Mathiesen & Perry, 2006, p. 148
***from Thyer & Myers (2003)
****from Barker & Thyer (2005)

tion, and the American Sociological Association *are* highly reputable periodicals with high impact factors.

There are some other signs that the journals of NASW and CSWE have problems with important factors such as the low quality of the peer review commentary provided to submitting authors, unduly long delays to provide authors a decision, and excessive lag times from publication until print (see Pardeck, 1992, Epstein, 2004). Again, the dues-paying members deserve better from their professional associations.

Why do these problems exist (and almost everyone who belongs to NASW and CSWE know they exist)? I can identify several factors. One is that the process of selecting the Editor in Chief for the NASW and CSWE journals is the prerogative of the President of these associations. Each organization does have a publications committee with some policy-making role, but these members too are appointed by the President. These editorial appointments, as well as appointments to serve as members of these journals' editorial boards or as consulting editors, are very much a function of patronage, personal relationships, favoritism and political correctness. The process is a pretty closed one, with no little opportunity for unconnected but competent individuals to receive such appointments. As a result, the scholarly achievements of these editorial board members are typically rather low, as empirically documented over the past three decades by Lindsey (1976), Lindsey and Kirk (1992), Pardeck (1994, 1992) and Pardeck and Meinert (1999), among others. The consequence is that the quality of peer-review suffers, with deleterious consequences for all other aspects of a journal's operation and reputation.

Another structural problem with the operation of our organizational journals is the use of a centralized review system. In the approach used by most journals (but not those sponsored by NASW or CSWE), when an author submits a manuscript to a journal it is initially seen by that journal's Editor, who then assigns it to two or more blind peer reviewers, most often members of the editorial board, with demonstrated expertise (not merely an interest) in the topic of the paper. In due course, a month or so, the reviewers send their commentary and recommendations to the Editor. The Editor assimilates these remarks with his/her own appraisal, makes a decision, and then communicates this directly to the author of the submitted paper. This model is direct and relatively rapid.

The journals of NASW and CSWE use a different system. When a paper is submitted it is received by a staff member within the publications office of the association. This staffer is unlikely to be either a social worker or an experienced author. They are likely to only devote a portion of their administrative duties to journal operations. In due course the staffer sends the manuscript to various members of the journal's editorial board. These reviewing assignments are often undertaken with little regard for the reviewer's expertise, but on the basis of the number of reviews they have recently completed, and if their name now appears at the "top" of the list of reviewers due to be assigned manuscripts. At best, the submission is assigned to editorial board members on the basis of the key words provided by the author for their paper. If the editorial board member uses some words to reflect their own interests (e.g., mental health, addictions, domestic violence), the organizational staffer may use these to match a given submission with a specific editorial board member. This is a very blunt way to assign reviews. Usually, Editors are very familiar with the professional qualifications of their editorial board members, and are much more qualified to assign reviews than a non-scholar, non-social work staff member.

Another problem that occurs with the NASW journals is that members of the Editorial Board of the various journals often receive several, sometimes 8-10, manuscripts to review at one time, and are given a very brief period of time (e.g., 2 weeks) to complete their reviews. This practice suggests that the part-time staffers in the NASW publications office only periodically attend to new submissions, otherwise the flow of manuscripts would occur more smoothly. This practice also makes it more likely that the reviews provided will be brief, with less attention to detail and perhaps less courteous in tone.

In due course the reviewers' completed commentaries get sent out, not to the Editor, but to the journal's staffers. If fewer than the desired numbers of reviews are received, the staff sends the paper out to a new reviewer. When sufficient reviews have been received, the staff, in due course (when his/her other duties permit), sends all the reviews and a blinded copy of the manuscript to the journal's Editor, who then determines the fate of the paper. S/he notifies the association's publication office of this decision, and in due course (when the staff's other duties permit), the author is notified. This centralized process used by NASW and CSWE is much less efficient and effective than the decentralized one employed by most other journals. It introduces individuals into the stream who are not necessarily competent to judge the content and methodology of a paper, and are hence less able to make knowledgeable decisions about the selection of reviewers. Using a centralized staff to receive, solicit and process reviews adds a layer of bureaucracy that is unnecessary. This has negative repercussions throughout the remainder of the review process.

During a meeting of social work journal editors held at a SSWR conference, I once asked the Director of NASW Publications why they continued to adhere to this inefficient model. We were told that changing the current system might violate the NASW staff members' union contract! Is this any way to run a professional organization, with best professional journal practices being held up by intractable union contracts?

There is another subtle factor at work which conspires to make CSWE and NASW journals less than efficiently run and produced and that that is the lack of an economy of scale. The American Psychological Association publishes over three dozen journals, while Sage Publications produces over 500. This makes possible vast economies of scale in terms of marketing staff, copy-editing, the processing of reviews, using state-of-the-art electronic submission portals to process submissions and the review process, physically printing and mailing journals, etc. CSWE with its one journal (it also recently undertook to publish the *Journal of Baccalaureate Social Work Education*), and NASW with its five, makes their production of a small number of journals an extremely expensive operation.

What can be done to improve the situation?

- Enhance the requirements for individuals being eligible for appointment to be a journal editor, member of a journal's editorial board, or member of an organization's publications committee. Establish some minimum number of research articles appearing in peer-reviewed journals such individuals must have published, within recent memory, as a precondition for appointment.

- Open up the nominations process with a published call for nominations for any such appointment, outlining the minimum qualifications. Invite everyone to self-nominate, as opposed to leaving it as a closed system dependent upon inside information, favoritism and personal relationships. A deeper pool of nominations will increase the possibility of selecting genuinely well-qualified individuals.

- Take the President out of the loop in making editorial appointments. Certainly in the case of the NASW the President often lacks a doctorate, and is rarely a strong scholar well informed about journal publishing and the role of an Editor. Place editorial appointments solely within the purview of the strengthened publications committee, itself comprised of exceptionally strong scholars.

- Track the quality and timeliness of reviews provided by editorial board members, and dismiss (after warning) those who fail to carry out their agreed-upon responsibilities.

- Provide the Editors of our organizational journals with financial compensation for the time required to be devoted to their editorial responsibilities. Those with full time academic appointments could "buy-out" a portion of their regular academic assignment. Being the Editor of a major organizational journal is not a task to be lightly undertaken, using one's "free time" in between teaching, administration, services or the pursuit of one's own scholarship. The Editor's time and talent deserves financial compensation.

- Provide the Editor with financial resources to hire a local assistant to help with the processing of manuscripts. This might be a graduate student. By decentralizing the review process, fewer (part-time?) staff at NASW or CSWE publications office will be needed and the resultant cost savings used to provide funding directly to the (currently unpaid and unsupported) Editor and his/her assistant.

- Allow editorial board members to choose which new submissions they will review by providing them with the title (at least) and abstract of new submissions. This will ensure that the reviewer has more of a sense what the paper is about and be in a better position to judge if they can provide a competent review.

- Decentralize the submission and review process by having submissions go directly to the Editor, who in turn assigns reviewers, receives completed reviews, makes a decision and informs the authors, and in due course sends in accepted papers to the copy-editing and production staff.

- Promote greater transparency in organizational journal operations by providing them with annual budgets, with an annual accounting of profit or loss for each such journal, and share this with all organizational members. Those journals consistently operating at a loss should be either improved, outsourced (see below), or discontinued.

- Outsource the operation of NASW and CSWE journals to either widely respected commercial publishers, a university press, or to the presses of other professional organizations which produce a large number of journals. The American Psychological Association, for example, publishes over a dozen non-APA journals. However, this really should be unnecessary since many social work journals with very small circulations make a tidy profit for their commercial publishers.

- NASW and CSWE journals should adopt the publication recommendations of the Presidential Task Force on Publications sponsored by the Society for Social Work and Research (see Holden et al., 2008).

- Permit individuals who are not members of CSWE to purchase an individual subscription to the *Journal of Social Work Education.* Currently this journal is only received by individuals who choose to belong to CSWE. This is shortsighted. Most social work academics do not belong to CSWE, but many would like to receive the journal. It could enhance subscription revenue for CSWE to allow non-members to subscribe to their journal.

Conferences

For many years NASW held an annual national conference, attended by thousands of members and non-members. This was a valuable membership benefit for the professional development of all social workers, and also afforded a useful and to some degree prestigious venue for social workers to present scholarly papers. In the face of budgetary restrictions in the 1980s, NASW foolishly decided to discontinue holding its annual conference, thus depriving its members of a significant benefit to belonging to this group, but of course NASW did not reduce its annual dues assessments to reflect this diminished range of member benefits. This left the major professional conference venue for social workers to be CSWE's Annual Program Meeting (APM), the discipline's sole remaining national conference, and one with lesser appeal to practitioners and social work researchers, since its focus on social work education meant that many diverse papers on practice or non-pedagogical research projects were unacceptable for presentation.

It is mind-boggling that NASW discontinued its annual conference as a cost-cutting move, when most other associations earn substantial income from hosting annual conferences, even very small ones. From its inception, SSWR has generated significant revenue from hosting its annual conference, whether it had only a couple of hundred attendees (as in its first conference), to well over a thousand, like recent ones. It is a sign of dreadful fiscal ineptitude for a massive organization such as NASW to lose money sponsoring an annual conference. If nothing else they could have subcontracted out the whole operation to one of the many conference organizing firms who would have been delighted to coordinate such a meeting, in return for retaining any profits earned, perhaps with a small percentage being provided to NASW. Thus conferences could have been continued at no fiscal risk to NASW.

Convening an annual conference is a major activity of most professional associations. Even most of the smaller social work organizations successfully hold them, usually at pleasant venues, and at some profit. In this manner they can help hold down the cost of annual dues for all members. NASW recommended that it "Establish a national conference for practitioners, researchers, educators, and policy sectors within social work" during 2008-2010 (NASW, 2005a, p. 6). This is what they used to do. It may be a good thing for them to resume this practice, not as a one-shot effort but as an annual one, providing they take some lessons from SSWR and other successful groups on how to coordinate a well-run and low-cost conference that will make a profit and prove reinforcing to its members.

CSWE's APM apparently loses money. According to the Annual Report of CSWE (which actually was mailed out in March of 2009!), the 2007-2008 conference revenue was $758,192, while the annual program meeting had expenses of $840, 632, resulting in a loss to the Council of over $82,000 (CSWE, 2007-2008). Concerns also exist about the APM's awkward organization, poor quality of papers selected for presentation and very high cost for conference registration fees and lodging. For example, the 2007 APM charged a $365 advance registration for members and the conference hotel cost $208 per night. These expenses seem difficult to justify, especially relative to those charged by other groups. For its 2008 conference (3 months after the APM), for example, SSWR charged a $250 advance registration, and its conference hotel cost $150 a night. Both conferences were in attractive venues (APM = San Francisco, SSWR = Washington DC), so the differential was not caused by SSWR meeting in some backwater place.

This burdensome financial disparity also exists with respect to dues. In 2007 a MSW paid $100 for a one year regular membership to join SSWR which included a journal subscription and a reduced conference fee), vs. $188 for CSWE (also getting a journal and a reduced conference fee), vs. $190 to join NASW (a journal, and no conference). In general there is a sense that CSWE does not take into account the burden these higher annual dues and conference costs levied on its individual members. It only costs $175.00 annual dues for an attorney five years out of law school to join the American Bar Association (a much larger group than CSWE), or $125.00 annual dues to belong to the Clinical Social Work Association (a much smaller group), for example. Lowering annual individual membership dues may increase the numbers of social worker who can afford to join CSWE and NASW.

Recently, the CSWE began requiring that ALL authors of papers being presented at its annual program meeting must pay the substantial conference registration fee, *even if that author was not presenting at the conference!* What this means is that if, for example, Karger, Stoesz, Carrilio and Thyer have a paper accepted by the APM, and we arrange for Karger to attend the APM, while Stoesz, Carrilio, and Thyer remain home to teach, write, or care for ill family members, the CSWE nevertheless now *requires* Stoesz, Carrilio, and Karger to pay the conference registration fee, even though they do not attend, nor cause the conference to incur any costs. Failure to pay these conference registration fees will result in Stoesz, Carrilio, and Thyer being dropped from the APM program as legitimate co-authors of this paper, or the entire paper being pulled from the program! This practice is problematic for several reasons. First, I am aware of no other social work conference which has such an outrageous policy. I asked the then-President of the CSWE what was the justification for this policy, and I was told that SSWR did it also. I did not believe this and when I subsequently checked with the President of SSWR, I was told that this was not true, there was no such policy, ever. It seems to have been implemented solely as a method to increase CSWE conference revenue. A second problem is that it is unethical. According to the CSWE's own *National Statement on Research Integrity in Social Work*, "Authors and co-authors should be determined on the basis of the type and amount of work completed" (see CSWE, 2009). If Stoesz, Carrilio, and Thyer cannot pay the registration fee, then Karger may be listed as the sole-author in the APM program of what was legitimately a co-authored piece of scholarship. It is unethical for such a co-authored work to be presented as a sole-authored piece. According to the NASW *Code of Ethics, statement 4.08 on Acknowledging Credit:*

"(a) Social workers should take responsibility and credit, including authorship credit, only for work they have actually performed and to which they have contributed.

(b) Social workers should honestly acknowledge the work of and the contributions made by others." (see http://www.naswdc.org/pubs/code/code.asp)

In the above hypothetical example, it is unethical for Karger to *claim* sole—authorship, and for Stoesz, Carrilio, and Thyer to *not claim* co-authorship of the paper, yet this is the position the CSWE policy mandating the payment of conference registration fees can place authors in. This policy can also *discourage* the authors of multi-authored works from submitting their papers for presentation at the APM, which would not be to the CSWE's long term best interests, despite any possible short term financial gains.

What Can be Done?

- NASW needs to resume holding an annual conference. This was an important membership benefit and the members deserve to have it reinstated. If NASW cannot afford to do this independently, they should consider piggybacking such a meeting onto another established venue, such as the CSWE's APM, or to more simply outsource the logistics (and financial risk) of convening such a conference to one of the many other organizations that have a successful track record in this regard, such as the Society for Social Work and Research, or the American Psychological Association. Many commercial firms also do this.

- CSWE needs to sharpen its pencils to find ways to reduce the costs of attending the APM, including hotels, registration fees, and travel expenses. The current bloated financial costs place an excessive burden on members, especially those lacking institutional travel support funding. There are many attractive venues less expensive than the usual high-cost destination cities chosen to host the APM, and there are cheaper but still high quality conference hotels available.

- Slim down the costs associated with bringing in expensive entertainment and speakers. Most CSWE members are perfectly capable of arranging their own entertainments during conferences (indeed they have an extensive history of doing so!) and there is no need to inflate conference registration fees by tacking on excessive entertainment costs.

- Focus the APM on social work *educational* issues. It is not (or at least should not) be a conference for the presentation of research findings not linked to social work education. A few years ago I attended an APM and saw a paper about the psychosocial needs of male Vietnamese manicurists! Such research, while perhaps of high quality, has little to do with social work pedagogy, and weakens the attractiveness of the APM for social work educators. Similarly, reduce the time devoted to songs and dances (these can be found by members on their own within a few blocks of the hotel), quilts-sharing, poetry, and other warm and fuzzy official activities, appearing on the official conference program. These all cost money and are directly subsidized by the conference registration fees paid for by everyone, even those uninterested in such activities. Reduce the amount of time on the conference program devoted to invited speakers and events, and enhance the resources devoted to presenting competitively selected papers.

- The CSWE should abandon its recent practice of requiring the all authors of accepted APM papers from being required to pay the conference registration fee, even if they do not attend the conference.

Concluding Remarks

Space does not permit delving into the problems related to social work research, centered around NASW and CSWE. Suffice it to say that

NASW betrayed the promises made to the Social Work Research Group (SWRG), induce them to amalgamate with the newly forming NASW in 1956 (see Graham, Al-Krenawi & Bradshaw, 2000). SWRG disbanded and joined with the new NASW only after the new group agreed to establish a Research Section within the NASW structure. In 1963 the Research Section was designated the Council on Social Work Research, with research still considered to be the third pillar of NASW's internal structure. Nevertheless, by 1974 the Council on Social Work Research was dissolved and research activities became considerably less conspicuous within NASW. So much so that a few years ago, when I attended an Executive Committee meeting of the SSWR held in San Diego, the Executive Director of NASW said to the group that NASW was not involved in research! This is despite the fact that the very bylaws of NASW continue to assert that a major purpose of the association is "to expand through research the knowledge base ... (and that) ... the corporation shall have power...to conduct appropriate study and research..." NASW, 2005b, p. 2). The appalling lack of attention paid to research by NASW necessitated the establishment in 1993 of the Institute for the Advancement of Social Work and Research (largely an advocacy organization) and in 1994 the Society for Social Work and Research, a now thriving membership organization. Both steps were damning indictments of the existing organizations.

Neither will I address the social injustices continuing to be experienced by social work students and academics on the basis of their religious beliefs which may be at variance with the preferences of selected faculty and administrators, as this critique has been addressed in a related paper (Thyer & Myers, 2009).

I will conclude this chapter at this point, having raised several critical issues that seem to me, at least, as a long-term member of CSWE and NASW, to present friction points between the needs of their members and the current operation of these two groups. Many important issues have not been addressed, such as the unwieldy and expensive governance structure of NASW. I have hopes that improvements can be made among these two major social work organizations. Some of the suggestions provided in this chapter would be good places to begin.

Biographical Note

Bruce A. Thyer, Ph.D., LCSW, is professor and former Dean with the College of Social Work at Florida State University. He is a past member of the CSWE Board of Directors, the Steering Committee of the Group for the Advancement of Doctoral Education in Social Work, the Executive Committee of the Society for Social Work and Research, and of the Council of Representatives of the American Psychological Association. He is a current member of the Social Welfare Editorial Board of the Campbell Collaboration. He can be contacted at Bthyer@fsu.edu.

References

Barker, R. L. (2003). *The Social Work Dictionary.* Washington, DC: NASW Press.

Barker, K. L. & Thyer, B. A. (2005). An empirical evaluation of the editorial practices of social work journals: Voices of authors published in 2000. *Journal of Social Service Research, 32*(1), 17-31.

Council on Social Work Education. (2000). *Affirmative Action Policy and Plan.* Alexandria, VA: Author. Retrieved August 24, 2007 from www.cswe.org.

Council on Social Work Education. (2007-2008). *Annual Report 2007 – 2008, Strengthening the profession of social work: Leadership in research, career advancement, and education.* Alexandria, VA: CSWE.

Council on Social Work Education. (2009). *National Statement on Research Integrity in Social Work.* Alexandria, VA: Author. Downloaded from: *http://www.cswe.org/CentersInitiatives/CurriculumResources/22252/NationalStatement-HTML.aspx* on 3 December 2009.

Epstein, W. M. (2004). Confirmational response bias and the quality of the editorial processes among American social work journals. *Research on Social Work Practice, 14,* 450-458.

Ginsberg, L. (1994). *Social work almanac (2nd edition).* Washington, DC: NASW Press.

Graham, J. R., Al-Krenawi, A., & Bradshaw, C. (2000). The Social Work Research Group/NASW Research Section/Council on Social Work Research, 1949-1965: An emerging research identity in the American Profession. *Research on Social Work Practice, 10,* 622-643.

Holden, G., Thyer, B. A., Baer, J., Delva, J., Dulmus, C., & Williams, T. (2008). Suggestions to improve social work journal editorial and peer review processes: The San Antonio response to the Miami State. *Research on Social Work Practice, 18,* 66-71.

Lindsey, D. (1978). *The scientific publication system in social science: A study of the operation of leading professional journals in psychology, sociology, and social work.* San Francisco: Jossey-Bass.

Lindsey, D. T. & Kirk, S. A. (1992). The role of social work journals in the development of a   knowledge base for the profession. *Social Service Review, 66,* 295-310.

National Association of Social Workers. (2005a). *Social work imperatives for the next decade.* Washington, DC: Author. Retrieved August 24, 2007 from www.socialworkers.org.

National Association of Social Workers. (2005b). *Bylaws of the National Association of Social Workers.* Washington, DC: Author. Retrieved August 24, 2007 from www.socialworkers.org.

Pardeck, J. T. (1992). Are social work journal editorial board members competent? Some disquieting data with implications for research on social work practice. *Research on Social Work Practice, 2,* 487-496.

Pardeck, J. T. (1994). An exploration of the factors explaining the distinction and achievement levels of social work editorial board. In R. G. Meinert, J. T. Pardeck & W. P. Sullivan (1994). *Issues in social work: A critical analysis* (pp. 147-164). Westrport, CT: Auburn House.

Pardeck, J. T. & Meinert, R. (1999). Scholarly achievements of the *Social Work* editorial board and consulting editors: A commentary. *Research on Social Work Practice, 9,* 86-91.

Thyer, B. A. & Myers, L. L. (2003). An empirical evaluation of the editorial practices of social work journals. *Journal of Social Work Education, 39,* 125-140.

Thyer, B. A. & Myers, L. L. (2009). Religious discrimination in social work academic programs: Whither social justice? *Journal of Religion and Spirituality in Social Work, 28,* 144-160.

10

Reinventing Social Work Education:
A Call to Action

As previous chapters have demonstrated, social work and the educational institutions that support and replicate it are beset with long-standing systemic problems. Weak leadership and low levels of professional and academic performance have resulted in social work's compromised identity; instead of employing state-of-the-art research to advance social justice, the field has been populated by those maintaining the status quo through a *de facto* patronage system. In refutation of its Progressive Era legacy, social work finds itself sitting on the curb, watching events go by as opposed to driving them, essentially allowing others to engage in the important conversations while it is focused instead on internal status matters. Further subverting social works stature within the academy, the profession's emphasis on values while demoting research makes it vulnerable to the assaults on its very foundation. Social work and its educational infrastructure, developed within the very different social context of progressivism, pragmatism and industrialism, require a reevaluation in order to meet the challenges of the twenty-first century.

Running in Place

Uncontrolled growth in social work education has been aggravated by a relatively stagnant student applicant pool, forcing many social work programs to adopt open enrollment, which in turn, has led to a weaker student body as evident in abysmally low GRE scores. Social work programs are managed by deans and directors who are often weak scholars, while journal editors lack the scholarship necessary to vet contributions to the field's literature, subverting the profession's knowledge base. Faculty enthusiasm for idiosyncratic, subjective methods, such as postmodernism and constructivism, impede the exchange of information with other empirically-based disciplines. Social work students incur tuition debt that is burdensome in light of the low salaries for BSW and MSW graduates. Increased competition from other disciplines is eroding social work's traditional turf. The practice arena into which students emerge is deteriorating as a result of political disinvestment, poor management, low practice standards, and weak leadership. Despite having success-fully lobbied for licensing laws, title protection and status have eroded with most master's level graduates making significantly lower salaries than graduates of sister disciplines such as nursing, public health, and education.

Social work as a profession has been incapable of developing a viable strategy to address these problems, in part because of the control exerted by special interest groups whose use of patronage deflects the organiza-tion from issues of larger public interest. The ineffectiveness of national professional associations to arrest the profession's slide toward mediocrity and the failure of multiple state licensing authorities to galvanize and lead social work education through the gauntlet of these problems por-tends poorly for the profession. The Council on Social Work Education deserves special scrutiny since it holds a monopoly on the accreditation of social work programs.

Maintaining the status quo is not an option if social work is to re-main viable with respect to traditional competitors, such as psychology, counseling, nursing, and public administration, as well as newer ones, including family studies, child development, and human resources. Nor will the status quo keep social work education in good stead as more universities use objective rankings, like Academic Analytics, to determine where and how to allocate increasingly scarce resources, an issue driven home by the worst recession since the Depression. When compared to other disciplines, most social work programs rank badly. Applying ob-jective measures to social work programs—both within and outside of the discipline—demonstrates the underperformance of many faculties in terms of scholarship, research and publications. It also partly explains why social work programs typically have such low status in the academy. Given this, it is not surprising that despite the rapid growth of social work programs, no *fully autonomous* (i.e., based on a deanship model) school of social work has been started since the 1970s. On the contrary, many older programs, such as Arizona State University and UCLA, have either been demoted from an autonomous dean-led school of social work to a department with a director or chairperson, while being consolidated into interdisciplinary academic units. Moreover, the vast majority of new social work programs are in middle-range, masters-only universities and colleges. Only four (East Tennessee State University, Morgan State University, North Carolina State University, and the University of Toledo) of the 20 MSW programs in candidacy in 2007 were in a doctoral-granting institutions, and only one (North Carolina State University) was in a Carnegie-ranked "very high research-intensive" university.[1]

Many social work programs have evaded institutional scrutiny because they deliver the student numbers at a low cost, thereby generating revenue for the university. However, since social work's high enrollment is declining in many places due to market saturation, more programs are vulnerable to the impact of metric ranking systems. Without high student numbers, social work education programs are an albatross around the neck of institutions desperate to ration resources in order to support high-visibility, prestigious programs. Unlike education programs that are necessary to feed the public school system, social work programs are by comparison more easily discarded. For instance, public school systems require certified teachers who graduated from accredited education programs. In contrast, public social services usually do not require social work graduates from accredited programs who have passed a licensing examination. In part, this is because social work abandoned public social services decades ago.

Social work education is replete with ironies. While CSWE exerts a high degree of control over curriculum issues, it exerts little influence over program growth or quality. Having become dependent on the accreditation fees that programs pay, the organization has become an engine of inertia. What CSWE has to show after a half-century of monopoly on social work accreditation, is educational mediocrity, which contributes to the questionable quality of the performance of social agencies and social work practice in general. Thus, rapid growth in the numbers and size of social work programs has been commensurate with a loss of social work's stature both within academia and in the larger community. Social work generates little empirical research that bears on bedrock issues, especially social and economic justice, relying on research from other disciplines. Absent the essential research, social work resorts to rhetorical pieties and impressionistic narratives, promoting what is essentially a moral metaphysics to advance its social mission. While social work education takes pride in its diversity, its educators are less prepared to reverse or meaningfully address in actual "real life" settings the discrimination and oppression of which they complain. Students are taught *about* diversity but actually cannot practice it! While social work educators complain about the low salaries of the predominantly female profession, CSWE has been loathe to collaborate with labor unions, which are most likely to enhance salaries and opportunities for social workers. It follows that social work and social work education cannot continue without major reforms.

The route to professional prominence in an affluent, technological society is straightforward: First, a discipline selects important problems to address then it cultivates methods that not only demonstrate the profession's efficacy, but does so in a manner that is comprehensible to other disciplines. Its most accomplished scholars vet submissions to the professional literature, thus replenishing its knowledge base. Professional education is at the apex of the discipline since it trains the next generation of practitioners while identifying leaders who will chart the profession's course. Oftentimes, capable scholars are sought to serve as deans of professional schools, and preeminent scholars are selected for leadership positions in the profession's association of educators. Fearful of compromising the profession's hard-won accomplishments, new programs are accredited only after a thorough review. At the same time, the profession encourages educational programs to develop their own specialized niche, institutional specialization evolving from faculty accomplishments. In turn, specialization serves as a magnet that attracts the most promising students who matriculate to specific professional schools in order to study with prominent researchers and educators. Professional proficiency translates directly into enhanced incomes and professional prestige for students who graduate with special, recognized skills. Because the number of graduates is regulated and their knowledge is current, their career path is promising. Some of them elect to return to the academy in order to pursue research and teaching, a handful become deans of professional schools, and a few rise to lead professional education. Merit is the norm by which various successful professions have thrived, including medicine, economics, and public health.

Over a century after its creation, little of this happens in social work education. Social work education selects leaders without regard to scholarly contribution to serve in decision-making capacities, refereeing contributions to its literature as well as directing its professional schools.[2] Instead of adopting more rigorous research methods, social work education promotes approaches of dubious epistemic theories, such as constructivism and postmodernism. Consequently, much of the professional literature consists of articles that advance a socially irrelevant romanticism that denigrates scientifically credible research methods. As a result, social work's literature is not only irrelevant to the issues of social need, but it is inferior to that of more rigorous disciplines. In the absence of credible research methods, and consequently valuable findings, social work's literature has become marginalized, an internal conversation among social work academics. Under the guise of diversity, ascribed status has been equated with oppression and subsequently, committees established to advance the agendas of aggrieved groups have proliferated at CSWE. The absence of academic merit among leaders in social work education perpetuates a patronage system; as one example, participation in social work's accrediting authority rather than scholarship has become an important means for career advancement. The loss of academic rigor in professional education has attracted weak students and faculty members to social work. This failure of professional education explains much of the profession's low public regard; when pressing social problems might invite comment by expert social workers, they are nowhere to be found.

The status quo of social work education is reinforced by actions of multiple stakeholders: Doctoral programs continue to proliferate, unregulated by an accrediting authority. The Group for the Advancement of Doctoral Education (GADE) meets annually to discuss issues, but shies away from establishing firm standards for doctoral programs. Instead, GADE relies on its vague "Guidelines for Quality in Social Work Doctoral Programs."[3] The organization fails to differentiate between legitimate, adequately-funded doctoral programs and those so seriously under-resourced as to be non-viable and ultimately deleterious to the health of social work education.

Deans and directors of social work programs continue to be tenured, often holding their administrative positions for decades, and produce little research or scholarship. Leadership positions within CSWE continue to be filled based on ascribed status, often a single demographic criterion. The control of decision-making by weak scholars at CSWE and deans and directors of schools of social work reinforce the patronage system through which leadership positions are gained by demonstrating fealty to the status quo. Challenges to mediocrity in professional education are either ignored or, when that is not possible, the critics vilified, despite the validity of their claims. Committed to postmodernism and constructivism, social work faculty fail to generate empirically sound knowledge; the research capacity of social work is degraded in direct relation to the investment in anti-empirical methods. As a result social work educators continue to depend on substantive theory and research from other social sciences and professions. Students shoulder tuition debt that would require years to repay due to static professional salaries. As the economic viability of social work deteriorates, schools of social work are forced to admit even weaker students to fill classes. The interaction of these factors contributes to a vicious cycle, a gradual descent from professional to vocational status.

Three Futures for Social Work Education

Given the disjuncture between pressing social problems and the performance of social work education, three future scenarios are plausible: (1) a status quo degrading into vocational education, (2) incremental reform culminating in organizational consolidation, and (3) more fundamental reforms to bring social work up to par with the professional education of other disciplines.

Vocational Education

Contemporary vectors in social work education may point to it becoming more a vocational activity than a profession. In Europe, for example, social work education follows various models, from basic post-high school training to university study.[4] Moreover, as current trends in American social work education increase the number of accredited BSW and MSW programs thereby outpacing the capacity of doctoral programs to produce high quality faculty, there may be fewer people able to teach social work in a university setting.

Certainly, there is value in folk wisdom that helps people in need; any additional knowledge could be imported from other disciplines. There are other benefits in moving social work from a university setting to a vocational venue, not the least of which is the lower costs of vocational education. Since vocational education does not require a four-year degree, the less time a student spends in school the lower the student loans and the less burdensome the training.

Vocationally trained social workers would still serve essential functions. Expanding disparities in income and wealth among Americans will likely translate into greater inequalities, fueling resentment, dysfunction, and dependence, problems that will require management by agents of the state and its contracting agencies: vocationally trained social workers could complement this regime. Rather than commit to costly training and research protocols, social work faculty could more economically download and apply the knowledge developed by others. Their instructional materials would consist largely of manuals at relatively low levels of abstraction; apprenticeships with agencies would complete vocational training. Administrators need not be scholars since they would simply manage vocational training programs, thereby losing their claim to university standing. Without the pressure for publications and funded research, faculty could focus on teaching, supervision and advising, in the process enhancing vocational training. Vocational education would also reduce the need for more and larger doctoral programs since skilled practitioners could be used more widely to provide training and expertise. Social work graduates of vocational programs might not command high salaries or rapid career advancement, but they would enjoy some lateral mobility. Established within the working class, vocational education would incline social workers to embrace unions; collective bargaining could be a source of empowering social workers. Within American vocational education, plumbers, electricians, dental hygienists, and correctional officers typify the ranks of those who do not claim professional status, but earn a living wage and provide important services to the public. In some instances they earn more than social workers, and the unions or professional associations representing these groups are powers to be reckoned with.

Given the quality of training and graduates' incomes, it could be argued that social work education already approximates vocational training. Social work education has not been able to demonstrate its efficacy, students are trained from knowledge derived from other disciplines (even those with an MSW are expected to be consumers rather than producers of research), educational materials in social work often resemble training manuals; textbooks are often packaged with study guides; and social work educators rarely publish books in which a theory is validated by original data, a common event among the academic disciplines and professions.

Within the labor market, social workers approximate the income and skill level of the skilled trades; in many cases, the income, benefits, and career mobility of social workers are actually inferior to unionized workers. Given these factors, social work's professional pretensions notwithstanding, it may be better understood as a skilled trade that prepares practitioners within institutions of higher education.

Incremental Reform

Any incremental reform strategy that relies solely on CSWE and NASW runs the risk of replicating the problems that currently typify social work's deteriorating prospects. Such a strategy would endeavor to shore-up the essential features of professional education: The editors of refereed journals would be recruited according to their scholarly achievements, and minimal requirements for deans and directors would be established. CSWE would encourage schools of social work to develop their own unique signature programs. Research activities by faculty and research content within the curriculum would be enhanced by pursuing strategic opportunities through government contracts and foundation grants. The inadequate salaries and career mobility of graduates could be partly addressed by engaging in discussions with labor organizations, such as the American Federation of State, County, and Municipal Employees (AFSCME) and the Service Employees International Union (SEIU). Through concerted efforts on several fronts, the economic prospects of social work graduates might begin to approximate those of other professions, such as nursing and teaching. Additional incremental reforms might include those suggested by Thyer, such as the re-initiation of a professional conference and making the CSWE annual meeting more relevant to an educational and pedagogical agenda.

Despite their inherent appeal, incremental reform strategies are problematic. The dominance of weak BSW and MSW programs in CSWE reinforces existing standards; increases in their numbers lessen the likelihood of instituting more rigorous standards since representatives of weak programs would continue to dominate CSWE. CSWE is, itself, self-regulating, so alterations of its committees and their membership would require changes in its governance documents which would likely be fought by the very groups that now benefit from the status quo. The proliferation of newer programs provides the dues that are vital to CSWE, so the organization would be reluctant to reduce the number of accredited programs. That so many faculty and educational administrators are tenured senior professors further impedes educational change; their long-term appointments serve to embed them in professional education; different orientations to professional education are likely to emerge only after they retire. The aptitude of students entering social work education is also unlikely to improve insofar as schools of social work have already experienced diminishing enrollments despite reducing admission standards and accepting larger percentages of applicants. Even the strongest remediation and retention strategies cannot be expected to compensate for the little knowledge, weak composition skills, and ephemeral commitment to social work that many students bring to professional education. Despite aggressive outreach, the low earnings and limited career options of social work graduates diminish interest by stronger applicants who are likely to opt for other professional opportunities instead.

Thus, the suggestion by Kay Hoffman and Alberto Godenzi that the many organizations that have evolved within American social work should be consolidated into one professional entity is unlikely to address these problems. Hoffman and Godenzi are at least candid in their assessment of social work's prospects, citing stagnant membership bases in CSWE and NASW. "Why are agencies willing to hire non-social work persons for social work jobs, in particular, why has the profession lost so much ground in health care and child welfare?" they ask. "Why have social work salaries remained constant when other professions have experienced sizable public and private investments?"[5] Significantly, they cite social work education's loss of stature within the university, which, compounded by the disconnect between education and practice, means that social work programs "will continue to be—most of the time and at best—junior partners in collaborations with other professions and disciplines."[6] Without attending to the specific problems that plague social work education—limited scholarship by educational leaders, faculty denigration of scientific methods, weak students, failure to regulate doctoral education, among others—there is little that would come out of organizational consolidation except metastatic mediocrity.

Radical Reforms

Fundamental reform requires honest self-appraisal and a reconsideration of the purposes and function of social work and professional education. If domestic difficulties, such as a severe recession, are not ominous enough, increasing globalization challenges current social work structures and educational practices.[7] A profession and educational structure emerging from and responding to, an industrial economy and culture needs to adapt if it is to prosper in a new socio-cultural context. American social work education evolved as a closed, monopoly model congruent with the industrial era of the twentieth century but out of step with the information age of the twenty-first.

In the rigid system of American social work education, the monopoly held by CSWE has produced contradictions that impede professional training. A classic example is CSWE's fixation on the MSW as the common denominator for professional educators. Instructors who teach practice courses must have an MSW from an accredited school of social work, plus two years of practice experience. Field instructors are expected to have a CSWE-accredited social work degree. Field directors are expected to hold the MSW degree and have two years of practice experience. Social work program directors are expected to have an MSW degree from a CSWE-accredited program, although a doctoral degree is preferred. Theoretically, a dean or director can apply for a Commission on Accreditation (COA) waiver, but it is not encouraged; only a handful of deans and directors of schools of social work lack an MSW.

Social work education is controlled by a monopoly, an archaic organizational form; arising in the industrial era, monopolies are antithetical to values prized by the information age: product customization, flexibility in structure, and responsiveness to stakeholders. As organizational forms, monopolies are closed systems. By the end of the twentieth century, closed systems had become associated with inflexible, wasteful bureaucracies that were not only dismissive of consumer preferences but averse to innovation. The collapse of communism made the case internationally; domestically, a renewed appreciation for democratic-capitalism as the nation's political-economy contributed to deregulation of industry as well as contracting out government services. In *Reinventing Government*, David Osborne and Ted Gaebler divided the roles between agenda setting and execution by employing a boat metaphor: government should steer the course, but not do the rowing.[8] Technological transformation complemented the political case against monopoly.

In computer technology, open architecture systems evolved as manufacturers publicly released specifications for their computer or hardware, not only allowing other companies to customize and enhance the hardware, but also including peripherals designed for it. Open source software evolved similarly while encouraging the public to view the source code, alter it, and then redistribute it. Since open source software is typically free, it has invited public collaboration. Conversely, in closed architecture only the original manufacturer can enhance the hardware; in software, only the original software developer has access to the code. Microsoft Windows is an example of proprietary software while Linux is open source.

In contrast to the monopolistic, closed source approach, social work programs in other countries utilize a more open orientation. For example, some countries have adopted a social work and applied human services model, which opens up faculty appointments to those in other disciplines. Other schools, like Oxford University, use a designation like "Department of Social Policy and Social Work." Faculty in these departments are often titled based on their discipline, such as professor of demography, professor of child and family psychology, or professor of social policy.

Many Australian universities, such as the University of Queensland, do not limit faculty hiring only to doctoral-degreed social work graduates.

While open architecture systems certainly contain their own set of problems, these are eclipsed by significant advantages. For one, this orientation could help to remedy the isolationism that typifies American social work by attracting top-flight applied social scientists from other disciplines. It would also open internships to non-social work students. Since social work education in the United States has limited most internships to traditional agencies that have MSW-degreed field instructors, students are denied exposure to the more dynamic organizations that are characterized by cutting-edge social policy analysis and advocacy. Plus, many social work students are assigned field placements in understaffed agencies where they are regimented and given rote tasks. While individually tailored internships may require more work, the benefits are greater. In an open architecture system, applied social scientists would be invited to teach courses social work courses in human development (HBSE), research, social policy, group work, and so forth. Such openness would bridge the distance between social work and other disciplines upon which it has become dependent for its knowledge. Since social work borrows so heavily from the other disciplines, the profession might as well go straight to the source. Bringing in a diverse range of academics could also help reinvigorate and challenge social work educators. An open architecture approach would reestablish social work's connection to areas of policy and programming innovation involving child welfare, health care, welfare reform, and retirement security, among others.

Bringing social work education into the information age would require radical reform of professional training. The objective of radical reform would to evolve a network of high quality educational programs. Fundamentally, this requires divesting CSWE of its monopolistic control over social work education.

Deregulate CSWE: An open orientation would deregulate CSWE. As Anne Neal, President of the American Council on Trustees and Alumni, notes, "accreditors have been able to apply intrusive prescriptive standards and have enforced ideological tests and other criteria unrelated to educational quality."[9] Decommissioning CSWE's educational monopoly by opening up the accreditation process to a competing body would reverse CSWE's more pernicious practices, such as micro-management, while at the same time encouraging innovation, particularly the creation of unique signature programs. CSWE's excessive preoccupation with curriculum tweaking has deflected the organization from examining other important issues, such as raising the criteria for student admissions, including a requirement for minimum GRE or MAT test scores. If existing GRE or MAT tests are not deemed useful, an accrediting organization could develop its own objective test, similar to the Law School Admissions Test (LSAT) or the Graduate Management Admissions Test (GMAT). Regardless, an aptitude floor should be set for student admissions. While variances will always exist around student abilities, the current non-process does nothing to ensure a minimum baseline of student ability across programs nationally.

Deregulating CSWE's monopoly over accreditation could release the creative potential that is being squashed within social work education. Deregulation will also help curb the growth of cookie-cutter programs that now dominate social work education, thereby encouraging more innovation. An added benefit of removing key curriculum decisions from CSWE would be the reduced power of the special interest groups that have affixed themselves to the organization. Echoing Barack Obama, it is time for professional educators to recognize that we are not Black social workers, or White social workers, or Latino social workers, or Asian American social workers, or Native American social workers, or female social workers, or male social workers, or Gay social workers, or Lesbian social workers, or Bisexual social workers, or Transgender social workers, or Queer social workers, or (dis)abled social workers, or urban social workers, or rural social workers . . . we are *all* social workers!

Recognize the doctorate as the terminal degree: Any accrediting body should acknowledge the doctorate as the terminal degree in social work education instead of the MSW. This would have several benefits: increasing the scholarship in smaller programs since doctoral-degreed faculty are more inclined to engage in research and publications, bringing social work in line with other disciplines and professions that have identified the doctorate as the terminal degree, and enhancing under-resourced educational programs which would be required to implement significant upgrades to attract and retain doctoral-degreed faculty. Certifying the doctorate as the terminal degree would also help those doctoral graduates in social work who lack an MSW to teach the full range of the curriculum.[10] In stark contrast to social work, no other profession values the master's degree more highly than the doctorate. At minimum, the MSW could be offered as part of the PhD program, which more would closely resemble other disciplines where a master's degree is assumed to be earned as part of the doctoral process.

Reduce the number of low quality doctoral programs: The proliferation of low-quality doctoral programs should be discouraged by establishing concrete standards for doctoral education (which GADE has been unwilling to develop), by nationally reviewing doctoral programs, and by restricting the application of BSW and MSW resources to doctoral education. Balkanized programs with inadequate faculty, support staff, and low institutional resources is a zero-sum-game and subverts efforts to enhance professional education. Without significant new resources, adding a new doctoral program detracts from the other social work programs. Equally troubling, low-quality and under-resourced doctoral programs weaken social work education by graduating students who are ill-prepared to successfully assume teaching positions let alone contribute to research and publish in refereed journals.

Rescind unnecessary restrictions on faculty permitted to teach in social work programs: The two-year practice requirement for teaching core social work practice courses should be dropped. To date, no credible research exists to demonstrate whether this practice requirement ensures higher quality social work education. Moreover, it is ironic that a faculty member whose practice skills may have atrophied after years in the classroom is allowed to teach a practice course while someone with more contemporary non-MSW social service experience is forbidden to teach the same course. As currently configured, the practice requirement not only discriminates against newly-minted doctoral graduates, but it also discourages gifted researchers from entering social work education.

Regulate Program Growth: Contrary to normal marketplace rules, unchecked growth of social work education has not resulted in less expensive, more efficient or higher quality programs; instead, it is leading to a race to the bottom. More social work programs have not resulted in more applicants, and programs often cope with increased competition by admitting weaker students to meet their enrollment requirements. Consequently, CSWE or another accrediting body should limit the growth of accredited social work programs. Guidelines should include the size of the demographic area as well as the number of existing programs. A larger part of the accreditation process should focus on how many programs a given region can support over time without cannibalizing other programs. While CSWE currently requires needs assessments, they are often insufficiently scrutinized as to their regional impact on social work.

Increasing the number of social work graduates without regard to its labor market impact or the adequacy of salaries illustrates the collusion between social agencies and social work education. Social agencies are content with the rapid growth of social work programs since they are assured a constant supply of cheap labor and interns with which to staff their agencies. In turn, social work programs have a built-in justification to argue for programmatic expansion. Unfortunately, this collusion is built on the backs of beginning level social workers who in many cases earn little more than community college graduates. The continued overproduction of social workers without regard to marketplace conditions will only further aggravate the salary differential between social work and other professions, making a career in social work unattractive.

Alternative Accreditation

Given the inherent problems with the CSWE monopoly, the quality of social work education would also be enhanced if educators were encouraged to pursue alternative forms of accreditation. While CSWE provides for "alternative reaffirmation" this is restricted only to those schools that have already conformed to normal accreditation requirements. In effect, alternative affirmation through CSWE is designed for programs that have proven compliant with the substandard expectations that have marked social work education with mediocrity. CSWE's alternative accreditation policy allows social work programs with stable curricula that want to commit some of the resources they would normally use in the self-study process to different program improvement activities. The option involves two independent activities: (1) the completion of a reaffirmation compliance audit to demonstrate program compliance with accreditation standards; and (2) a special project which addresses a subject of significance to the social work profession or the social work program. Unfortunately, many programs are ineligible for alternative reaffirmation "Because programs must apply for the alternative to the reaffirmation at least two years and two months prior to the date of the program's scheduled review, eligible programs must be in at least their eighteenth year of accreditation."[11] CSWE, in other words, allows departures from its hegemonic control only after a program has adhered to its monopoly in social work education for two decades.

Alternative reaffirmation is not a form of alternative accreditation since programs must still comply with basic CSWE standards. As such, it is not designed to foster innovative programs but to lessen the burden of the self-study process for older, established programs. Not surprisingly, few programs have expressed interest in alternative accreditation; by 2009 only eight had taken advantage of the option:

- Case Western Reserve's Mandel School of Applied Social Sciences is developing "an assessment based curriculum designed around clearly identified outcomes that would become the basis for assessing student competence and program outcomes."[12]

- The School of Social Work at San Diego State University proposed infusing its curriculum with evidence-based practice.[13]

- The Social Work Program at Skidmore College planned on using "community-based and action research" in order to further "the promotion of empowerment and social change along with the acknowledgment at communities are the experts on their own strengths, needs, and capacities."[14]

- The University of Denver School of Social Work proposed to mount three empirical studies of distance education and "the elements needed for developing effective blended social work education."[15]

- The School of Social Work at the University of Hawai`i at Manoa received alternative accreditation for "exploring and developing concepts, processes and applications of indigenization in relation to the School."[16]

- The University of Michigan School of Social Work planned on focusing its curriculum on "Privilege, Oppression, Diversity, and Social Justice" in order to prepare students for "socially-just practice."[17]

- The Helen Bader School of Social Welfare at the University of Wisconsin-Milwaukee proposed integrating its generalist BSW curriculum with content on alcohol abuse.[18]

- The Department of Social Work at West Virginia State University planned to "integrate health and wellness theory and activities into the curriculum" in order to promote the health of West Virginians.[19]

Alternative accreditation under CSWE is a symbolic gesture toward educational innovation. By 2009, of the 656 BSW and MSW programs accredited by CSWE, only 1.2 percent had received alternative accreditation.

Performance-Based Accreditation

At the turn of the millennium, leaders of undergraduate institutions embraced evaluation, conceding that higher education lacked accountability with respect to its primary functions. These assessment projects are now deployed extensively throughout higher education; they have common characteristics: they are voluntary, comprised of measurable indicators, and are consistent across participating institutions. Notably, social work educators have been absent from these ventures; indeed, CSWE's most recent EPAS is retrograde by comparison, evidencing a studious avoidance of measurable indicators.[20]

In 1998 the Pew Charitable Trust convened a planning group to develop what would become the National Survey of Student Engagement (NSSE); by 2000, 276 campuses were using NSSE to evaluate five dimensions of student experiences: level of academic challenge, active and collaborative learning, student-faculty ratio, enriching educational experiences, and supportive campus environment. In its 2008 report, NSSE included responses of a random sample of students on 769 campuses, augmented by student records, and data from the Integrated Postsecondary Education Data System. As freshmen and during their graduate year, students are evaluated on a Likert-scale on items such as the frequency with which they made a class presentation, e-mailed an instructor, had discussions with students from other backgrounds, applied theories to new situations, the number of books they read, the number of papers between five and 19 pages written, their engagement in extracurricular activities, the extent of institutional support, among others. NSSE revealed positive findings, such as between two-thirds and three-fourths of students discussed ideas with faculty members outside of class, 60 percent of seniors engaged in volunteer service, and the amount of writing correlated positively with collaborative learning, student-faculty interaction, and "deep learning." Negative experiences were also reported by students, including 20 percent of students frequently did not complete readings prior to class, and only half of seniors had been encouraged to interact with students from different economic, social, and racial backgrounds. Several institutions found the NSSE useful in documenting their accreditation requirements.[21]

For the 2004-2005 academic year, the Council for Aid to Education, a nonprofit founded in 1952 to encourage corporate support of higher education, instituted the Collegiate Learning Assessment (CLA), a written evaluation of critical learning skills acquired during an undergraduate education. The CLA consists of three measures—make-an-argument, critique-an-argument, and performance task—that are administered to a sample of students enrolled in subscribing institutions. By 2008, 357 institutions were participating in the CLA, representing 27,083 students. To augment CLA, the Council for Aid to Education mounted the College and Work Readiness Assessment for high schools, the Community College Learning Assessment for institutions offering associates of arts degrees, and CLA in the Classroom to integrate the CLA with course activities. In promoting the CLA, the Council for Aid to Education notes that it uses no multiple-choice questions in evaluating students' critical analysis skills.[22]

In 2006 a discussion about the quality of undergraduate education sponsored by the American Association of State Colleges and Universities and the National Association of State Universities and Land Grant Colleges prompted the development of the Voluntary System of Accountability Program (VSA). From an initial grant from the Lumina Foundation, VSA convened an oversight board of ten administrators of public universities; by 2009, VSA had 317 institutions committed to develop institutional portraits according to VSA's template. In order to evaluate student performance, VSA adopted three instruments: the Collegiate Assessment of Academic Proficiency, the Collegiate Learning Assessment, and the Measure of Academic Proficiency and Progress. In light of public concern about the rigor of higher education, universities were quick to adopt VSA indicators. In a few years the following university systems had agreed to participate in VSA:

- All 33 universities of the Texas public universities,

- All 23 of the California State University system,

- All 16 institutions of the University of North Carolina system,

- All 14 of the Pennsylvania State System of Higher Education campuses,

- All 14 of the Ohio public institutions of higher education,

- All 13 of the University of Wisconsin system,

- All eight of the University of Louisiana System campuses,

- All seven of the Kansas public institutions of higher education,

- All six of the South Dakota Board of Regents' system,

- All four of the University of Missouri campuses,

- All three of the Iowa public universities.[23]

The rapid development of VSA demonstrates that leaders in higher education are willing to become accountable for the performance of their institutions.

The higher education accountability movement, illustrated by NSSE, CLA, and VSA, presents poignant issues for social work accreditation:

first, an array of public universities has embraced the concept of accountability through a range of empirical methods; second, the initiative has become established throughout undergraduate education. The universities that have subscribed to NSSE, CLA, and VSA, host a large number of undergraduate programs in social work, so they will soon be reporting on the performance of BSW students. With their adoption, it is likely that graduate programs will eventually be evaluated as well, thus including MSW programs. This raises an obvious problem for social work education: in the absence of social work educators developing comparable instruments, the evaluation of social work programs will be left to evaluators from other disciplines. Rather than complementing the efforts by national leaders to hold higher education more accountable, CSWE's 2008 Educational Policy and Accreditation Standards actually confuses the matter by proposing an "explicit curriculum" (specific courses of the curriculum) and "implicit curriculum" (the educational environment), neither of which are evaluated by empirical measures.[24]

Until social work educators craft an empirically-based assessment for social work education, they could start reporting essential indicators related to the quality of professional education. By identifying variables against which schools can be compared as well as explicating standards of scholarship for leaders, Performance-Based Accreditation would be superior to the subjective standards currently mandated by CSWE. Significantly, with Performance-Based Accreditation, the responsibility of data collection would be placed with member schools, reducing the staffing required by accreditors. Performance-Based Accreditation presumes that decision-makers with greater responsibilities should be more accomplished scholars. The most consequential decision-makers within professional education make policy while serving on the boards of accreditation authorities and vet the professional literature while serving on editorial boards; accordingly, they should have a record of achievement above that expected of program administrators.

Performance-Based Accreditation would not only enhance the autonomy of schools of social work but specify the variables through which they could be judged. Generated through any decent information system, these indicators would be posted on a school's web site annually, allowing stakeholders to compare schools. Accreditation based on such a strategy would free schools of the untold hours consumed by current accreditation procedures, allowing faculty and administrators to invest resources in activities, such as knowledge-generating research and community-related program innovations, which would burnish social work's reputation. The performance of schools could be compiled in an annual report, "The State of Social Work Education," which would track basic indicators of social work education, allowing prospective students to identify the strengths and weaknesses of programs to which they plan to apply while at the same time providing a longitudinal portrait of professional education.

Free of the restraints imposed by CSWE, schools of social work would be able to craft their individual educational signatures and affiliate with schools with similar priorities. Like the regional authorities that accredit institutions of higher education nationally, schools of social work in the Southwest, for example, may develop a focus on border issues and immigration; those in the Northeast may opt for expertise in community development and unemployment; those in the Northwest and Alaska would emphasize First Nations; while schools in the Southeast could specialize in African Americans in rural and urban communities.

Performance-Based Accreditation would encourage diversification among schools allowing them to establish their own curricula, requiring only that they report basic performance indicators to an accreditation authority. Like open-source software, accreditation would be transparent, customized, not only assuring that social work education was congruent with local circumstances but also affording comparison with social work programs across the country. Unlike accreditation as controlled by CSWE, Performance-Based Accreditation would provide the data to evaluate the performance of schools of social work, individually and collectively, over time providing a longitudinal portrait of professional education. So configured, Performance-Based Accreditation would bring social work education into conformity with the Congressional intent behind the Higher Education Act of 1992 and amended in 1998, which called for institutions to report according to indicators such as student achievement including "course completion, state licensing examinations, and job placement rates."[25] More recently, the Higher Education Opportunity Act of 2008 requires the Department of Education to begin reporting in 2011 not only on the top five percent of high-cost colleges and universities but also a range of performance measures—admission data, test scores, minority representation, grant aid, and graduation rates—for institutions participating in Title IV programs.[26]

The variables constituting Performance-Based Accreditation would not be standards with which programs must comply, but indicators of educational performance. To illustrate Performance-Based Accreditation, a handful of variables are suggested under four headings:

Students:
   Tuition (out-of-state if applicable)
   Acceptance rate of applicants
   GRE, MAT or other standardized scores of applicants
   Scholarships, number and amount
   Percent of students completing a research thesis for graduation
   Graduation rate
   Percent attaining licensure
   Percent employed, salaries
   Percent contributing as alumni
Faculty:
   Number full-time, rank, and course-load
   Number of adjuncts and percent of courses taught
   Publications in SSCI-cited journals+books
   Research grants, number and amounts
   Training grants, number and amounts
   Foundation grants, number and amounts
Administration:
   Courses taught
   Publications in SSCI-cited journals+books
   Ratio of administration to instructional expenditures
Instruction:
   Concentrations and enrollments
   Certificates and enrollments
   Class size
   CEU courses and enrollments
   Community projects

A list of variables useful to stakeholders could be limited to a single page, although schools would be free to elaborate beyond the basic template.

Through Performance-Based Accreditation schools of social work could choose to evolve their collective affiliations into separate accrediting authorities sanctioned by the Council for Higher Education Accreditation. Depending on their foci, social work schools could then elect to affiliate with multiple accrediting authorities. The staffs of accrediting authorities would be small, sustained by the nominal dues of member schools, their primary purpose being facilitating the activities of their members. Those accrediting authorities developing a better track record in educational development would attract more institutional members, enhancing their service capacity. CSWE might continue, but it would have to compete with other accreditors for membership.

Performance-Based Accreditation in social work education would follow precedents set in other fields. There are two major accrediting bodies in teacher education–the traditional National Council for Accreditation of Teacher Education (NCATE) and the small upstart rival, the Teacher Education Accrediting Council (TEAC). Each body has a different philosophy regarding accreditation. Like CSWE, NCATE's philosophy is that teacher education programs should be evaluated based on how well they conform to a uniform set of standards for the profession. TEAC's more controversial approach is based on allowing teacher education programs to set their own goals, and then requiring them to produce rigorous evidence that they are being met.

Enhancing Leadership

Performance-Based Accreditation could also provide prescriptive standards to upgrade the quality of professional education. Publications have primacy since they are the means of generating and transmitting knowledge not only within the professional community but to other disciplines as well. The schedule below illustrates how scholarship could become a basis for upgrading professional education throughout the vertical dimension of academic leadership. While compliance would be voluntary, schools adhering to such a schedule could claim scholarship as a basis for leadership. With respect to the accrediting authority, clarifying scholarship would reinforce the quality of decisions relating to educational policy. Applied to editors and referees, similar expectations would upgrade the quality of professional journals.

Schools of social work:
    Deans—12 SSCI-cited articles + books
    MSW Program Directors—six SSCI-cited articles + books
    BSW Program Directors—three SSCI-cited articles + books
    Doctoral Program Directors—nine SSCI-cited articles + books
    Field Directors—three SSCI-cited articles + books
Boards of accrediting authorities:
    Chairs: 15 SSCI-cited articles + books
    Members: 12 SSCI-cited articles + books
Editors:
    Journal Editors: 15 SSCI-cited articles + books
    Referees: 12 SSCI-cited articles + books
    Consulting editors: six SSCI-cited articles + books

Ultimately, such indicators would change the normative expectations of social work education, bringing it in line with more established academic disciplines and professions.

The Future of Social Work Education

A century after its inception, social work has failed to fulfill its promise, and this failure is reflected most conspicuously in the dysfunction of its educational establishment. Social work deserves a more honorable fate than that orchestrated by CSWE. Under the guise of accredited professional preparation, social work education attracts some of the weakest students, dabbles in frivolous methods, elevates non-scholars to deanships and referees of the professional literature, constructs a patronage system, and burdens its graduates with unconscionable debt, all the while portraying itself on the side of the angels. In fact, decades of miscues make social work education one of the most vulnerable academic units in higher education.

It has been almost a century since Flexner determined that social work was not a full-fledged profession. Since then, several factors have augured well for social work: the inception of the welfare state, the emergence of the service economy, the proliferation of technology for generating and distributing knowledge, and the expansion of higher education. These are the ingredients of professional ascendance, and some disciplines have exploited them commensurately. Yet, social work education has not prospered from these propitious circumstances largely because of the overly-prescriptive, ideologically-laden, and bureaucratic accreditation procedures mandated by CSWE. Six decades of CSWE's accreditation monopoly has actually subverted the quality of professional education. Instead of being poised to achieve full-professional status in the twenty-first century, social work more resembles the inert, industrial vocations of the twentieth.

This is paradoxical in light of The Great Recession, an economic downturn that has resulted in the highest rates of foreclosures, unemployment, and poverty in recent memory. Coupled with disabilities, deployments, and death attendant with prosecuting two wars, social work should be expanding to address increasing levels of need. At the very moment the nation requires effective assistance with problems not unlike those of the Great Depression, social work education offers a mediocre educational network maintained by an accreditation monopoly. Rather than prepare students for the challenges of dealing with global social justice in an age of information and entitlement, social work educators have promoted solipsism and self-absorption in the guise of identity politics; instead of posing solutions to problems attributed to economic collapse, social work has become largely irrelevant. At best social work educators offer a cosmetic assurance that the educational project is, in fact, delivering what it promises: a professional education capable of enhancing the public good. "But while it is easy to talk about the 'public good' or the 'public interest,'" noted Gordon Davies, "it is equally easy to turn such phrases into euphemisms."[27]

In retrospect, social work education's rush to credential practitioners with insufficient focus on issues of competence or their economic prospects is more than ironic, since the profession was created a century ago during the Progressive era, a time in which research, planning, and management were the hallmarks of social engineering and the means used to advance the public good.[28] In rejecting this legacy, social work education has created a bubble, expanding the number of accredited programs, in the process creating an artificial demand for graduates.

Conservative critics argue that social work is beyond reclamation and should be left to die an ignominious death. But if social work dies, what, if anything, would replace it? Which other discipline even mentions the term "social justice"? As moribund as it might have become, social work still has a social and moral compass, something absent from other pretenders in human service education. If social work is gone, who will perform those essential social functions: amelioration, social adaptation, and social reform, while recognizing the complex interaction of the person within the social environment? Social work education should not reject its Progressive promise because it has been hijacked by a cadre of self-serving academics, ineffective organizations, and special interest groups. Simply put, social work brings to the twenty-first century a noble legacy and, even if it has spent recent decades curbside watching, it has made substantive contributions to the nation's well-being; social work education *is* worth reinventing.

References

1.   The Carnegie Foundation for the Advancement of Teaching, The Carnegie Classification of Institutions of Higher Education. Retrieved June 5, 2007, from http://www.carnegiefoundation.org/classifications.
2.   John Pardeck and Roland Meinert, "Scholarly Achievements of the *Social Work* Editorial Board and Consulting Editors: A Commentary," *Research on Social Work Practice* (9)1(1999), pp. 86-91.
3.   Jeane Anastas, Denise Bronson, Wendy Crook, Howard Doueck, Rena Harold, Fariyal Ross-Sheriff, David Tucker, Rowena Wilson, "Guidelines for Quality in

Social Work Doctoral Programs," Revised, 2003, Group for the Advancement of Doctoral Education (GADE). Revision approved by the GADE membership October 18, 2003.

4. Council of Europe, Steering Committee on Social Policy, "The Initial and Further Training of Social Workers Taking into Account Their Changing Role, " Strasbourg, France, 1995.

5. Kay Hoffman and Alberto Godenzi, "Increasing Our Impact through Unification," *Journal of Social Work Education*, (43)2 (Spring/Summer 2007), p. 182-83.

6. Hoffman and Godenzi, p. 184.

7. K. Porter, "Globalization issues—globalization: What is it?" retrieved August 13, 2003 from http://globalization.about.com/cs/whatisit/awhatisit.htm and N. Rzack, "A critical examination of international student exchanges," *International Social Work*, 45, 2, pp.251-265.

8. David Osborne and Ted Gaebler, *Reinventing Government* (Reading, MA: Addison Wesley, 1992).

9. Ann Neal, "Dis-accreditation," *Academic Questions,* vol. 21, no. 4 (Fall 2008), p. 432.

10. Prohibiting faculty with doctorates in social work who lack an MSW from teaching the entire spectrum of the curriculum not only discriminates against those who have attained the highest credential in the field, but it also may require them to go back for an MSW after they complete their doctorates, a backwards career trajectory.

11. Council on Social Work Education, Alternative Reaffirmation: Compliance Audit and Project, Alexandria, VA, December 20, 2006, p. 1.

12. "Ability Based Learning," Mandel School of Applied Social Sciences, Case Western Reserve University, Cleveland, OH, December 2006, p. 2.

13. Sally Mathiesen and Melinda Hohman, "The Infusion of Evidence-Based Practice into a Social Work Curriculum," (San Diego, San Diego State University, n.d.).

14. Crystal Moore, "Enhancing College-Community Collaboration," (Saratoga Springs, NY: Skidmore College, n.d.), pp. 4-5.

15. Catharine Alter, et al., "Distance Education for Social Work Education," (Denver: University of Denver, 2007).

16. "Alternative Reaffirmation Project," Manoa, Hawai`i, n.d., p. 5.

17. "Promoting Socially-Just Practice in the Field," (Ann Arbor: University of Michigan, 2005).

18. "Alternative Accreditation Proposal," University of Wisconsin-Milwaukee, School of Social Work, n.d.

19. "Social Work Health and Wellness Project," Institute, WV, Department of Social Work, December 1, 2006, p. 1.

20. "Rationale and Guiding Principles Used to Draft EPAS," (Alexandria, VA: Council on Social Work Education, n.d.).

21. Promoting Engagement for All Students: The Imperative to Look Within," (National Survey of Student Engagement, 2008).

22. "Collegiate Learning Assessment," (New York: Council for Aid to Education, 2008).

23. "VSA Participating Institutions by State," downloaded January 14, 2009 from http://www.voluntarysystem.org/index.cfm?page=background

24. Stephen Holloway, "Some Suggestions on Educational Program Assessment and Continuous Improvement," (Alexandria, VA: Council on Social Work Education, 2008), p. 1.

25. Neal, "Dis-accreditation,", pp. 437-38.

26. "The Higher Education Opportunity Act and You," (Washington, DC: American Council of Trustees and Alumni, 2009).

27. Gordon Davies, "Accreditation for the People," *Chronicle of Higher Education* (May 4, 2007), p. B13.

28. Howard Karger and David Stoesz, *American Social Welfare Policy* (5th edition) (Boston: Allyn and Bacon, 2006).

Index